THE NEW EPOCH
FOR FAITH

BY

GEORGE A. GORDON

MINISTER OF THE OLD SOUTH CHURCH, BOSTON

BOSTON AND NEW YORK
HOUGHTON, MIFFLIN AND COMPANY
The Riverside Press, Cambridge
1902

TO FELLOW-STUDENTS OF THE TIMES WHO
ARE YET FELLOW-SERVANTS
OF THE ETERNAL
THIS BOOK IS INSCRIBED
AS A TOKEN OF GRATITUDE FOR INSPIRATION
RECEIVED FROM AN UNSEEN HOST

PREFACE

THE occasion of this book was an invitation received nearly three years ago, to deliver a course of lectures before the Lowell Institute in Boston. The writer's sincerest thanks are due to the Trustee of the Institute for the honor of this appointment, and for the time granted in order to prepare to meet it. In the fulfillment of this duty last autumn, the substance of about one half of this volume was delivered as lectures.

The title of the book, which has not been selected without care, may seem to some persons to be excessive in its optimism. Even if this is so, there is really no help for it. It is the expression of a conviction, which, for the writer, has the force of truth. And when one thinks of the revolution in all matters of faith in which men are now living, it is not unwise to hope for great issues. In an unpublished address the late Professor C. C. Everett, of Harvard University, referred to the last third of the nineteenth century as having witnessed a greater revolution than took place under Luther. "That was a transition," said Professor Everett, "from one form of the letter to another; this has been a transition from the letter to the spirit." If one might venture to add anything to these weighty and admirable words, it would be that the transition has made evident the true place of the letter in the service of the spirit. It has been shown that while the spirit is master, it cannot live in this world without the letter as servant. The variations of the letter as the organ of the spirit, from the vagrant whispers about God and his divine order, found among all peoples and in all tongues, up to the full-toned and mighty utterance of the Hebrew seers and the supreme music of the speech of Christ, have also become apparent. The world's speech about God is related to its object, as the world's speech is related to thought. The one runs through many variations from the lispings of the child to the utterance of the man; the other runs a similar course from the fugitive words of the spiritual childhood of the race up to the expression of divine maturity in Jesus Christ. The place of the letter has thus been made more secure.

Ideas in abstraction from their highest historic expression are not for this age, any more than dead mechanism usurping the place of insight and love. With this double movement in full force, this primacy of the spirit maintained, however, through the service of the letter, this recognition of history as the fruitful soil of all valid thought, this discernment of idealism in the facts of existence, this high conjunction of God and his world down to its least detail, its cup of cold water, its widow's mite, its unconscious humanity and inhumanity, as in the Judgment parable of Jesus, there rests upon the modern believer an obligation to hope.

The purpose of the volume is to discover and announce the chief significance for faith of the nineteenth century. It is believed that the great witness of that century is the witness to man. In the second chapter the attempt is made to justify this position.

Assuming that this justification has been made good, Christianity, as the religion of the Divine man, comes into the presence of this new consciousness of humanity for new appreciation. Doubt, however, of the sincerest and most searching sort is one of the moods of the cen-

tury; and this doubt means the falling of man from confidence in the witness of humanity, and in the high vocation of his kind. It is claimed that this negative mood is educational, and that it issues in a fresh assertion of humanity, that is, in a new return to faith. During the last hundred years history has acquired an immensely increased importance; and the association of the permanent and yet growing beliefs of the race with history would seem to result in a profounder assurance of their reality. As the first chapter is upon things assumed, the final one is upon things expected. The book is thus a consideration of what are believed to be the sovereign moods of the century, intervening between fundamental assumptions and final issues. Assuming the validity of the religious view of the world, it seeks to appraise for that view the value of the century.

For such an undertaking it is obvious that knowledge is necessary. This essential preliminary is indeed appalling in its extent. It may well seem that an adequate knowledge of the period under review is beyond human attainment, or that only a specialist in history can compass it. Against criticism of this kind the

writer has nothing to say. He is forward to confess that such knowledge as he should be glad to possess he has found beyond his power. He has consoled himself with several reflections. It has seemed possible that ideal knowledge might lie beyond the widest learning. "Only one who is ignorant of the complexity of all historical phenomena could cherish the delusion that he could give an exhaustive and adequate account, or a final and authoritative estimate, of the intellectual situation of any age." [1] Inadequacy thus falls alike, if not equally, upon the specialist and the non-specialist. Investigation has been made as wide and deep as could be done in the circumstances. Books have been read of many sorts, but chiefly those great books that constitute the watershed of the century's opinion and feeling. Genius is the lawgiver in every age. The few men of original genius, and those who are great in the reproduction of ideas, thus abbreviate undertakings like the present one. For the writer, the last third of the century has meant opportunity, struggle, and life ; and its atmosphere filled with many significant voices has been his chief source of knowledge. The

[1] *The Ritschlian Theology*, p. 5. Alfred E. Garvie.

time in which one has lived, the changes that
one has witnessed, the faith and the struggle in
which one has shared, are an unconscious discipline both in knowledge and in insight. The
writer has also tried to investigate symbolically;
he has endeavored to find the whole in specially
significant parts; and by way of comfort he has
reflected that if one falling apple served Newton
for his great generalization, certain facts may
be presumed to include within their own meaning that of their entire class.

This book would be absurd without a solid
basis in fact; yet the fact is but the beginning.
The attempt is at valuation. The search is for
the meaning of ideas and events, the appraisal
of moods and achievements. And here again
abundant fault may justly enough be found.
The criticism as to the adequacy of the basis in
fact may be matched by that which questions
the competence and disinterestedness of the insight. The writer's weights and measures may
seem to be all wrong. His mood may appear to
be too confident, too dogmatic; or even that of
one committed to a side. Such criticism cannot
be obviated. If it is entirely true, the truth
cannot be concealed by a polemic phrase. If it

is not wholly true, the truth may still be, like
the foreign accent upon speech, unobvious to the
writer, although ludicrously plain to others. Let
it be considered what the design of the work is.
It is an interpretation. A history of ideas and
events is not written but presupposed. Knowledge has been sought for the sake of wisdom.

That a writer should take sides, in a work of
this kind, would seem to be essential. The person who has no interests at stake is at the
greatest disadvantage in understanding any part
of the world. One thing is certain, and that is
the stern straightforwardness of the universe in
which men live. Play is incidental, purpose,
high and serious, is the soul of the world. The
inevitable is on every hand.

> " But heard are the voices,
>   Heard are the sages,
>   The Worlds and the Ages:
> ' Choose well; your choice is
>   Brief, and yet endless.' "

It is believed that there is a movement in history
subduing the world's divisions into eternal unity;
but up to date the end is unaccomplished, the
dualism is still extant; and the camps of truth
and falsehood, right and wrong, hope and de-

spair, life and death, confront one another in deadly battle. In this state of affairs, the writer has no desire to become "president of the heaven-and-hell amalgamation society." If what he has written is of any value, it is because it is an honest and emphatic opinion concerning crises upon which he has looked through his own eyes, and through all other available eyes. That the situation is greater than his vision and that its meaning is vaster than his judgment are freely and, indeed, gratefully confessed; and yet it is believed that his work may be of some slight help both to knowledge and to wisdom.

There should plainly be a sequel to this discussion to indicate, in an orderly way, the conceptions of faith that come out of the nineteenth century. Such an outline was at one time contemplated as the conclusion to this book. It was found, however, to be foreign to its essential design; and it is the writer's hope that another volume will follow, in the near future, upon Ultimate Conceptions of Faith, and dealing with the theology that rises out of this day of crisis, freedom, and necessity.

GEORGE A. GORDON.

OLD SOUTH PARSONAGE, BOSTON.

CONTENTS

CHAPTER I

THINGS ASSUMED

CHAPTER II

THE ADVENT OF HUMANITY

CHAPTER III

THE NEW APPRECIATION OF CHRISTIANITY

CHAPTER IV

THE DISCIPLINE OF DOUBT

CHAPTER V

THE RETURN OF FAITH

CHAPTER VI

THE NEW HELP FROM HISTORY

CHAPTER VII

THINGS EXPECTED

THE NEW EPOCH FOR FAITH

"It is the end of the earthly life of the human race to order all its relations with freedom according to reason."

" From this principle we arrive at five great and only possible epochs, exhausting the whole earthly life of the human race : First : That in which human affairs are governed by reason as instinct without violence or constraint. Second : That in which this instinct has become weaker, and now manifests itself in a few chosen individuals, and thereby becomes an external ruling authority for all the rest. Third : That in which this authority is thrown off; and with it reason in every shape which it has yet assumed. Fourth : That in which reason in the shape of knowledge appears among men. Fifth, that in which art associates itself with knowledge in order to mould human life with a firmer and surer hand into harmony with knowledge, and in which the ordering of all the relations of man according to reason is, by means of art, freely accomplished, the object of the earthly life attained, and our race enters upon the higher spheres of another world." — FICHTE, *Popular Works*, vol. ii. pp. 69, 70.

" At last the kingdom and the power and the glory of God must surely come." — *Ibid.*

THE NEW EPOCH FOR FAITH

CHAPTER I

THINGS ASSUMED

THE ultimate premise of thought is not proof. It is insight or assumption in accordance with sane reason. This familiar idea runs back through all the books on logic to Aristotle's "Posterior Analytics," where the ultimate judgment of infinite fruitfulness is described as a function of the mind itself. In perception there is seen at work a native discriminative power. Rational experience is possible because the soul is of such a nature as to be qualified for it. The home of the original principles of knowledge is the mind.[1] The organ of knowledge must be assumed ; its essential trustworthiness must be taken for granted. Back of this position it is impossible to go. That there exists in man intellect, critical and constructive, with an eye for reality and with the power to reach it, is not something that has been proved. It

[1] *Post. Analytics*, ii. 19.

lies deeper than all proof. It is an assumption made in accordance with sane reason.

The temptation is to linger for a moment to fix the reality of this subjective ultimate. Plato remarks, with an exquisite touch of humor and pathos, that the insane man is only somewhat more emphatically out of his head than the rest of society.[1] There is in all men an original uncertainty of mind. Paul calls it the carnal mind, which in all high matters is incompetent. This apostle describes the dualism in his soul, the conflict between the sane and the insane moods of his spirit.[2] The old thinkers called this original and persistent uncertainty in vision and in feeling and in preference depravity; to-day it is known by the softer names of prejudice, eccentricity, abnormal development, excessive sensibility. The fact is the same, however, under the old names and the new. Man is originally like turbid water; the beginning of wisdom is to wait for the settling of this sediment of insanity.

This result the great Greek thinkers described as the emergence of ὀρθὸς λόγος, right reason. It meant something like rational transparency, clear and sure insight. It was the fountain of all speculative power, no less than of all valid practical judgment. It was a power that grew through use, that acquired mastery through the

---

[1] *Laws*, 929, D.　　　　[2] Romans vii.

experience which it tested. It became at length
the philosopher's sane vision, and the sure discrimination of the man of the world. It is the
origin, in all ages, of genuine critical power, and
of valid insight. It is the last and best resource
of the highest thinker and the humblest man.
It is this faculty against which the system of a
Spinoza goes to wreck. The philosopher's intox-
ication with God is sublime; but his treatment
of human life runs against right reason; and
the God who thus reduces human life to a mere
and miserable mode of his own infinite and irre-
sponsible existence is himself discredited in
the presence of right reason. There has been
no argument with the philosopher; perhaps the
critic is altogether incompetent clearly and
elaborately to expose the latent incoherence and
unwarrantable assumptions in the system that
he rejects. The great system goes because right
reason is against it. The system of Jonathan
Edwards is a vital American example. Much
as there is in it to admire and to accept, there
is much in it to deplore and reject. And this
result is reached not only by the competent
critical thinker, but also by the average layman.
Elaborate refutation is unnecessary; right reason is the spear of Ithuriel that lays open the
hidden error. It is this priceless gift that enables the furnace tender of whom Tennyson
speaks to offer availing comfort to his wife,

whose mind had been unbalanced by a sermon
on everlasting torment in the fire of hell; it is
not true, "no constitution could stand it." The
same instinct enabled Father Taylor to maintain
the integrity of his faith under the influence of
Emerson, whom he deeply admired and loved.
He was sure there was a screw loose in Emerson, although after listening a year he had been
unable to hear it jar. The sense of that loose
screw, undetected although it was, protected the
smaller mind against the undue domination of
the greater.

The presence in man of the possibility of a
right mind is abundantly recognized in the
teaching of Jesus; but nowhere more strikingly than in the poor madman whose dwelling
was in the tombs. After his subjection to the
influence of Jesus his friends found him clothed,
and in his right mind. The sediment of insanity had settled, and again the water of life was
clear and calm. Here the insight is the issue,
not of rational, but of moral discipline; and the
resulting vision is not so much for speculative
purposes as for ethical ends. And here one
comes upon the inmost secret of Jesus. He is
himself absolutely sane; the rational and the
moral vision are in him one, and the discovery
is as true and sure as the order of the world.
The power of Jesus over the mind is always in
the interest of sobriety and fidelity. He affects

the judgment and the will through the heart, yet his final work is in giving wisdom. The school of Christ is the great discipline in mental health. There, as nowhere else, men learn to see straight. The Christian view of the world is addressed to the mind previously recovered to sure judgment. The ecstasy of Christ is the lifting men out of the insanities born of the animal nature, into the insight and love of his own pure humanity. The Pauline ecstasy is of this kind. It is not a wild whirl of feeling; it is the resolution of the soul into extraordinary clearness and range and sureness of vision. It is the unwonted expansion of the right reason, the high inspiration of the right mind, that as possibility lives in every man. It helps to fix attention upon the subjective ultimate, without which there could be for man neither truth nor righteousness in the world.

In like manner, there is an objective ultimate, which, however, beyond the statement of the fact, need not detain us. The basal premise of science is the reality of the external world. Of this reality there is no proof. None is needed. Every one knows that the world is real. This conviction is the result of insight; again it is an assumption made in accordance with sane reason. Insight does not determine the nature of the reality; that remains to be investigated. Assumptions do not interfere with the work of the sciences. But the question comes, Is the object of science real? The universal answer is that it is real. This answer is, however, not the result of proof. In the light of reason the reality of the external world is seen, and the truth of the insight is taken for granted.

The fundamental ideas of faith are of this order. Their reality for the life of man is discovered by their own light. They are not the issue of demonstration. They are the subject of verification, but not of proof. The certainty to which men come concerning them is the certainty of insight, of sane reason, of repose upon the ultimate conditions of the life of human beings. For example, if one shall exclude God from life, and then try to find him by logical process, the quest will be vain. One may as well try to construct a flight of stairs to enable one to touch the sky. The attempt is fruitless and unnecessary; fruitless because as fast as one rises the sky recedes; unnecessary because the sky is with one now. It is the condition of one's physical existence; it is in one's blood and sinew and brain. There is no need to mount to heaven to find it; walk abroad in it, and it will renew the revelation of its reality in the wonder of renewed life. God is not reached as the last conclusion of the intellect from premises that exclude him. No logical flight of stairs can convey the mind from a godless earth to anything other than a godless heaven. God is known as the supreme condition of spiritual life. Men know him through the life that he first makes possible and afterwards real. They live and move and have their being as men in him. He is in the blood and substance of character, and from him spiritual existence is renewed day by day. The being of God, the moral order of the world, the worth of history, the immortality of man, and the social life beyond time are fundamental assumptions. They are best discussed when they are discussed in their own light as they stand in the service of human life.

In this book they are not discussed; they are taken for granted. At another time the basal things of faith may occupy the writer's attention; here they are assumed, and the discussion goes forward upon the assumption that they are valid. This is the background against which the writer's work is to be judged. Has he read aright the signs of the times? that is the question which his book should raise. And the answer should be made with a clear sense of the things which he has assumed. He has indeed read the ideas and events of the nineteenth century in the light of certain fundamental conceptions. The meaning of the times does not lie in the times themselves, but in the ideal forces behind them and that work through them. The test of this work must therefore lie in the

responsiveness or unresponsiveness of the facts
with which it deals to its fundamental assumptions. In the light of these assumptions this
book is written ; it is waste of time to read it in
any other.

It is assumed that the religious view of the
universe is true. It is the manifestation of the
Supreme being, to whom men are bound by the
sense of obligation and by the sense of privilege. The basis of nature and the ground of
humanity is the Eternal spirit. The universe
has its meaning in the ancient insight : —

> " The eternal God is thy dwelling-place
> And underneath are the everlasting arms."

There is the Infinite behind nature and above
man and in them. Nature is for industry, art,
science, and for something more. She is the
condition of physical life, and one of the conditions of the highest life, and she may be something for herself. But these are stages in the
journey toward her ultimate meaning; they do
not constitute the journey's end. Nature has
something to say for God, not a great deal to
be sure, but nevertheless an authentic and significant utterance. She is not her own ; she
belongs to another ; of her Owner she is a
manifestation, and her final meaning is found in
the terms of his life. Man is for knowledge
and achievement and love ; he is an end unto
himself, a value for himself. In a certain sense

the significance of man lies within the circle of his own activities and experience. But in the last analysis he is forced beyond himself for the full account of himself. Like nature, only in a sense immeasurably higher, he is for God. The religious view of the universe is given with great power in the one hundred and forty-eighth psalm. The universe has its primary meaning as a value for God. The heavens are called upon to praise him; all angels, all hosts, sun and moon and stars of light, all the fullness of power that floats in the upper air; the earth is called upon to praise him; "fire and hail, snow and vapor, stormy wind fulfilling his word, mountains and all hills, fruitful trees and all cedars, beasts and all cattle, creeping things and flying fowl." And in unbroken continuity the summons is served upon man : —

> " Kings of the earth and all peoples ;
> Princes and all judges of the earth :
> Both young men and maidens ;
> Old men and children :
> Let them praise the name of the Lord ;
> For his name alone is exalted :
> His glory is above the earth and heaven."

The ultimate view of the universe is the religious view. Its worth is ultimately worth for the Supreme being. Here is the note of permanent value in Edwards's great essay upon the end of creation. Edwards finds the final value of creation in its value for God. The universe becomes at last transfigured in the life of God; and in the fact that it is for him lies its distinction, its permanence, its hope. The Christian conception is but the highest version of the religious view of existence. According to Christianity God is love, and as such he is the origin, motive, path, and end of all that is. "For of him and through him and unto him are all things."[1] All phenomenal existence is filled and fixed with the Eternal presence; and its original meaning is its worth for his infinite wisdom and love.

It is assumed that God is obviously present in human life. It is taken for granted that in a special way he is in the constitution of human reason, in the structure of society, in the moral articulation of being which is deeper than all conscious will, and which is the condition of the life proper to man. There is a network of relations in the constitution of mankind. In this order men appear as persons confronted with ideals and obligations. Society is thus originally organized in parenthood and childhood, in citizenship and in brotherhood. All social conventions disclose their worth and their defect in the light of this aboriginal order. All schemes to set it aside, or to ignore or suppress it, are reforms against nature, or rather warfare against God in the constitution of man. Individuals are

[1] Romans xi. 36.

in themselves incomplete and essentially without
meaning, like a hand wrenched from the wrist
and from the body to which it belongs. The
Platonic ideal of self-sufficiency for the good
man is the reverse of true.[1] Not less than others
but more is he in need of his brethren. Humanity is indeed an organism, where the individual is
at the same time both end and means. Individuals complete themselves in society, and society
completes itself in God. This is the moral organization of human life to which Paul has given
frequent and profound expression.[2] This is the
deepest meaning of Hebraism. Individuals
have their life and significance in the nation,
and the nation has its life and significance in
God. Here one sees the permanent distinction
of Aristotle's political philosophy, and its fundamental defect. Human life naturally involves
the family and the state ; men are men in and
through society ; but the thinker who sees so
clearly the essentialness of society to the individual fails to discern the essentialness of God
to society. As there is nothing in the individual
that does not concern society, so there is nothing
in society that does not concern God. Society
is the full expression of man, and religion is the
complete expression of society. The fields of
industry, art, science, philosophy, government,

---

[1] *Republic*, bk. iii. 388.
[2] 1 Cor. xii. 12–31 ; Eph. ii. 11–22.

and family love lie in the light of the Divine presence in the conscience of man. The reign of conscience is over all human interests; and through it the moral order of the world is reached. The ethical view of the race and its environment is the valid view; and this human moralism is an expression of the Infinite conscience, and the eonian operation of it is the attestation of God's presence in human life.

In this Divine order the voluntary life of good men becomes a new witness. Upon the basis of what God has done for all, many are able to do something for themselves. Born upon the common elevation of manhood, they climb " to a height that is higher." The shame of life is but the shadow of God, the aspiration of life is but his inspiration. Moral grief and hope betoken the nearness of the Infinite rectitude and pity. The good ethical habit is a new possession in God; the wiser and nobler mind bears witness to something above itself. The discipline through which vision comes is a transaction in the Divine life, and its goal is the beatitude : " The pure in heart shall see God." Prayer, obedience, experience, and the hope that is born of experience lift one into a higher human world. As a witness of Immanuel, to the moral organism of humanity there must be added the moral life of good men.

It is assumed that God works for ends. In

this assumption there is a necessity of thought. In this way only can man know God, since man is himself a being of ends. There is a gradation of ends in human life that must be taken into account in the quest for its meaning. Like the depths in the sea, human needs sink into one supreme need; like the earth's elevations, human ideals rise into one highest ideal. The thirst for the living God is the need, the clear hope of reaching the river of God is the ideal. Thus man as a being of ends insists that his ultimate end shall match his highest power. His *summum bonum* must be on the level of his essential endowment as man.

In no other way can man think of God. To him God is necessarily a being of ends. Teleology is in the warp and woof of humanity; it must be in the warp and woof of Deity. Evolutionary science has but strengthened this view. Natural selection is but a mean disguise for ignorance, if it does not imply cosmical purpose. The movement of life from lower to higher is a movement upon ends. Will is the last account of the universe, and will is the faculty for ends. The moment that one concludes that God is, it appears certain that he is a being of ends. The universe is alive with desire and movement. Its organization is in desire and movement. Fundamentally, it is throughout an expression of will. And it follows that the ultimate ends of

God in human history must be worthy of himself. For Christian faith God's character is love, and his ends must equal his character. As he is, so must be his goal. He cannot deny or discredit himself. Details are beyond the range of our vision. We know what we are, "sons of God," but "it is not yet made manifest what we shall be." This much, however, is clear, that God's purpose must cover humanity here and elsewhere. His object must be a moral universe wholly in accord with himself. His achievement in those who love him must indicate his intention for those who turn away from him : "We know that, if he shall be manifested, we shall be like him ; for we shall see him even as he is." [1] Nothing other than this and nothing less can match the absoluteness of God's love. In the rational life that he has made his ideal must be to become all in all. For this the world was made, for this it moves, for this it lives in hope ; and to this end God is bound by the immutable pledge of his perfection.

It is assumed that progress is real. Mere change does not express history. That is something more than the shifting of the scene of action from Egypt to Assyria, from Assyria to Persia, from Persia to Greece and Rome, and from these to the nations of modern times. Nor is the impulse of this movement properly

[1] 1 John iii. 2.

read as the domination now of one ambition and again of another. History is something more than the record of the successive dynasties of human passion. The emergence of the new is one feature of history, the richer development of the old is another feature, and still another, and most fundamental of all, is the conception of better and worse. The idea of worth is essential to the history of man, and the tide of time is a rising tide of human values. Unsurpassed epochs there are in the past, perhaps there are in it men unsurpassable in genius and in character; but the question of progress does not deal with single instances. It is concerned with the comparative condition and character of the whole. The question is not whether there is discernible in every section of the sky a few stars of the first magnitude, but whether to the eye of historic time there is traceable a universal movement from darkness to light. Loss there had been, still the chief note of history is of slow but sure gain. Ideals vanish in the presence of higher ideals; and in the teeth and eyes of all fashions and fads it may still be said that permanence is sure only to the best that man can think and do and be. Man is best known through the value that he puts upon his supreme monuments. Something can surely be said for the race that has conserved in the wreck of three civilizations the Old Testament,

Greek literature, and Roman law. The New
Testament is the book revered above all other
books in the western world. It is the supreme
instance of the permanence that belongs only to
the best. The few are indeed still the custodians of the world's highest things; but these
few custodians are more and more visibly servants of the race. More and more the race
struggles upward to a share in the world's noblest ideas and achievements. The gods still
hold their banquet upon the heights, but the
invitation to it has gone to the ends of the
earth; and since it is irrevocable, the sinews of
the multitude grow, in the ample opportunity,
into equality to the task of ascension. Upon
the whole, and over the wide expanse of time,
the historic movement is slowly but surely away
from the brute, and upward to the attainment
of manhood according to the measure of the
stature of Christ.

It is finally assumed that the finite world of
man has enduring worth. It is not, as in the
idiom of pantheism, a passing phase of the
Eternal, a prophetic spring, a glorious summer,
a golden autumn lost at last in winter's ice and
death. Not as the endless succession of the
seasons to the abiding life of nature is man's
relation to the Infinite. Man's world is not
mere and temporary expression, a token of an
evanescent mood, pathetic or amusing, sad or

sublime, of the Ineffable. It is not a chance and brief composition of forces, as in the materialistic view. The human world is a structure of thought, a building of love, an edifice rising more and more in response to righteousness; and it cannot rest upon a non-mental, an unloving, an unmoral foundation. The architect of the temple of intelligence and passion and conscientious life cannot be blind chance. Nor is man's world an unprogressive multitude of souls, to be swamped in hell or carried to heaven, in accordance with the issues of existence here, as in the terms of traditional theism. "The assumption that this course of human life is strictly the probation of the individual in his mature development, and that the terminus of this probation is in the incident of the death of the individual, and that the location of heaven and hell is beyond the earth, and that the object of salvation is transportation to the one and escape from the other, and that human life is evil, and that the few who have a conscious faith, which has yet in itself no ethical ground, are alone saved in the ultimate assize, to which all are summoned; this is the staple of the various religions of the world." [1] Somewhat unsympathetically, as respects its motive, and yet with essential justice as regards its general results, does Dr. Mulford here condense into a single

[1] *The Republic of God*, pp. 258, 259. Dr. Elisha Mulford.

descriptive sentence the characteristics that have
made traditional theism, for an enlightened
mind, an impossible belief. Humanity as a
whole is an imperishable value for God, and
the final significance of God for man must ever
be God in man. Of man's universe the Incarnation is the centre; and God in history, in
society, in the redeemed but progressive life of
mankind is the permanent aspect of the Infinite
love. Whatever insights are possible into the
being of God for himself offer themselves only
to those who know God as the life of man. But
beyond our human world, which had a beginning
in time, and whose destiny is always to pursue
a growing ideal, and which can, therefore, never
be complete, is the life of God for himself.
That surely is a fundamental truth. By itself,
however, it is barren truth. Man's imperishable and endlessly growing world can never give
one the whole Deity; yet must this world and
our God stand or fall together. For rational
and Christian theism the extinction of man
would be the cessation of God; for in and
through man only is God known. Break the
association between God and human society
and you abolish your Deity. The other side of
God is nothing when once the hither side has
been destroyed; God for himself is an empty
phrase when God for man has been rendered
meaningless. The absolute God, who is eternal

society in himself, may indeed be seen and
known somewhat, and more and more, but always as Archetype of human society, always as
the ground of our social humanity, always
through the knowledge of God as man's Maker,
Redeemer, and Sanctifier, always by means of
the benedictive process of Christian experience:
The Grace of the Lord Jesus Christ, and the
Love of God, and the Communion of the Holy
Spirit.

CHAPTER II

THE ADVENT OF HUMANITY

I

CANON LIDDON is authority for the story of a Presbyterian minister who, in behalf of Queen Victoria, and in her presence, offered this prayer: "Grant that as she grows to be an old woman she may be made a new man; and that in all righteous causes she may go forth before her people, like a he-goat on the mountains." [1] There could not be a better example of the saving strength of the ideal. There could not be a more faithful symbol of the mixture of high intention and immeasurable ludicrous impropriety on the part of mankind, as it thinks its best thought, does its best work, and utters its best life under the shadow of the Infinite Majesty. Between the Peloponnesian war and the work of Thucydides, the tragic beauty of life and the dramas of Sophocles, the truth of things and Plato's philosophy, mediæval faith and the Divine Comedy, the fifteen centuries of human struggle and the image upon Gibbon's vast can-

[1] *Collections and Recollections*, p. 125.

vas, the modern world and the plays of Shake-
speare, the French Revolution and Carlyle's great
and burning picture, there is an infinite incommensurateness. Even the classic achievement
of man is pathetically and ludicrously inadequate ; it is saved by the truth of its ideal and
the sincerity of its spirit. Of man's best work,
no less than of himself, it is true " by grace
have ye been saved." The incommensurateness
between the ends of science, art, philosophy,
government, and religion, and their achievements
is the sad humor of history. The race was made
to laugh at itself in its pursuit of the highest,
and at the same time to feel the immeasurable
dignity that the highest bestows upon it through
that pursuit. The comic and the serious belong
together, and the ludicrous aspect of life is inseparable from the religious.

Reflections like these are inevitable, and they
are a comfort when one undertakes to find and
announce the chief significance for faith of the
nineteenth century. The ideal is the despair
and the hope of the greatest minds ; and both
its rebuke and its encouragement may sober and
sustain the humblest enterprise that is honest.
One who has lived in this century, to whom its
doubt and its faith have been profoundly real,
and its achievements objects of wonder and serious study, and who conceives the value of the
past to consist in the illumination of the present,

is likely to be possessed by two convictions. The first will be the spiritual impression which the century has made upon him, and his desire to record it. The second thing will be the emergence upon him through his wider studies of the hopeless greatness of his task. Learning and insight equal to this undertaking exist in no man, much less in him. Still here is the great section of time repeating the impression of its consequence, and calling for witnesses. It is the last requisition upon courage that one should be willing to become a fool for the ideal.

Another period of time has become centenarian, and calls upon men to listen to its final words. It repeats the language of Burke with the added weight of its own impressiveness: "What I say I must say, at once. Whatever I write is in its nature testamentary. It may have the weakness, but it has the sincerity of a dying declaration." [1] The voice of an age speaking from the edge of the grave is charged with peculiar power. When a full hundred momentous years cry, "We who are about to die salute you," it is impossible to remain unmoved; when a century repeats its *nunc dimittis* only shallow souls are insensible to awe. This time of ours, this century now vanished has seen many wonderful things. It has looked upon the bright face of genius, watched the high servants of all human

[1] Regicide Peace Letter, i. p. 99.

interests, considered all aspects of the universe, — the lilies of the field, the birds of heaven, and yet more, the heart of man. The earth was fresh upon the tomb of Washington when it was born, and the grass is scarcely green upon the graves of Gladstone and Bismarck now that its race is run. Its young face greeted, as among its prophetic souls, Emerson and Bushnell, Tennyson and Browning, Darwin and Wallace, Maurice and Mill; and with care-worn countenance it bade them adieu. It honored and educated more or less to its own use great names received from its predecessor — Scott and Byron, Shelley and Keats, Coleridge and Wordsworth, Fichte and Hegel, Goethe and Carlyle. It discovered Lincoln and shortly afterwards buried him among the kings with infinite regret. To all the men now in power in all departments of activity it has been both sun and shield. At last it has welcomed into the temple of time the children who are to be the world's ruling spirits, the Lord's anointed ones for the coming generation; and we can hear the voice of a great century in the treble of extreme age lifted up in pious supplication : —

" Now lettest thou thy servant depart, O Lord,
  According to thy word, in peace ;
  For mine eyes have seen thy salvation,
  Which thou hast prepared before the face of all peoples;
  A light for revelation to the Gentiles,
  And the glory of thy people Israel." [1]

[1] Luke ii. 29–32.

More than twenty years ago a student in Harvard University, wearied with the task of the week, and vexed with the eternal problems of thought, sat doubting and dreaming in the dear old college chapel before the usual Sunday morning service began. The question returned with an unwonted intensity, For what purpose is this mental toil and trouble? Why continue this hopeless quest for truth? What will it profit a man to conquer the whole world of learning? Is there an ultimate and everlasting motive for the scholar who is at the same time a man? Can anything fill the universe with living beauty and bestow upon it power and charm? The question was forced from our student with his back against the wall. The report is that the answer came, as from the Infinite Watcher of men, "All things are for life." The rumor is that in greater detail it ran thus, "Rejoice, O young man, in thy youth. Keep inviolate your sense of life. Wonderful instincts are at work in your nature, fountains of power are every month opening in your heart, strangely beautiful ideals are appearing overhead. Your life is conscious of elemental energy, and there beats in it the prophecy of a new heaven and a new earth for itself and for mankind. Hold fast to this great, central, substantial, and teeming fact of life. Range the universe round this mighty consciousness of being with its unappeas-

able appetite for more. Test all customs, traditions, beliefs, literatures, religions, by the fact and
the necessity of life. Relate the past achievement
of your race, and its present many-sided and won-
drous activity to your own soul, and see if there
does not open before you a path into peace. If
you have been born into certain religious beliefs,
if custom has reduced this inheritance to a life-
less mass, if you move about in it like a som-
nambulist with staring eyes that see nothing,
here is the remedy. Relate the inheritance to
life, convert the tradition into a servant of character, draw upon the history for support in the
struggles of the spirit, declare a war of extermination against the total evil of the world;
and then raise new armies and organize into
fighting force every belief available in the faith
that has descended to you. Thus the essential
and serviceable will appear, and the unessential
and useless. The cowardly things that leave the
field when your manhood is hard pressed, and
the imbeciles that remain only to block the way,
will become manifest through this stern test.
The sun is the same whether it floods with its
light the dead moon or the living, responsive
earth. The living universe can do nothing for
the dead man but gild his tomb; it can reveal
its eternal life only through life. Pass within
the gates of moral life, and see if the faith that
has sunk to a tradition, a ceremonial, an insti-

tution, does not rise and inaugurate a new day."

In no other century since the world began would such an answer have come to a bewildered student with such obvious and large significance. And the reason for this is the fact that slowly and in spite of all opposing forces life itself has been winning the chief place in thought. For the first time in history, in the nineteenth century, the people have made their appearance. They have put in their claim, and in their majesty they have stood up to see that it is recognized and allowed. Thought has come back to man, in order that with the acknowledgment of man as the first interest of man it may the better understand nature and God. The chief concern of the nineteenth century is a concern for man. It compels science, art, philosophy, government, social reform, and religious purpose to approach men with the serious announcement: "We come that you may have life and that you may have it abundantly." In secular phrase it has been admirably said that "the creed of the nineteenth century is collectivism. We have seen that this creed was begotten in the eighteenth century. We have followed its successive stages of growth, in Winckelmann's conception of Greek art as an outgrowth of Greek life; in Lessing's view of a continuous development of religious ideas throughout the ages; in Herder's vision of the organic unity of all mankind; in Kant's exaltation of the moral law; in Goethe's and Schiller's idea of a perfect, all-embracing personality. But if collectivism was begotten in the eighteenth century, it was born only in the nineteenth. Only in this century has it ripened into a principle of its own, affecting national life at large, revolutionizing science, art, religion, politics, changing the mental, moral, and social aspect of all Europe." [1] This statement is made from the point of view of the history of German culture. The word humanism is preferred to collectivism by the writer simply because of his different point of view. Beneath both words the general fact is the same. The one best word for the distinctive character of the nineteenth century is humanity; and the century's high distinction is that within its limits there has been a surpassing advent of humanity.

II

It is interesting to note that the two greatest ideas of the modern world, the idea of a universe and that of a humanity, both had a religious origin. Long before Newton had discovered the balance of all material things, their exactly proportioned affinities and repulsions, and their

[1] *Social Forces in German Literature*, p. 399. Kuno Francke, Ph. D.

union under the omnipresent force of gravity;
ages before modern physics had reduced the het-
erogeneous forms of matter to essential, indestructible energy, and had gathered the worlds
of space into one infinite kingdom, religious
insight had dated all things from the Divine
will, and grounded all things in it. The idea of
a universe came as the inevitable consequence
of the idea of God. Through large inductions
and wide generalizations modern science has
vindicated this idea of unity; it has given unexpected richness and range to the religious intui-
tion; still it must be said that it was religious
genius, and not scientific investigation, that first
gave to the race this great conception. The
earliest philosophers of Greece were theosophists.
For Plato all things became one through the
sovereignty of the good, and Aristotle found no
universe until he found God. The same remark
would seem to hold true of the profound but
fantastic, often insane speculations of the Indian peoples. Their sense of unity is primarily
a religious conception; its development is apparently a religious necessity. Modern philosophy
owes more, as respects origin, to the religious
impulse than to the scientific. The Cartesian
philosophy is avowedly religious in its primary
motive, and Spinoza, the thinker who gave the
most impressive expression to that philosophy,
is rightly described as a " God-intoxicated man."

Even English empiricism becomes an enthusiastic idealism in Berkeley, whose philosophic passion from first to last is supplied by theistic faith. Hume and Kant are exceptions; but again the idealistic movement in Fichte, Schelling, and Hegel, the most fruitful movement in the nineteenth century, is inconceivable apart from religious necessities. The Hebrew seer, therefore, would seem to give the true historical and psychological genesis of the idea of unity when he says: "In the beginning God created the heavens and the earth."[1] This should dissolve the strife between the religious interest and the scientific. The fact that reason would appear to have disclosed her deepest demand, her final ideal to religious insight, should be enough to reconcile in one body all genuine students of science and all worthy students in theology.

For the origin of the idea that is our present concern, the idea of humanity, one must go to the same high source. Industrialism, travel, international interests, history, science, and the ideals of the intellectual life generally, are in the service of the great conception. And one cannot be too thankful for this service. Any idea that is to prevail must be able to impress into its service a vast variety of instruments; indeed it can be carried into controlling influence only by the concurrent action of all the

[1] Genesis i. 1.

better forces in our civilization. Until that hour shall arrive the new idea can do nothing but stand at the door and knock. The world is host, the great idea is guest; the host cannot originate a guest; creation is not his task. He assumes the independent reality and presence of the guest; and in the same way the other civilizing forces of the world look to religious insight for the discovery that God " made of one every nation of men for to dwell on all the face of the earth." [1] The Christian apostle was justified by the historical fact when he connected the idea of a human race with the conception of men as sons of God. The Greek faith " we are his offspring " is the source of whatever sense of brotherhood that people possessed. The Hebrew faith that men are made in the likeness of God is the ultimate source of the idea of humanity. Men and races are one because in God they have a common archetype. Monotheism is the priceless gift of the Old Testament to the modern world. Of this tree of life the two great branches are that all worlds and all men are one in the one perfect God.

III

Some account must now be taken of the forces in society that have opposed with a success so tragic the speedy realization, and even the sin-

[1] Acts xvii. 26.

cere recognition, of the brotherhood of man.
For the explanation of the persistence of human
selfishness the old notion of a fall in Adam has
been made to do heroic duty. The German philosopher Hegel has consecrated anew the story
of the fall.[1] He found in it a striking symbol
of some of the deepest facts of moral experience ; and in the Hegelian sense the wonderful parable has obtained a fresh lease of life.
The original innocence of instinct did dissolve
into discord in the first man because he was
man, and this resolution of animal content into
spiritual discontent has been repeated in all his
descendants. The Paradise of instinct is but
the beginning of history for the first man and
for all men ; the expulsion from this Paradise is
a universal experience. Milton reads a chapter
from universal human history in his famous description : —

> " They, looking back, all the eastern side beheld
> Of Paradise, so late their happy seat,
> Waved over by that flaming brand ; the gate
> With dreadful faces throng'd, and fiery arms.
> Some natural tears they dropt, but wiped them soon :
> The world was all before them, where to choose
> Their place of rest, and Providence their guide.
> They, hand in hand, with wandering steps and slow,
> Through Eden took their solitary way." [2]

The harmony of the child intelligence breaks

[1] *Logic*, pp. 54–57. W. Wallace.
[2] *Paradise Lost*, bk. xii. lines 641–649.

up into the discord of the man; still it remains
as the symbol of that concord which he must
win through the toil of the spirit. " The har-
moniousness of childhood is a gift from the hand
of nature ; the second harmony must spring
from the labor and culture of the spirit." [1] Man
cannot live in his first Paradise, nor can he live
without the hope of a second. To recover
through the wealth of experience the lost Paradise, to see it reconstructed by the energy of
the spirit, greatened out of the fullness and
conquest of life, is the ideal aim of manhood.
In this sense the fall of man is the first act in
the drama of human history particular and universal.

The notion of inherited depravity is true but
one-sided. It needs to be supplemented by the
notion of inherited excellence. The historic
stream is double ; and its twofold character is
indicated with philosophic precision in Paul's
great words : The first man is of the earth
earthy ; the second man is of heaven.[2] History
is the record of both these men, not only in the
symbolic Adam and the real Christ, but also in
universal experience ; and inheritance is thus a
compound issue of earth and heaven, or, in plain
words, of depravity and excellence. In pro-
nouncing the idea of the fall as an insufficient
explanation of the origin of evil, and in the

---

[1] Hegel's *Logic*, p. 55.   [2] 1 Cor. xv. 47.

literal meaning of it incredible, the truths to which it has borne witness must not be overlooked. It has served to remind the world that men are not merely individuals, that they have race connections, and that the character of the past is written in the flesh and fibre of the present. It has stood as a sign of racial union for better and for worse, of partnership in a common calamity and a common hope. It has been associated with great truths, while itself untrue. It emerges in the parallelism of Paul in a form that must ever carry with it the Christian reason of the world : " For as in Adam all die, so also in Christ shall all be made alive." [1] But taken in the letter, and according to the traditional understanding, it is past belief that two human beings created in moral integrity could by one act of disobedience dissolve themselves and their descendants in a universal sea of depravity. The notion of the fall can no longer serve as an account of the source of moral disorder.

Another way has been found in our time of regarding this resistance of man to his own higher development. Man has been discovered to be of a twofold origin. He begins in God as a mind or spirit, and he begins in the brute as an animal organization. It is held that it is the persistence of the brute in man that is the origin of the trouble ; what Tennyson calls " the

[1] 1 Cor. xv. 22.

ape and tiger," the unsanctified bequest through an insufficient number of intermediaries, from the primeval dragons

"That tare each other in their slime."

This is the first mother of the fierce egoism that has drenched the earth in human blood, the original source of the Ishmaelitism that has seen in other men not friends but enemies, the awful fountain of the savage individualism that has gone through history as a blasting presence. The ancient Hebrew did not muzzle the ox and the ass as they were treading out the corn on the primitive threshing-floor. It was a humane custom. The brute in the service of man has its rights. The ox and the ass were not muzzled, but they were harnessed. So much cannot be said of the animal in man. In him the ox and the ass, and all other forms of the brute, domesticated and wild, have not only been unmuzzled but uncontrolled and uncontrollable. Nothing here said is meant as a censure upon the existence in man of a passionate individualism; the contention is that it has no business there on its own account; it is as a servant and not as a master that it has its place in the human economy. In the strength of the brute, it is therefore held, lies the ultimate and most obstinate resistance to the kingdom of man. For the opinion that found the source of moral evil in the lapse of a perfect person there is substituted the view that regards the person as from the beginning a compound of discordant forces, and that goes behind him for explanations. The new doctrine of original sin goes deeper than the old; it passes below the first man in his primary estate, about which it has, as has been intimated, its own judgment, descends into the arena of the beast, and finds there the home of the antagonism to the moral ideal which by the weapon of heredity continues to fight its eonian battle.

The second great obstruction to moral progress lies in the weakness of human reason. In taking the animal into partnership, it has formed ideals not for itself but for the animal. As one surveys the life of man one is saddened by the poverty of his conception of the good. From the dawn of history the moral ideal, for the masses of men, has been a poor thing. Prohibitions have been served upon excessive murder, lying, and lust, largely on economic considerations. Certain restrictions have risen about the family because the human heart was strong in its demand here. The ideal of social union has been formed in a prolonged compromise with the beast in man. Only in the rare moments when the voice of the beast was struck dumb, and his vote taken away, have the genuine ideals of the moral reason been able to put in an appearance. Exceptional experience in exceptional persons has given the truth; the average life and custom have begotten and perpetuated the lie.

There is the element of exclusiveness in the historic ideal. Government has been an oppression because the interest of the ruler has been conceived to be opposed to that of the subject. Conquest has been a ruthless slaughter, and not a militant missionary, for the reason that the conqueror construed his advantage as at war with the advantage of the conquered. Industry has been a prolonged duel rather than a genial and serious expression of brotherhood for no other reason than the predominance of greed. Greed has not been confined to the rich; but their example has too often provoked it and filled it with scorn in the ranks below them. About the only parts of the Bible that the great majority of the money kings have lived up to are the stories of Naboth's vineyard and the expulsion of the Canaanites. It is clearly discernible that there has been a malformation of the human ideal. The cry of the beast is, " Every man for himself, and the devil take the hindmost; " and the immediate and shining success which waits upon this maxim reduced to practice has a tendency to drive all humane ideas to the wall. The method of sacrifice against that of greed brings one to say : " The foxes have holes and the birds of the air have nests, but the son of man hath not where to lay his head." [1] The principle of love arrayed against that of brute power brings Jesus to his cross. In numberless instances there is this temporary defeat of the best. Is it not strange, therefore, that in the economic struggle humane feeling should be regarded as a hindrance? When men see their economic competitors feeding the beast, tipping his horns with spears, training him to gore the enemy and trample upon him, there is nothing extraordinary in the fact that the resort to the aid of the beast should become general. Powerful rascals, especially in trade and in politics, force into general use inhuman methods. This would seem to be the point in Kipling's "Truce of the Bear." The man lays down his arms in the presence and at the call of the beast; the result is that the man is clawed to the bone. The hopeful thing in this gloomy situation is that it is an outrage upon human nature, and one that outraged humanity will not always allow to go on. When self-interpretation is self-reduction the power to redress the wrong is generated by the wrong itself. It is true that the idealizing faculty has been to a painful extent the organ of human selfishness. That accounts for the delay in social progress; it likewise calls out the protest that avails more and more as the centuries pass.

[1] Matt. viii. 20.

In the briefest account of the main forces that have so long delayed the kingdom of man, to the persistence of the animal and the weakness of the opposing reason there must be added as a third obstruction the element of perversity. In almost all the disasters to the moral life the strength of the animal nature is obvious. The havoc that ignorance works is also plain. But it is impossible to crowd back into these two sources of animalism and ignorance all the streams that run through the consciousness of moral insolvency. The personal will is the centre of conduct, and the doings and misdoings of men obstinately refuse every reference as a finality other than this. The basis of all true philosophy is the full and naked integrity of real life ; and the scheme that does not accord with the essential facts revealed in the normal human consciousness can have but a provisional value. As far as it goes, the Socratic doctrine that vice is the issue of ignorance is true.[1] It is based upon a genuine ethical insight. Still, the insight is limited and insufficient. The Platonic observation, that the beast in man in alliance with weak or ignorant reason is the source of the moral difficulty, is a richer observation.[2] But not until Aristotle indicates will as the centre of moral experience does the adequate analysis appear.[3]

[1] *Protagoras.*   [2] *Phædrus.*   [3] *Ethics*, bk. iii.

The difficulty in making out a clear case for this third and final source of moral trouble lies in the fact that it nowhere operates alone. The moral renegade is at once under the combined influences of the brutal and the blind and the perverse forces of his nature. The treason of Judas is an example. There is the animal desire for gain to which the thirty pieces of silver are an appeal; there is the moral ignorance that does not take in all the facts, that does not properly value the facts that are apprehended, that does not permit a sane judgment upon the situation; and there is the perversity that will not entertain the whispered suspicion concerning the real character of the contemplated act, the dim surmise that it is diabolic. When the act is done it is willed into existence under protest. The confession is: "I have sinned in that I have betrayed innocent blood." [1] The attempt to reduce this confession to the acknowledgment of misfortune would be mockery. The confession is the confession of a personal will that has acted in the face of a real, and perhaps a tremendous, protest. The shame lies in the fact that the protest that should have been availing was unavailing.

The believer in human progress must reckon with the fact of wickedness. Until he has recognized the fact of self-induced irrationality, the

[1] Matt. xxvii. 4.

force of sheer perversity, the reformer has not measured the strength of his enemy. Indeed, will is the reality of life; and wherever will is real, and confronted by the conflicting goods of the flesh and of the spirit, to whose appeals it is constitutionally sensitive, perverse choice and perverse habit are always possibilities of the case. "Not this man but Barabbas" is an ignorant choice; it is more. It is a choice against an inner protest. It is perverse. This point is of fundamental importance. Without the reality of the will the confessional literature of the race is either cant or insanity. On this basis human accountableness for the delay of the kingdom of justice is an illusion; it is no longer a normal feeling, but a form of disease. One must seriously amend Plato's comparison wherein the soul is seen to be composed of the black horse of passion and the white steed of love harnessed to the chariot of life with the reason as charioteer. Reality goes with the will. The chariot and the horses and the driver that remain are a mechanical device, a wax-work semblance of reality. But nothing that breaks down the consciousness of reality should be accepted as true; and the pious dreams that see no perverse will in the way of human progress are the worst kind of wild-cat currency. They are the notes for mighty sums of spiritual bankruptcy; they can never be redeemed by those who issue them. If they should be coined at length in the flesh and blood of real persons, in the character that can be won only by the agony and the bloody sweat, it will be because the signature of freedom and responsibility has been written upon them.

Brutality, ignorance, and perversity have invaded the institutional life of mankind. The evil in men's hearts has gained immense influence through expression in custom, law, government. Inhumanity has fortified itself in the institutions of trade, society, politics, and religion. As an example of institutional antagonism to the spread of humanity there may be named the failure of the church to understand the idea of election or vocation. It is believed that next to the family the Christian church has done more for the welfare and freedom of man than any other institution or agency. Still, it is true that the mistakes of the great are calamities. And because of the general high distinction of the Christian church its error upon the vocation of man has been one of the greatest enemies to human progress, and may well serve as the type of all other enemies in their institutional form.

The central sin of Israel was its misconception of election or national vocation. The nation traced its origin to a man to whom the promise was made that in him and in his seed the whole earth should be blessed. This divine election is the foundation of the national existence of the

Israelites. The idea is supreme in their literature, constantly influential in their history, always potent in their forecast of the future. That
Israel had a special vocation as the peculiar people of God is a conviction universal as her life.
The fact is admitted ; the meaning of the fact is
the great question. The first Hebrew was chosen
for his descendants and for all the families of
man. The nation that drew its life from him
was elected for universal service. Its isolation,
its unique endowment and history were privileges
whose termination was the good of mankind.
And this idea of the national vocation never
took any strong hold upon the popular mind.
Their distinctive history inflated the pride of the
people ; it became the ground of the bitterest
exclusiveness. Election understood would have
been the saving strength of the nation ; election
misunderstood was its ruin. The nation felt
that the election of it meant the rejection of
other nations. This interpretation left it without a vocation, served to check humanity as a
sentiment at war with the Divine decree, and
degraded it and its deity by encouraging it in
the notion that Israel was a pet of Jehovah.

Upon this fundamental error Israel went to
wreck. All that the world has held precious in
the literary and religious bequest of that great
race was of little account to her. The nation
was like a ship that founders at sea. Her great

records, her monumental writings were saved ;
the nation herself perished. She was out of her
course from the beginning; she sailed upon a
misconception, and could never reach her destination. The wisdom which was disowned was
rescued ; the civilization itself went down.
Jesus Christ is the vindication of the Hebrew
prophet, the conserver of his unheeded message,
the renewer of his unavailing protest against
national pride and infatuation. He went forth
the authentic interpreter of his people's vocation, the correction of their vast mistake, the
substitute for their measureless failure, the sublime consummation of the thwarted but unde-
feated purpose of God in their historic career.

The Christian church has repeated Israel's
mistake. It has set the seal of divinity upon
Hebrew inhumanity ; and it has signally failed
to appraise at their true value the really great
things in that civilization. The church has
assumed that Israel understood herself ; and
then theologians have proceeded upon this
assumption to gather from the four winds of
the immemorial mistake texts in proof of God's
restrictive purpose concerning mankind. The
Christian church inherited and repeated an historic tragedy. Election has meant the same
thing to the Christian that it meant to the Jew.
It is the doctrine that to-day lives under the
phrase "survival of the fittest." The fittest are

Nature's elect; the unfittest are her reprobate offspring. The ancient error is quick to seek scientific shelter. But it should be clear that inhumanity in God must be fatal to the recognition of humanity among men. Upon this issue the choice is between ecclesiastical theology and the reality of the moral character of God. It is true that this is but a single philosophical position. The debt of the world to the church is very great. Still, when one asks for the fundamental reason for the failure of the Christian church in her witness for humanity one must point to her deplorable misconception of the divine election. Not since the voice of Origen died away, and not until the great voices of the nineteenth century began to be heard above the perennial Babel, has there been within the pale of ecclesiastical orthodoxy the conception of a redemption for humanity, ordained by the sincere purpose of God, mediated by Jesus Christ, and held forth by the institution that has borne his name. The humanity of the Incarnation was discounted for fifteen centuries.

When one considers how great an influence Hebraism has had upon civilization, and reflects upon the uncritical way in which it has been taken up into traditional Christianity, the force of its fundamental misconception will be apparent. And when one recalls the fact that as men think about God so they come to think about themselves, the obstruction which the ecclesiastical doctrine of election has presented to the development of the Christian idea of man is beyond description great and terrible. For the sources of moral motive are not in man; they are in the character of God. The vigor of the individual, the energy of a people, comes out of the heart of moral faith. Fundamental ideas about life ultimately rule life. The character of men and nations is to be found in their theory of the universe. Conceptions about the Infinite are the most prevailing forces in human history. Theology is the hand that fashions existence. Man is a reasonable being in the long run; and philosophies of the world, explicit or implicit, as clear ideas or as solutions in feeling, exercise an elemental power over moral motive. Hindu character conforms to Hindu pessimism; Mohammedan fatalism is the mother of another great type of life; and in the Christian world the ideas of a Divine election and rejection have to an unimaginable extent controlled the fountains of moral energy and hope. The watershed determines the course of the river; and it is the ultimate belief about the universe that shapes the character, directs the power, and fixes the issues of human beings.

Nothing has been said of the metaphysical origin of the brutality and the ignorance and the perversity that have opposed the full advent of man. The relation of the Divine will to the moral evil of the world would seem to be an impenetrable mystery. The writer has no gospel upon this subject except a negative one. Moral evil must be acknowledged as real, as something that ought not to be; and faith demands that, both as respects its origin and its continuance, God shall be held to be its absolute enemy. This position does not pretend to explain how moral evil entered the world; it does claim to save for living faith the moral integrity of God. As between Mill's position of a limitation upon the Divine power in the interest of his perfect goodness, and the Calvinistic view, championed so chivalrously by John Fiske, that takes the world as it is as the expression of the Almighty will, there seems to me but one choice for moral faith. Mill's God one can worship and help; the Calvinistic God one can only abhor. If at this moment the world as it is suits the Deity, it is plain that it suits no good man. And upon that scheme the good man is higher authority than the Almighty deity. But there is a third position, that which postulates the absolute perfection of God, therein clearing him of all complicity with the moral evil which all good men hate, and thereby securing the support of the Infinite for the swiftest possible elimination of the shame whose origin under the reign of eternal goodness it is at present powerless to explain.

Mr. Fiske finds the origin of evil in the essential constitution of man.[1] Moral evil is indispensable in the drama of human history; it cannot but be. It is part of the order of nature. And this conclusion is an inference from the law of human intelligence. For example, contrast is necessary to knowledge ; the fundamental one of subject and object, and all the derivative contrasts implied in the subjective and objective worlds. This is the premise of Mr. Fiske's argument ; this is the fact which he thinks supports his conclusion.

That conclusion is that a contrast equally fundamental is necessary to moral experience. As in reason there is no knowledge without this, and not-this, so in conscience there is no moral knowledge without goodness and badness, without virtue and vice. If this inference is valid, it makes absurd a further conclusion of Mr. Fiske. If sin is essential to holiness, if the one can exist only with the existence of the other, if they are a sort of Siamese twins whose being is inseparable, then it follows that there can be no elimination of moral evil through evolution save by the elimination of moral good. The co-essentialness of virtue and vice in moral experience makes both eternal or both temporal. Indeed, if sin belongs to the moral life as such, it must belong to the nature of God ; and thus

[1] *Through Nature to God*, pp. 34–47.

he is both divinity and devil in one person, and from everlasting to everlasting.

It is clear from this issue of his logic that there must be a fallacy somewhere in Mr. Fiske's argument. Contrast is essential to knowledge, and it is part of reality; but contrast is not antagonism. The contrasts that make real the moral life need not be contradictions; for example, sin and holiness, high moods and base ones. They may be the unlikenesses involved in an ascending series of goods; for example, a man's love for his family widening into friendship, patriotism, philanthropy, religion. It may be like the extension of vision of one climbing a mountain, where expansion presents contrasts but no contradictions. This must be possible for the moral life; otherwise Mr. Fiske's optimism is vain.

It is not difficult to see that moral evil is not a metaphysical necessity, something without which moral experience could not be. For the bare possibility of infinite sin is sufficient antithesis to the absolute perfection of God; and the moral life of Jesus Christ would seem to have been of this order. He knew no sin; it was simply the dark possibility which lay over against the perfect actual of his soul. And in holding this type of moral life to be the truth for the race, the ultimate truth, and therefore, in the Divine order, the aboriginal truth, one would seem to be doing only bare justice to the best moral insight of mankind.

Mr. Fiske's purpose is commendable, but his conclusion is a consecration of the wickedness of the world, an authorization of it in the name of the fundamental and unalterable law of being. That holiness may be real, it must have an antagonist; that holiness exist, it must fight this antagonist to the death. But if holiness shall succeed, it will be a Samsonian victory; the defeat of moral evil will be the end of the moral world. Dualism of the worst kind is involved in Mr. Fiske's fundamental position, and nihilism upon the supposed reduction of the dualism. Such are some of the infelicities that annul the usefulness of Mr. Fiske's brave essay. Evil is indeed a mystery; but one can fight it on the assumption that it is not an essential part of the moral order of the world, and that God has no complicity in it.

Principal Caird in his Gifford Lectures discusses "The Origin and Nature of Evil" in a richly suggestive manner.[1] He disposes successively of the Augustinian theory, and the idea that moral evil is negative, or that it rises out of the conflict between the flesh and the spirit. The origin of evil is in the will itself, and Principal Caird's account of it " stated generally is

[1] *Fundamental Ideas of Christianity*, vol. i. pp. 196–232; vol. ii. pp. 1–73.

this, that in a spiritual self-conscious being, the will is the capacity of realizing the true ideal or end of his nature ; and that the good will is that which finds its satisfaction in seeking this end, the bad will that which seeks its satisfaction in lower ends ; in briefer terms, that goodness is true, baseness false or perverted self-realization." [1] The related topics are admirably, if somewhat diffusely, discussed in these volumes. The nature of spirit in the Infinite and in man is treated with abundant insight. The distinction is made plain between the false self and the true, the individualistic self and the universal, selfishness and self-realization. Under new phrases and modes of treatment, for which Principal Caird is indebted to Hegel, his German master, whom he translates and even transforms so admirably, lie in fresh clearness wide expanses of important truth. The nature of moral evil and the character of moral good are faithfully drawn. Suggestions of great value abound, bearing upon the relation of the human spirit to nature and to society, and through both to God. But the origin of evil remains undiscovered, or at least undeclared. The Augustinian theory breaks down under moral criticism and under the pressure of reality. The idea that moral evil is essentially negative is " a virtual evaporation of the existence of evil." Sin

[1] *Fundamental Ideas of Christianity*, vol. ii. pp. 56, 57.

is not in the flesh but in the perverse spirit; all
this Principal Caird tells admirably well, but
why it is there, upon the assumption of the
infinite moral perfection of God, he does not tell
us. And this is the real question concerning
the ultimate origin of evil. The theories that
make God all in all take an inadequate view of
human wickedness; and the theories that gain
the deepest insight into this wickedness are un-
successful in adjusting it to the absolute perfection of God. That moral evil is here, and that
it is at war with every human interest, are facts;
that God abhors it and that he works against
it, also are facts; that he is free from the contradiction of originating that which he seeks to
destroy is not matter of demonstration, it is the
position of faith.

IV

The idea of mankind as forming one brotherhood in the presence of the Eternal Fatherhood
is not an explicit teaching of Hebraism. It is
implied in the ethical idealism of the great prophets. The demand, "Have we not all one
father? hath not one God created us?"[1] refers
doubtless to the people of Israel; still, the premise is here that justifies the conclusion of universal brotherhood. The Hebrew belief in one
God made inevitable the ultimate confession of

[1] Mal. ii. 10.

one humanity. Still, Hebraism did its great work for man indirectly. Its ideas of the human conscience, individual and social, and its conceptions of the Divine character and government were the forces in it that told for the rights of the race. It was a great servant of human fraternity, but only by the logic of its central thoughts and not by express proclamation. Indeed, there is much in the Old Testament, taken as a whole, that is a witness against humanity.

It is here that the Jonah story has its interest. It was written when the Hebrew heart began to be enlarged, when the suspicion arose as to the right of Israel to a monopoly of the Divine favor, and the dim surmise had dawned that perhaps Gentiles might have relations with the Eternal not only in judgment but also in mercy. The conviction had somehow gained strength that the Hebrew race was called to be the missionary of forgiveness and hope to the doomed heathen inhabitants of the adjacent nations. Genuine humor and true religion are inseparable, and the Jonah story has gone through history as a kind of test in both departments. The purpose of the writer is one of tenderest humanity, and into this human passion he poured the strength of his religion. But he was no dreamer or blind devotee of impractical schemes; he was a person of wide observation of the customs and feelings of his own race. He had seen and measured, and he was able to characterize the immense obstacle in the way of his new gospel of humanity. And here his humor came into play. In the construction of his story his sense of the immediate hopelessness of his idea found vent. The plot was formed in the interest of his religious passion for man as man ; but the peculiar character of the plot was the creation of his humor. He put a great fish into his story, and when he did this it would seem as if he must have known what he was about. The church has fought over his whale and paid little heed to his humanity. The purpose of the story, the new national psychology that flowers in it, the overflow of the religious interest of the devouter Hebrews to all the world that is part of its unique value, and the blow which it delivers, in the name of God, full in the face of inhumanity, have received scant attention. The whale has been nearly everything and the humanity nearly nothing.

One can imagine the writer of this immortal parable following with infinite zest the fortunes of his little work. The people of God have lost their sense of humor because they have lost the truth of their religion. Never mind about Nineveh overhung by doom, but go on contending that the whale was a genuine whale, that the prophet tabernacled in it for a season, and that he has left the world his log in the psalm that he afterwards inserted in the story. Nothing could better exhibit the dullness and duplicity of man in his religious struggle than the way in which the teachers of Christianity have fallen victims to the high faith and divine humor of this prophet. He put his best vision and his purest passion into conflict with the stupidity and insincerity of the time; he had come to the double conclusion that the ideal must never be surrendered, and that the hope of immediate victory was vain. He put both conclusions into his parable, and for more than two thousand years only a handful of scholars have seen either.

When genuine laughter is present tears are never far away; and the two main reasons why religious teachers have missed the purpose of this precious booklet are the pathetic side of the venerable blunder. One of these has been reverence for Christ; as if the great Master of parable could not borrow one from the religious literature of his people, without thereby meaning that it is actual fact. That spirit of dead prose has left unappreciated much that is highest in the Bible. The other reason has been the fear lest in the loss of the most grotesque of miracles there might be the surrender of the supernatural; as if the mind that entertains the heavenly vision of the Infinite pity, and a humanity everywhere capable of recovery to the lost ideal, and personal character open to the tides of love from the unseen, did not already possess the supernatural in its supreme form. Miracles have their place in human history, but even when most authentic and serviceable they are only back doors in God's house, opening into the lanes and alleys of existence where the victims of sense and passion gather. They who live forevermore in that house have only a sympathetic and secondary interest in these accommodations to human weakness. Now that the Jonah story is alive with interest for Christian people, assuming, as it is, the function of a tract for the times, it looks as if sanity and seriousness, genuine humor and true religion, were upon the eve of a revival.

The idea of humanity is foreign to Greek civilization. It never occurs to Plato that God made of one every nation of men for to dwell on all the face of the earth.[1] According to him there is among human beings a racial and irreducible difference.[2] His ideal commonwealth is composed of three classes, answering to the three functions into which he divided the soul, — the appetitive, the passionate, and the rational. The lowest class are made for menial service and nothing else ; the middle class are the standing army of the state, good only so far as they are governed by the born rulers, the rational head of the commonwealth.[3] It is true that there is an escape possible to genius from the lowest

[1] Acts xvii. 26.   [2] *Phædrus*, 248.   [3] *Republic*, bk. iii. 413.

rank, and for privileged stupidity there is a
way to hell even from the gate of heaven.[1]   Still,
to Plato democracy was a hideous thing.   And
with all his genius and goodness the claim that
all men are brothers would have struck him as
supremely ludicrous.   The same remark applies
to his greatest disciple.   The slave is no part of
human society.[2]

It is therefore no part of the direct teaching
of the highest wisdom of Greece that men com-
pose one kind.   Nevertheless, Greek civilization
has been an amazing force working indirectly
toward this end.   The Odyssey is the shadow,
pathetic and beautiful, of the fortunes of men
as men.   Its hero is indeed an ideal Greek ; but
he is more.   He is a magnificent man.   And
whether defying Circe and her swine, cherishing
his pure, inalienable love of home in Calypso's
isle, covering himself with leafy boughs when
cast ashore in reverence for the young women,
conquering the brutal strength of the Cyclops,
or in dearest memory and desperate fondness
grasping at the ghost of his mother in Hades,
Odysseus stands as a witness for humanity.
This is true of the great tragedians and come-
dians of Greece.   Their greatness lies in the
human situations that they depict, in the human
passions of love and sorrow, humor and mirth,
that they portray ; and their reign is less owing

[1] *Republic*, bk. iii. 415.   [2] *Politics*, bk. i., iv.

to the fact that they are high examples of Greek literature, and infinitely more to the way in which their wonderful art continues to mirror the heart of man. The indirect service of Greek literature and Greek philosophy to the sense of manhood is great. Greek art dealt with the enduring feelings, and Greek wisdom stated the essential problems of man and contributed toward their solution ; and, therefore, in both man was raised into a higher self-recognition.

Rome at her best was a witness for unity, and, therefore, for man. The gathering together under one mighty government of all the peoples that made up the civilized world was a great event for human progress. The fact of outward unity could hardly fail to produce a larger sense of inward unity. The forms of Roman law must have operated powerfully in the same direction. Roman sovereignty was the essential condition of the missionary career of Paul ; and the Roman empire must be regarded as a John the Baptist in the cause of humanity. The common love of Greek literature, the common pride in the empire, the common sense of justice and protection under its mighty shield, the passion for travel, and the prevalence of an unprovincial type of intelligence made admirable material for the staging of the temple of humanity whose foundations were then laid in the strength of the divine love in the gospel of Christ.

In the Protestant Reformation one beholds
the play of many forces. There is the play of
culture, the bolder confidence of the scientific
spirit, the increase of adventure and commercial
enterprise, the recent discovery of the character
of the planet that men inhabit, the allurement
of the great hemisphere sleeping in the sunset,
the birth of nations, the dawn of the modern
colonial era, the regeneration of the Christian
religion ; but best of all is the new sense and
the sublime assertion of manhood. The Reformation must be put down as the epoch in which
man began really to come to himself. It is to-
day the backer of every movement in the interest
of progress. Its momentum is as unspent and
full as that of Niagara. It is one of those periods in history when the organic structure of the
soul works with a terrible intensity, and when in
the sunlight of some man of genius it stands
revealed with an overwhelming majesty. Such
is the significance of Luther. He spoke for the
world's manhood ; he represents an epoch that
was an epoch for humanity.

V

The great mood of the nineteenth century is
the mood of humanity. In this century man as
man has meant more than in any other. The idea
of human brotherhood has been here from the
day in which Jesus began to preach his gospel ;

but it has been comparatively uninfluential. The world has not taken it up, or even seriously looked at it. And for this long and discouraging delay the teachers of religion must bear their part of the shame. The remark that the young Thracian woman is said to have made about the philosopher who fell into a well as he was looking at the stars holds true of them. She said that " he was so eager to know what was going on in heaven that he could not see what was before his feet." [1] A similar lapse has been the unfortunate experience of the thinkers who have ignored man on the pretense of discovering God. And the consequences of this fall have been as wide as they have been unhappy. It must, therefore, be repeated that while the idea of humanity has been here from the morning of time, it has been here as the western hemisphere is here. It has been, hitherto, practically an undiscovered country. It has slept for ages in a vast solitude. It has been isolated from the great currents of social interest. Granted that in Christianity the idea was once for all completely presented, Christianity itself has been the possession of the few. It has been but poorly understood, and still poorer has been the employment of it. Christianity has been waiting for man to come to himself; earlier than this its day of power cannot dawn.

[1] *Theœtetus*, 174.

The time arrives when the world takes up the great idea. Conceptions that stand at the door and knock, that no length of neglect can discourage, that have an everlasting confidence in their own persuasiveness, when they do gain admission to human life, come to stay. What Emerson says so finely of Burns may be said with equal truth of every great idea that has once really caught the ear and touched the heart of mankind : —

" The memory of Burns, — heaven and earth have taken too good care of it to leave us anything to say. The west winds are murmuring it. Open the window behind you, and hearken for the incoming tide, what the waves say of it. . . . The memory of Burns, — every man's, every boy's, and every girl's head carries snatches of his songs, and they say them by heart, and, what is strangest of all, never learned them from a book, but from mouth to mouth. The wind whispers them, the birds whistle them, the corn, barley, and bulrushes hoarsely rustle them, nay, the music-boxes at Geneva are framed and toothed to play them ; the hand-organs of the Savoyards in all cities repeat them, and the chimes of bells ring them in the spires. They are the property and the solace of mankind." [1]

Such has been the high destiny of the idea of humanity in the present century.[2] The thought

[1] Vol. xi. pp. 368, 369.

[2] " True humanity, the determination that the crying social

that seems to me the great burden of the time is the right of the people to be heard in all the occupations and concerns of man. In government, in literature, in science, in art, in philosophy, in religion, the people have met with a recognition such as they have never before received in the history of the world. It is the presence of humanity in them that has made all these old interests new. And therefore it is essential in any consideration of the religious meaning of the century to look at its humanity. That is the point from which its entire benign revolution in religion, and in all other high concerns, has gone forth. It is in order, then, to call up witnesses to the truth of this fundamental contention.

The first note of the new epoch of humanity is rung out by the fierce and far-resounding voice of the French Revolution. Many questions are still unsettled concerning that tremendous dissolution of society; but about the innermost character of the vast phenomenon there is now little room for dispute. Two books upon the subject,

evils of our time shall not continue, the certainty that they shall be abolished, an unwavering faith in human nature, have never been so strong, so vigorous, so rapidly growing as they are to-day. . . . The flowing tide is with us. We have great poets, great writers, great thinkers, to cheer and guide us; and an ever-increasing band of earnest workers to spread the light and help on the good time coming." — *The Wonderful Century*, p. 380. Alfred Russel Wallace.

both classics in our English literature, stand out
preëminent, one as the signal of essential misconception, the other as the interpretation of a
true prophet. Burke's famous book is a failure.
This is true notwithstanding all its high wisdom
in general remark, the wonderful sanity and
strength of much of its conservatism, its just
appreciation of many of the characters in the
drama, its fine scorn for notions that try to act
the part of realities, its magnificent command of
the English tongue, and the compass and grandeur of its imagination. Burke the statesman,
the lover of the antique, the chivalrous gentleman, the burning orator, was deeply moved
by the Revolution; but Burke the man was
hardly touched by it. The permanent value of
the work is, therefore, incidental to the main
purpose of it. It is, perhaps, the best text-book
in the language on political conservatism. It is
of great and enduring literary worth. It is a
monument to the genius and strength of the
author. It is all this and much more. But one
essential thing it is not. It is not a true reading of the character of the French Revolution.
And the reason for the failure is that Burke
thought too much about kings and queens, nobles
and clergy, and too little of the five-and-twenty
millions who in the judgment and practice of
the privileged classes "counted for nothing."
There is the secret of Burke's failure. The mul-

titudes who were worth everything for production, for national wealth and strength, had for generations counted for nothing. The anarchy of society in behalf of society, the insurrection against a conventional order in the interest of an indestructible human order, the revolution that was the despair and the hope of a nation gone mad under centuries of social and political outrage, Burke utterly failed to understand. His failure was foreordained the moment that as a student of the lurid event he laid aside his generous humanity.

Carlyle succeeded where Burke failed, because for him the French Revolution had a human interest. In its wild, waltzing whirlwinds he caught the voice of man. He cared little for the peculiar ideas that were working in the leading French minds at that time, and in the generation preceding. Rousseau, the great preacher of the rights of man, obtained but scant justice at his hands. Voltaire, in his campaign against the Infamous, does not strongly engage Carlyle's sympathies. The Encyclopædists, as a body, are oftenest the object of his humor and scorn. His political creed was in fundamental opposition to theirs; and his insight into the Revolution cannot be accounted for on the ground of his sympathy with the intellectual promoters of it. Carlyle's work may have faults of over-emphasis and lack of perspective. His book may be regarded as a series of brilliant pictures rather than a continuous history of his subject. When one listens to his unqualified praise of the Mirabeaus and Dantons of the period one is tempted to cry: "These be thy gods, O Israel." There are many merits of historical composition that may be denied to Carlyle's production; but there is one merit, and it is supreme, that no wise student of the Revolution will withhold from it. It regards the event as an event for man. The chief interest of the Revolution is not economic or political, but human. If it is an earthquake, it is a human earthquake. Its innermost meaning is moral. The rights of man that roll up in tides of fire from the volcanic depths, and whose utterance is so terrible, are the rights written by the finger of Destiny upon the human heart. They are the rights that conserve humanity. In the sad pretense of prayer for the debased and heartless tyrant, Louis XV., as he lies a loathsome mass upon his deathbed, the secret of Carlyle's success is told in a few short sentences: "Prayers! From a France smitten (by black art) with plague after plague, and lying now in shame and pain, with a Harlot's foot on its neck, what prayer can come? Those lank scarecrows, that prowl hunger-stricken through all the highways and byways of French existence, will they pray? The dull millions that in the workshop or furrowfield, grind fordone at the wheel of

Labor, like haltered gin-horses, if blind so much the quieter? Or they that in the Bicêtre Hospital, 'eight to a bed,' lie waiting their manumission?" [1] The history of the French Revolution is Carlyle's greatest work. Here he forgets himself, and walks among the awful scenes as Dante walked among the ever-deepening circles of hell, full of infinite pity, but sustained by the vision of eternal justice. His "desperate hope" becomes strangely bright and piercing as he sees in that terrible furnace whole worlds of immemorial inhumanity perishing, as he notes the signs of returning conscience and the resurgence of the divine in man.

It is interesting to find in a single song of Burns, written in 1795, five years after Burke's book appeared, and one year before the publication of the "Regicide Letters," the manly and magnificent utterance of the innermost meaning of the French Revolution. How bad the condition of social opinion then was may be judged from the fact that one of Burns's editors writes of this great song that " it may be said to embody all the false philosophy of Burns's time, and of his own mind." It is indeed the cry of essential manhood against all that is false and base in social custom. It is a better expression of Christianity than any utterance to be found in Scottish theology during the eighteenth cen-

[1] *French Revolution,* vol. i. p. 4.

tury.   It is the song prophetic of the triumph
of man over his inhumanity, and should be sung,
as Carlyle said of " Scots wha hae wi' Wallace
bled," " with the throat of the whirlwind."

" Is there for honest poverty
   That hangs his head, an' a' that?
   The coward slave, we pass him by —
   We dare be poor for a' that!
     For a' that an' a' that,
     Our toils obscure, an' a' that,
     The rank is but the guinea's stamp,
     The man 's the gowd for a' that.

" What though on hamely fare we dine,
   Wear hodden grey, an' a' that?
   Gie fools their silks, and knaves their wine —
   A man 's a man for a' that.
     For a' that an' a' that,
     Their tinsel show, an' a' that,
     The honest man, tho' e'er sae poor,
     Is king o' men for a' that.

" Ye see yon birkie ca'd ' a lord,'
   Wha struts, an' stares, an' a' that?
   Tho' hundreds worship at his word,
   He 's but a cuif for a' that.
     For a' that an' a' that,
     His riband, star, an' a' that,
     The man o' independent mind,
     He looks and laughs at a' that.

" A prince can mak a belted knight,
   A marquis, duke, an' a' that!
   But an honest man 's aboon his might —
   Guid faith he mauna fa' that!
     For a' that an' a' that,
     Their dignities, an' a' that,
     The pith o' sense an' pride o' worth
     Are higher ranks than a' that.

" Then let us pray that come it may
   (As come it will, for a' that)
   That Sense and Worth o'er a' the earth
   Shall bear the gree, an' a' that !
      For a' that an' a' that
      It 's coming yet, for a' that
      That man to man the world o'er
      Shall brithers be for a' that."

Such were the notes with which the last century closed ; such were the voices that sang their great annunciation hymn in the reddening dawn of the new time. In one sense the literary succession has not been true to this matin of the century. Scott was an aristocrat and a Tory ; Wordsworth and Coleridge lived to regret their first love for the Revolution, and partially, at least, to renounce their faith in it. Byron and Shelley and Keats count for beauty, hardly for the characteristic enterprise of the century, and not at all for ideas. Tennyson is no democrat ; Emerson, our own best voice, is mystic and beautiful, but somewhat vague and uncertain. Browning is the only literary genius of the first order that stands first and last and all the time for the inalienable rights and the sure progress of man. He is the century's one supreme humanist. The originality of his thought lies in its humanity, the total impression of his work is an impression for humanity. His human nature is the strongest thing in him, and more than any other writer in the English tongue he is the prophet of the century's deepest burden.

In an indirect way, literature in the nine-teenth century has been a new force for human-ity. Every great writer has written for the many rather than the few. Scott the Tory aristo-crat wrote for the people; and the people read, and while they read felt their humanity grow. With the exception of Wordsworth and Cole-ridge, all the leading writers aimed at becoming voices for the public; and even these two were restricted only by the manner of their message. John Stuart Mill set the fashion of writing phi-losophy for the average intelligence, and Her-bert Spencer and many others have continued it upon a very large scale. Similarly, all de-partments of history, economics, physical science, art, and theology have been written into a liter-ature for the people. Translation has become a new and an immense profession. The great clas-sics of the world have been done into English, and in many instances by scholars of first-rate attainments. The ancient Greek and Roman, the mediæval Italian, the modern Frenchman and German have been induced to speak in the English tongue. Sombre Egyptians from the yonder side of the Pyramids, wild Assyrians and penitential Babylonians from prehistoric times, stolid Chinamen, Persian fire-worshipers, and Hindu dreamers from before the flood, may be seen any day, in any good library, standing in such English dress as their queer mummy forms and skeleton shapes can be made to wear, and with a deep millennial pathos in their looks, waiting for readers. In the nineteenth century the whole higher literature of the world, along with a good deal of a different character, has risen as from an eonian sleep, and gone in search of the masses of mankind. This surely is significant. It is one great voice proclaiming the advent of democracy, and that too in an exceedingly aristocratic region. What can one see but a mighty regard for the people in the scholar who undertakes to make Aristotle and Spinoza, Kant and Fichte, Schelling and Hegel, so plain in an English form that wayfaring men though fools shall not err therein? There are humorous elements in the situation, no doubt. Still, when the voice of honest mirth has died away, it will be clear that, directly and indirectly, the literary activity of the century has been an impressive witness to the dignity of man.

For this is the fundamental meaning of the popular movement in literature. When all due allowances have been made for the hunger of authors, the ambition of publishers, and the necessity of creating the new profession of the translator to help in the settlement of the problem of the unemployed, one discovers a very noble remainder. Under this popular movement in letters one finds the working of a new insight, an insight into the universal human

capacity to share in the whole higher achievement of the race. The movement is an effect
of Protestantism, and had a religious beginning.
Wycliffe gave the Bible to the people; Luther
put the Scripture into the German vernacu-
lar. The highest literature in the world thus
went forth upon its mission to the multitude.
And this great innovation had its origin in the
insight of the Reformers; they saw that nothing
but custom and misfortune stand between the
humblest men and fellowship in the highest
wisdom of the race. This insight has spread
to all who deal in ideas. The great interests
show their greatness by their universality. The
problems of philosophy are human problems;
science deals with nature, and nature exists for
man; art is devoted to beauty, and beauty appeals both to the king and to the beggar; religion goes in the strength of the heavenly vision,
and that vision is for mankind. The race has
been set into all these great concerns of intelligence in a new way. The intellectual and spiritual achievements of the race are representative of the life of the race; and what owes its
existence to life must return to life in service
and solace. It would seem as if the great annunciation song were ringing out not only from
religion, but from art and science and philosophy, from all sides of the total nobler achievement of man: "Behold, I bring you good tid-

ings of great joy which shall be to all the people." [1]

Socialism is another great feature of the century. As to its worth there is the widest difference of opinion. The best-reasoned socialistic scheme may be open to insuperable objections. It may be that it does not reckon sufficiently with the laws and limitations of the physical world; that it is insensible to the necessity of the struggle for existence, imposed upon man both by his environment and his nature. It may be that in getting rid of all forms of individualism it would destroy character, stagnate enterprise, throw society into infinite confusion, make progress impossible, and suppress man himself. The debate must go on until political economists and social philosophers shall see eye to eye. But whatever one may think of socialism as a scheme, socialism as a sign of the times is worthy of all respect. The movement does not owe its origin to greed, or lawlessness, or idleness, or atheism. These forces have gathered round it, no doubt, as they do about every great enterprise. Let ten thousand soldiers march through the streets of any great city, in full uniform and arms burnished and bands playing; and another army twenty thousand strong, composed partly of the dignity and worth of the city, and partly of its waifs, its rags, and its

[1] Luke ii. 10.

crime, will accompany it. The army that represents the power and majesty of the nation must be distinguished from that which embodies the community's sad compound of honor and shame. The noble impulse of which socialism is one great sign should be clearly discriminated from all accompaniments. It moves by the authority of manhood. It is clothed with the dignity of all that is highest in human nature. It may be mistaken, but it is merciful. It may be wrong in its propositions for relief, but it sees and pities the sufferings of the multitude. It looks upon the tenant farmers of the old world, groaning under rack-rents, considers the marine, the mining, and the manufacturing enterprises of the world, and it sees everywhere conditions that make the heart sick. It cries out against the unnecessarily accumulated inequalities of society. In large sections of the industrial order there is beheld, working on a vast scale, and with a terrible cruelty, man's inhumanity to man. Whether this condition is or is not remediable or mitigable may be open to doubt. Whether socialistic propositions and remedies are wisdom or folly may lead to endless controversy. But that a deplorable state of things exists is beyond dispute ; therein lies the greatest service of socialism. It has been a mighty voice for a dumb world, a world that has borne in silence, and with infinite patience, and while

doing much of the best work of society, an immeasurable weight of suffering and wrong. Socialism has made men see and deplore this ancient horror. It has refused to believe that the
strong are made to drive the weak to the wall.
Through the whole range of its extravagances
there may be heard one clear and prophetic
note : " We then that are strong ought to bear
the infirmities of the weak, and not to please
ourselves." [1] It has borne consistent and tremendous testimony against the ethics inherited
from the first murderer : " Am I my brother's
keeper ? " It has been a rent in the rock of
inhuman custom through which have gushed
the springs that are deepest in man's heart.
Socialism is at least a witness to the power of
humanity.

In Jack and the Bean-stalk one of the things
that amazed the little man was the assimilative
capacity of the giant. The kinds and the quantities of food that the great creature devoured,
and the vitality by which they were converted
from their own character into the flesh and sinew
of the eater, were simply miraculous. Something like admiration mingled with horror
seems to have seized Odysseus as he watched
Polyphemus at his meals. Two men for supper, two for breakfast, and two more for a
second evening meal, without any of the refine-

[1] Romans xv. 1.

ments of dressing or cooking, and with endless quantities of milk and sweet wine added, constituted a new wonder for the mighty adventurer. The assimilative capacity even on a less extensive scale is indeed impressive. When one sees a flock of sheep eagerly and silently feeding in a piece of fine pasture, one can but wonder how it happens that the green always turns to white, and the white never to green ; one asks why it is that the sheep prevails over the grass, and not the grass over the sheep. When one considers what goes to make it, the whiteness of wool is a signal triumph of the power of assimilation. With little Jack one looks through an imaginative crevice upon the giants of these days ; upon the moose and bear that live in our woods, upon companies of elephants tearing through the thickets of the tropical forest, and the marvel is that these ravenous eaters do not turn into trees. A healthy human digestion is a standing miracle. The young Carlyle, in the drought and terrible fires of his dyspepsia, looks upon the old man Wordsworth eating raisins after dinner with the strangest compound of envy and wonder.

The feats of digestion, whether as exhibited in mythologies or in authentic history, reveal a great law of life. An organism may be called great in proportion to its assimilative power. And as there is, in addition to the physical

organism, an intellectual and a moral, it will
be seen that the capacity to take in, and to turn
into personal character, the resources of the
world, is of fundamental importance. The
power of Goethe lies in assimilation. He
turned the modern world into himself. This is
the leading characteristic of great intellect.
Whether through books or through contact
with nature and human life, or through all
three, the really great mind is forever adding
to its own substance. Emerson reads comparatively little ; he understands in detail the
thought of hardly any great master ; but he is
constantly brooding over a rich variety of ideas
gathered from all quarters of history. The face
of nature and the fresh countenance of man's
life are ever with him. In ways that the scholar
mocks at, in a manner that is the despair of the
systematic thinker, he yet builds his intelligence
upon the principle of assimilation into a structure solid and fine. Wordsworth turns away
from books, but all the more does he seek to
build his mind from nature and the human
heart. On the other hand, Carlyle, like Goethe,
reads books endlessly, and carries with him
through life the scenery amid which he grew
to manhood, the wide melancholy of the Scottish
moors, the bleak sad hills, the wild floods, the
mournful sky now beautiful with great white
clouds sleeping in the uncertain sunlight, and

again dark and pitiless as the coming of doom.
Ancient Greece lives in Plato and Aristotle;
mediæval Europe in Dante; the modern world
in Shakespere, Goethe, and Hegel, because of
the devouring eyes with which they looked upon
their respective environments, and the supreme
capacity which they possessed for consubstanti-
ating all things with themselves. The doctrine
of the Mass covers an important truth. Transubstantiation is the fundamental law of everything that lives. Industry, art, science, philosophy, religion, all are forms of transubstantiation;
they are the modes in which the universe ceases
to be a thing for itself, and in which it becomes
identified with man's existence, bone of his bone,
and flesh of his flesh. Because of the depth of
human appetite, and the various kinds of digestion with which man is gifted, owing to his
power to take over the universe into his life,
and to turn it, so far, into his own substance,
industry flourishes, art has risen up, science
pushes her dominion over ever wider spaces,
philosophy goes on her great mission of understanding, and religion lifts up her soul in rapt
insight and service. That Christianity should
have been able to take up into itself Hebraism,
Hellenism, and the really edible elements in
Roman civilization, has been universally regarded as a witness to its wonderful vitality.
An equally prevailing vitality this religion has

shown throughout its history. It has survived the fall of the ancient world and saved its monuments; it has encountered the rise of the modern era, mastered the most revolutionary conceptions of science, held its ground against pantheistic philosophies, and conquered them with its completer truth; it has come into conflict with the religions of the world, and again the prophecy is that they will be assimilated by it, and not it by them. Christianity might be called the Holy Spirit of assimilation. It has an organism of eternal vitality; it is able to take in all fact and all truth, to absorb the universe, and to turn it into its own substance.

A similar assimilative power has been shown in the last quarter of the nineteenth century by the idea of humanity. Evolution as at first preached was supposed to be the final blow to the unique dignity of man. After evolution was in control of the field, how one could still think of the human race as exhibiting a type of life essentially different from all other types, it was nearly impossible to see. The case seemed to be made out for the purely animal ancestry of man. For those who really understood the evidence the conclusion appeared unavoidable that all forms of life had a common and an extremely low origin. The old metaphor of the tree of life came back into human thought with strange implications. There is but one life;

there is but one organism of life. All forms of
being are nothing more than the different parts
and functions of this one gigantic mechanism.
The roots with their home in the darkness, and
the boughs beautiful with blossoms, or fruit-
laden, lifting up their heads toward heaven, are
kindred. The polyp in the pond, and man at
the summit of his intellectual and religious
achievement, are members of the one inclusive
family. Garden of Eden stories of special creation and special inspiration became incredible.
The idea of humanity had encountered the idea
of the brute, and it seemed to many, for nearly
a generation, that the man had lost and that the
brute had won. The conflict was not unlike that
of Horatius at the bridge. A few militant believers flung defiance into the faces of the whole
host of Tuscan scientists. When it was discovered that, unlike the Roman situation, there
was no bridge to be cut down, that the link was
missing between man and his prehuman fore-
fathers ; and when it was further seen that the
Tuscan side of the Tiber was becoming more
and more untenable, our defenders of the eternal
city sought the other shore. It was the beginning of wisdom on their part, and the dawn of
defeat to the enemies of the dignity of man
whom they had abandoned. The word differentiation had somehow been in the discussion
from the first. The last brute became the first

man by a considerable differentiation. And this original differentiation was the fruitful ancestor of a whole world of successively higher differentiations. Gradually under cover of these differentiations the territory which the man had lost, in his first desperate encounter with the beast, was restored. With allowances for a considerable difference in pedigree, human beings found themselves, after the conflict, in pretty much the same condition in which they stood before it began. The new theory showed a final willingness to be content with the simple demonstration of the sub-human origin of man. It abandoned all attempts to make further deductions from his dignity. It little thought that its demonstration of lowly origin would be used against itself, that its sinking of the pit in which man began would but render more impressive the elevation to which he has risen, that its supposed deduction from the dignity of human nature would turn out to be one of the most striking testimonies to its inherent worth and power. This is what has happened. John Fiske, Professor Drummond, and many others have impressed evolution into an unexpected service. In the light of this theory human history becomes a new thing, the achievements of man appear more and more marvelous; and the constant birth of fresh insights and sentiments and powers along the whole ascending path of development indicate, with resistless impressiveness, the high possibility and divine capacity of the original nature. If two thousand years ago one had been in California, and had witnessed the winds sowing the great spaces with seeds, one would have found it difficult to tell that out of which the giant tree of to-day was to spring and that out of which the shrub long since vanished was to grow. In the fists of the wind all the seeds looked pretty much alike; and yet in those differing seeds there was involved the promise of the whole mighty contrast that was evolved. In the light of their contrasted developments these nearly similar seeds fall into different classes; they stand apart from each other by the entire width and character of their separate histories. This is the work that evolution has done for the idea of man. It has unwittingly differentiated his beginning by the differentiation of his history. However similar in the mass of primitive life the seed that became man was to the seed that remained brute, under the mask of that similarity there was hidden the sure prophecy of the coming endless contrast. The romance of individual lives is nothing in comparison to the romance in the life of the race. Joseph taken from prison and made to sit upon the throne of the Pharaohs; Moses fished out from among the bulrushes and educated by the oppressor whom he was to destroy;

David found among the sheepfolds and anointed king; Martin Luther, the miner's son, raised to the greatest influence of his age; Oliver Cromwell, the obscure land-holder, lifted higher than any ruler that England ever had; George Washington, the surveyor, become the father of a mighty nation; and Abraham Lincoln, the rail-splitter, turned into one of the permanent and shining names of the world, are totally eclipsed by the race itself. Evolution that thought to cast man down to hell has raised him to heaven. The idea of humanity has met science in its extreme prejudice and enmity; it has turned the tide of prejudice in its own favor, converted the unbeliever to faith, and made its stoutest denier the confessor of its power. As the bell in the tower of the Cologne Cathedral that rings out the songs of divine love was cast from the cannon taken from the French in their attack upon the city in 1870, so the idea of humanity has captured the idea of evolution and turned the whole strength of its hostility into one vast, far-resounding pæan to the unique dignity of mankind.

To many minds, the greatest witness in the nineteenth century to the power of humanity is the wonderful missionary activity of the Christian church. Here it is necessary to rise above all private views and prejudices, if one would see the fact. When one has passed behind the limitations of theology, and discounted the presence and operation of morbid motives, the essential greatness of this astonishing missionary zeal is only the more clearly evident. It embodies a scheme, and the scheme is a stupendous one. It is nothing less than the plan of establishing the reign of Infinite love in all hearts, and among all peoples. It views all men as at least the possible children of God, and members of one great human family. It seeks the realization in society of something infinitely nobler than Plato's Ideal Republic or Augustine's City of God. It overhangs the race with an ethical idealism that is the sublimest and most precious possession of man. In the range and nobility of its conception, the missionary programme of the church has a right to the veneration of the world. It is a programme of the highest character, and it is for all human beings. Its scheme is simply an ideal for humanity ; humanity is the great note in the missionary intellect of the church.

This scheme has been adopted through faith. Its essential belief is brief. It is all contained in the words, " God so loved the world." [1] The ideal of the church for humanity is believed to have behind it the humanity of God. Its idea of Christ is equally explicit : " the love of Christ constraineth us." [2] The scheme is alive with the humanity of Christ. Because it is believed

[1] John iii. 16.　　　　[2] 2 Cor. v. 14.

that the Highest in the universe and the Best in history are for man, and not against him, the great missionary programme has been framed. The church finds itself in possession of a gospel for the whole earth, a gospel of divine sonship and human brotherhood. This is the audacious faith out of which the daring plan has risen. The humanity of God and the humanity of Christ and the humanity of the church together make up the great missionary chant. The limitations and the inhumanities of the traditional theology are disappearing before the irresistible logic of missions. The theology implicit in the missionary enterprise is conforming to its own human type the theology of the creed. It is not difficult to see what must be the scope, the freedom, and the vitality of the faith which is to support the movement for the evangelization of the world.

In a remarkable sermon Dr. T. T. Munger has given new expression to the range and character of pity.[1] He sees in it the last and finest result of the noblest nature. It is, in fact, the great nature absorbed with the poverty and the suffering of the little nature. It is the tribute, voluntary and involuntary, of the strongest to the weakest; at its best, it is the inevitable answer of God to man. The young athlete in the joy of his elastic strength experiences an

[1] *The Freedom of Faith*, p. 131.

involuntary pang as he sees the poor cripple
drag himself past. To those who are alive to
the magic of color and the beauty of the world,
the sightless eyes of the blind are most affecting.
The rich man who takes his heart with him and
makes a tour of inspection among the wretched
tenement houses of the city cannot suppress a
feeling of pain as he contrasts the narrow and
squalid homes of the poor with his own. Dr.
Arnold has said that the greatest rebuke that he
ever received came from the stupidest boy that
he had in his school. To his teacher's burning
sarcasm he replied with irresistible pathos of
truth, "I am doing the best that I can, sir." The
helpless pupil in his faithful and heroic endeavor
laid an immense hold upon the heart of the
accomplished scholar. The destitutions of men
always act in this way upon noble men of power.
This action of weakness upon strength is notice-
able to-day. Among the healthy for the sick,
the rich for the poor, the educated and wise for
the uninstructed and foolish, there is widespread
pity. As has been noted, the source of this
benign passion is the happy consciousness of
power looking down upon limitation and suffering. Pity comes with the development of man;
it is the badge of moral greatness. The pure
profound pity with which Dante looks upon
the horrors of the Inferno is an evidence of the
essential dignity and richness of his nature.

Devils have no pity for one another; rascals in proportion to their rascality are pitiless. The saving note in that greatest of all poems of despair, " The City of Dreadful Night," is the high and sacred voice of pity in it. It is the sad chant of a nature essentially noble and really great in its resources in the presence of vast suffering. The compassion of Burns for " Auld Nickie-Ben " does not rise from indifference to the eternal authority of righteousness, but from the greatness and happiness of the poet's heart. The thought that even the worst being in the universe should live in everlasting deprivation fills him with regret. From the wealth of his own heart, at home in every part of God's fair universe, he can but commiserate the outcast spirit. In the affluence and joy of his own existence he must needs pray : —

> " O, wad ye tak a thought an' men' !
> Ye aiblins might — I dinna ken —
>   Still hae a stake :
> I 'm wae to think upo' your den
>   Ev'n for your sake ! "

The pity of children is noticeably in proportion to the noble resources of their nature. The captive maid in the house of Naaman the Syrian general is the classic example from the Old Testament. Her own healthy flesh reflected in her happy mind made unendurable the sight of her master's leprosy. The cruelty of the world is inconceivable to children. Among the least fortunate among them pity is still easily reached. It is a spring in the desert, indicating that the destitute surface is not everything, proving that the forlorn life has a clear and unobstructed connection with the eternal deeps. It may be assumed, therefore, as a general truth that pity is an inevitable consequence in the rich and noble nature when it considers the weak and the suffering.

The pity of God is the eternal necessity of his nature in the presence of human need and suffering. Assuming that the Supreme being is infinitely wise and good, it follows that pity must be fundamental and everlasting in his character. Humanity must seem to him inexpressibly poor and weak. Its hand must be forever upon his heart. In all the universe the most moving sight to the strong and tender God must be man in his blindness and aspiration and suffering. It is this that, in the fine insight and phrase of John W. Chadwick, makes him "The Beseeching God"[1] The burden of the pitiful God is to get men to allow him to relieve their poverty and distress. The appeal of the universe is the ceaseless prayer of the Infinite strength for access to the needy soul. God lives in the eternal fullness of being; and the contrast between his ineffable life and man's is the

[1] "The Beseeching God," sermon in *Power and Use*, p. 87.

abiding assurance of his compassion. " He remembereth that we are dust." [1]

In the character of Christ pity is central for the same reason. The richness and the nobility of his spirit, the universe of love that lies open to him, the resources of his Father's nature that are at his command, lift him to an immeasurable height above the multitudes that follow him from town to town. And, therefore, when he sees them as sheep without a shepherd, he is moved with compassion. Pity is thus the passion that makes the lowest indispensable to the highest. It is the great conservative force in the moral world, the ultimate source of the patience and devotion that carry forward the total education of men.

This is the high passion out of which has risen the missionary activity of the church. It takes refuge in the strength of the supreme example: "Ye know the grace of our Lord Jesus Christ, that, though he was rich, yet for your sakes he became poor, that ye through his poverty might be rich." [2] Still the missionary community looks upon itself as rich. It has a command over the sources of wisdom and solace and moral power that makes its existence great. It is the thought of the nations lying in wickedness, the vision of them as outside the spiritual wealth of the world, destitute, afflicted, tor-

[1] Ps. ciii. 14.   [2] 2 Cor. viii. 9.

mented, when they might be in the temple of
peace, and in communion with the Infinite love,
that floods the stream of missionary zeal. The
deprivation of the Infinite is to the good man
the only intolerable poverty; and the spiritual
want and woe of the heathen nations appeal
overwhelmingly to those who are rich toward
God. The contribution of millions of dollars
annually to carry on this enterprise is the simple consequence of this inspired human passion.
A few may give from the force of tradition,
or early habit merely; others may contribute
as the only way of release from the foreign missionary beggar. Importunity is painful to the
person importuned, and the speediest end to
the pain may sometimes lie in surrender to the
appeal. But the great and generous supporters
of this cause have a profounder and infinitely
nobler motive. They are rich in their own
souls; the consolations of the Eternal are with
them, and they are not few. For them life has
risen into the consciousness of communion with
the Absolute Life, and therefore they are moved
by the whole strength of their rich possession to
try to cancel the deprivation of the nations.

Thus ideal and faith and experience together
work the great foreign missionary organization
of the church. The ideal frames its programme
of a divine life for all men; the faith supports
this programme with the nature of God and the

character of Christ; and the experience of the ideal, made more and more attainable in personal life by the faith, supplies the passion of pity that seeks to bring the race to the knowledge of the Infinite love. Whether as plan, or as religious belief, or as human tenderness, the missionary movement of the church is an impressive witness for humanity. The race stands as the object of its vast device, the concern of its great faith, the solicitude of its profound pity. Its ideal is for all, its God is for all, the treasures of its human heart are for all. This movement, originating in the highest thoughts and feelings of the Christian community, declaring its sincerity through thousands of lives of unsurpassed heroism and devotion, showing its power by the enduring organizations which it has called into existence, and by the multitudes whom it has interested in its cause, indicating its sanity by the countless acts of good to individuals which it has wrought, and yet more by the permanent connection which it has established between the nations of the earth and the richest and strongest force in human civilization, has but one meaning. It is one of the century's greatest voices in behalf of the needs, the rights, and the possibilities of mankind.

The last great servant to be named here, of the idea of humanity in the nineteenth century, is the United States of America. It is not unusual in these days to hear even from wise men criticisms upon the Declaration of Independence. One of the best and wisest of Englishmen, F. D. Maurice, found the special greatness of Lincoln to consist in the fact that he carried the policy of the nation back of the Declaration of Independence, and grounded it upon the theocratic faith of the Puritan commonwealth. And it is true that the humanity of Lincoln rested upon a divine basis. His best speeches have in them this high union of faith in the humanity of God with the purpose for the emancipation of the slave. Ever memorable are these words : " Fondly do we hope, fervently do we pray, that this mighty scourge of war may speedily pass away. Yet if God wills that it continue until all the wealth piled by the bondsman's two hundred and fifty years of unrequited toil shall be sunk, and until every drop of blood drawn with the lash shall be paid by another drawn by the sword, as was said three thousand years ago, so still it must be said that the judgments of the Lord are true and righteous altogether." [1]

There is, however, no real conflict between the Puritan belief in God and the view of human society embodied or implied in the Declaration of Independence. If there is any essential conflict, the right to victory rests with the great

[1] Second Inaugural Address.

Declaration.   Puritan theology in the eighteenth century had become formal and far from human. It was never an ideal theology; it never ceased to do violence to man's best thoughts about himself, and it fell infinitely short of an adequate expression of the mind of the righteous God toward mankind.   In the noble genius of its greatest representative, it has been well said that the great wrong which it did "was to assert God at the expense of humanity."[1] With all its high strength, Puritan theology was sadly in need of a broader and richer humanity. The Declaration of Independence can be so read as to make it the Bible of anarchy; but this is to commit outrage upon its spirit, and upon the ancestry of its political ideas.   The great document stands for the inalienable rights of man against the tyranny of power.   It embodies the ideas of French thinkers before the Revolution; but these ideas have proved a permanent addition to the political wisdom of the world.   When all is said against Rousseau and his political theories that honest and enlightened criticism must say, it remains that his political protest is the protest of human nature.   The significance for the American people of the Declaration of Independence lies in the fact that it was the faithful utterance of their aggrieved manhood. For the purposes of expression it was not bor-

[1] *Life of Jonathan Edwards*, by A. V. G Allen, p. 388.

rowed; it was original. As an assertion of principles and feelings it had its primary inspiration,
not in foreign political philosophy, but in the
popular intelligence and heart. Its ideas and
sentiments are indeed part of our native humanity. The Declaration of Independence is therefore the complement and correction of the Puritan theocracy. The nation began its existence
with a testimony to the rights and dignities of
man that shook the civilized world.

The modifications of government, within the
nineteenth century in the line of democracy,
seem to the writer to be due mainly to the example and influence of the United States. In
literature, science, philosophy, and educational
forms the United States has followed the great
European nations; as a witness for political
freedom it has led the world. The American
Revolution - preceded the French Revolution,
and if French ideas told here, American example told there. Great Britain may be slow
to admit it, but the fact is nevertheless evident,
that the greatest influence in carrying her from
a highly privileged monarchy to a practical
democracy has been the influence upon her
people of the United States. Where this influence has been resisted, as in Germany and in
Russia, it has still been felt; and no one can
measure the immense good that is sure to come
from steady progress in power and in self-con-

trol of the great Republic of the West. Throughout the civilized world, government at the close of the nineteenth century is a very different thing from what it was at the beginning; and in bringing about this vast change the influence of the United States has been predominant. When one considers that political institutions have a closer relation to the life of the nation than all others, and that more than all other forces they either improve or afflict the character of the people, preëminent and prevailing influence for justice and freedom in this chief sphere of popular concern must be set down as high honor. And this high distinction must be awarded above all competitors to the United States.

The receptivity of the people toward the leading writers and thinkers of the century, and the force of character with which they keep in circulation the ideas that make for human progress, deserve to be noted. Carlyle first gained his reading public in America, and notwithstanding his ingratitude, and all the savage things which he said about her, America continued her early recognition and admiration. Herbert Spencer has had a much more extended influence here than he has had in Great Britain. The wider religious implications of the evolutionary philosophy which Mr. Spencer has represented have been more broadly felt here than elsewhere, and this because of our larger intellectual hospitality. Browning is another great name that recalls the open-mindedness of the American people to merit, even when that merit comes in forms somewhat strange. Matthew Arnold, notwithstanding the pious contempt that never fails him when he writes about the United States, has had a wide and cordial welcome. The new biblical criticism has spread considerably even among our preachers. There is here a popular interest in physical science, in political economy, in large philosophical ideas, and in good literature of all kinds. Through the instrumentality of the universities of the country, and by none so conspicuously as by Harvard University, the best ideas and the best knowledge of the world are to find a new and promising field in the eager, receptive, and ambitious intelligence of the nation. This immense national hospitality has its darker side; but so long as the classics of the world have a larger popular market here than anywhere else, gratitude and hope must prevail over regret and fear. The national mind is, it is believed, more receptive and more sane toward the productions of genius and the thoughts of wise men, than any other equal body of intelligence in the world. The high receptivity, the noble sanity, and the abiding enthusiasms of the people of the United States have counted for much during the last hundred years.

The greatest war of the century was fought on American soil and by American citizens. This war is called the war for the preservation of the Union. That is its legal description. But it was something infinitely deeper than that. It was the conflict between the humanity of the nation and its inhumanity. It is one of the noblest struggles in human history. And when one thinks of the great future that lies before the United States, of the hundreds of millions that are to live their lives together here, of the procession of the generations and the centuries with their teeming populations, their unfigurable wealth and power, one must regard the war that preserved the Union, and that freed the slave, and that laid anew the foundations of the state in unrestricted humanity, not only as the noblest, but also as the greatest in history. It has not yet been written as some day it will be. We are waiting for the man of genius and of piety, who shall see its unique and permanent social significance, who shall exhibit its character and its issues in their own bright and everlasting light, who shall turn the great drama into an epic to be recited by our descendants down into the final sunset of time.

In the absence of a state church, in the toleration of all types of opinion, in the equal chance given to all philosophies of man's existence, the United States has placed religion upon a human

basis. It has shown its faith in noble ideas by
simply setting before them an open door. In
making religion optional it has allowed it room
for the disclosure of its everlasting necessity to
man. Temporary embarrassments have risen in
connection with this freedom. But they amount
to nothing in comparison with the total gain, in
comparison even with the single gain of honesty.
It is an immense advantage for national character when the real convictions of the people are
frankly uttered. Concealment of the ideas that
are really entertained is, when the habit concerns
large bodies of men, a public calamity. Freedom
of speech makes room for foolish speech as well
as for wise; but we have it on high authority
that so long as the fool is silent he is unknown.
The continuous silence of the fool may conduce
both to his own concealment and to the public
comfort; but this habit is hopeless for his con-
version. A nation that has the right of free
speech, and that uses it as this nation does, gives
itself away at once. The wise man sees his opportunity, the Christian has his task defined for
him, intellectually as well as morally. And here
comes in the gain to religion. If officially there
is less of it than in other countries, in reality it
is believed that there is vastly more. At least,
what there is of it is, on the whole, honest. And
all that an honest religion, an honest Christianity
asks is an equal opportunity with all other ideas

before the intelligence and conscience of the people. State churches have had the noblest and the most ignoble ideas urged in support of them. That man is depraved, that religion is not natural to him, and that unless he is coerced he will not attend to the chief concern of his existence, have been widely and seriously urged as the ground for state churches. The writer is aware that reasons infinitely nobler have been given.[1] But the most popular argument for them is the depravity of man. And Christianity has had, for a thousand years, to fight this mightiest foe in her own household. The conditions of religion in the United States are not artificial, they are human. It is assumed that religion is a universal interest, that it is the instinct of man to be permanently satisfied with nothing short of the best, that a fair field and no favor is essential to the discovery of the highest ideas, that Christianity is so surpassingly good, and so intrinsically desirable, and so fundamentally necessary to human life that it wants nothing, and will be embarrassed by anything more than an unrestricted and everlasting opportunity. Thus, in the ideas upon which it was founded, in the nature and scope of its political institutions, in the striking intellectual hospitality of its people, in the object and issues of its great war, and in

[1] See Maurice's *Kingdom of Christ* for a profoundly noble philosophy of state religion.

the human foundation which it asserts for religion, the United States has been, in this century,
the foremost servant of the idea of humanity.

For ages the civilized world has been enacting
the parable of the Prodigal Son. It has been
headstrong, revolutionary, bent upon pleasure.
It has taken its journey into the far country, and
there wasted its substance in riotous living. On
an enormous scale it has come to want. Under
the compulsion of hunger, it has hired itself to
many a base master; and in a thousand ways
the son has turned swineherd. But the story
does not close in sin and shame. The chief
thing in it is the fact that during this time man
has been coming to himself. This return of man
to himself has enabled him even in his disgrace
to see how far below him the swine and the
swine's fare are; how high above him his human
ideal is; how essential his own true nature is to
the appreciation of the Father whom he abandoned and toward whom he is now on the way
back. Because of the swiftness with which man
has been coming to himself during the nineteenth
century, despotic governments have fallen into
disrepute; the defenders of the privileges of the
few against the rights of the many have been
driven to the wall; the inhuman conditions of
labor have been assailed by a power that must
prove resistless; the brute world lifted by science into the circle of human kinship has been

unable to retain its new seat, and has now sunk to a lower depth than that from which it was taken; the nations in the great aggregate of their humanity, in the totality of their destitutions, and emphatically in their deprivation of the Infinite, have appealed to him with an inexpressible pathos; and he has begun to look up through his own nature into the clear sky and the eternal brightness of the Divine presence. And the peculiar passion of this return of man to himself, and the clear vision of the order of being that lies below him, of the unique order that he is in himself, and the world that is above him, and his own nature as the path into it, constitute the sovereign event in the nineteenth century.

CHAPTER III

I

WHAT nature is or means minus man no one has yet been able to say. If by nature is meant the physical and animate order, or the cosmos, what it amounts to independent of man would seem to be a hopeless puzzle. It would appear to be an instance of the lack of humor in philosophy, to ask for the meaning of one of two things in invariable relation, after the other had been suppressed or annihilated; to inquire for the significance of an outside that should have no inside; to demand a judgment upon the cosmos from man subsequent to his suicide. This is what the question concerning the meaning of the outward world, independent of the race, comes to. It not merely blindfolds humanity, and then bids it prophesy; it abolishes humanity, and afterwards calls upon it to discover and declare, in terms of that abolished humanity, the character of its great companion, the cosmos.

Still the admission may be made that the

cosmos is something for itself, that it has a character to exhibit to man. It follows that for appreciation, if not for existence, nature must look to human thought. The pageant of nature, supposing it to exist, is lost upon the brute. The cosmos had no lover, no worshiper looking up into her face with inspired wonder, until man appeared. The whole creation was in pain, in the pain of an unappreciated life, beating upward in an incessant aspiration toward the manifestation of the sons of God. Understood by the spirit in which it originates, the creation longs to be understood by the spirit in which it culminates. It may be conceived as feeling that when the sons of God should come, they would look back upon the vast process of which they were the consummation with insight and sympathy. The wonder of color, for example, waited for the development of the human eye. The fact of order remained unappreciated until man came. The sun had risen and set times without number, the moon had been the faithful witness in the sky of nights and months, the great constellations had swung themselves from horizon to zenith in an immemorial succession, the earth had put forth her tender leaves, brought the promise of the year to harvest, from a dateless past covered herself with the snows of winter, and the countless forms of pre-human life had been wholly oblivious of the varied and endless wonder. So, too, with the fact of progress. The ascent of life was ancient history before it began to be read. On the hither side of her life, nature depends for appreciation upon man. The song of the morning stars is unheard until the sons of God appear and answer it with their shouts of joy.

Now, as nature waited for the living appreciative senses and intelligence of man, so Christianity has waited for the coming of man to himself, in order to declare its character. Man is the interpreter of nature ; Christianity is the interpreter of man. Christianity would be thrown away upon the savage. Until man becomes aware of his manhood he cannot fathom the heart of the gospel. Thus far Christianity has been obliged to become a John the Baptist for itself. It has spent much of its force in preparing the way for the wider and deeper insight into its own character. Like some mighty original genius, it has had to create its own audience. In the world, and among the race that belong to it, it has been a stranger. So far its strength has gone into a preparatory discipline. Its purpose has been to lift man to his manhood in order that it might disclose its glory to him.

For man, the paths to the Infinite are nature and society. Both these paths or approaches are given in the nineteenth psalm, which may be called the song of two worlds. The outward world and the inward, the glory of the firmament and the great and solemn process of the social conscience unite in a declaration of the character of the Infinite as power and righteousness. These are the two worlds of Butler's "Analogy." There is the constitution and course of nature, and there is the order of human society under what Butler calls natural light, and again under what he regards as supernatural light. These are the two constitutions, and they amount to two manifestations of the Supreme being. These are the order of the physical universe and the character of human society into which modern science and common sense divide reality. They are the two things that impressed Kant with ever-deepening wonder. They form the nature and the spirit of Hegel as the twofold sphere of the Absolute; the extension and the thought of Spinoza that declare the one eternal substance; the sensuous image and the intellectual reality that together constitute Plato's universe.

These two fundamental aspects of reality become significant for religious thought according to the relation which each is made to bear to the other. There is the view that regards the cosmos as essential, at least in its elements and laws, and man as incidental. On this basis, inference to a cosmic mind is valid; but no higher character can be attributed to the deity thus reached than power. If the cosmos is greater

and more authoritative than man as a manifestation of the character of the Infinite, it follows
that human history must rank second to natural
history, the teachings of the social conscience
must be subordinated to the laws of chemistry
and physics, the significance of love must fall
below the higher meaning of force. This is the
view to which Mr. Spencer has given wide currency during the last thirty years. Human
society, human history, human existence is but
an incident in the measureless process of the
cosmos. It is a late comer in the immemorial
play of the physical order; it is the remembrance of a guest that tarrieth but for a day.
The aims of the cosmos are essentially non-
human ; they are human only in the way of incidence. Men appear at a given place and time
as part of the train and equipage of nature ; but
the vast procession soon has done with them,
and heedless of their vanished life, and with all
memory of them forever extinguished, goes forward on its endless way. This view has received
monumental expression in the poem of Lucretius.

There is, however, the opinion that defends
the opposite extreme, that looks upon nature as
beginning, and upon man as consummation.
Evolution has been turned into a teacher of this
conception. Which gives the higher revelation
of the life of the tree, the seed or the fruit ? It

has seemed that the best judgment upon the character of the ultimate life of the universe is that delivered by its best and highest expression. It has appeared as nothing more than obedience to sound logic to seek for the regulative conception of the Infinite in his best work. All things depend ultimately upon the creative impulse, and if out of that impulse have come thought and the world that thought has organized, love and the world to which love has given birth, individuality and sympathy and the social whole which they have brought into being, it seems only fair to allow the light of these worlds to fall backward upon the face of the great primal Inspiration. If Zeus made all things the Odyssey is a better expression of his genius than Olympus. If there is one life out of which all that is has come, human society is a higher revelation of its character than the cosmos. The path to God through nature can result in nothing higher than a religion of nature ; the approach to God through man must come to a conception of God as essentially human, and to a religion of the eternal humanity.

This is the proper place, perhaps, for a few remarks on natural theology. And the first thing that impresses one is the ambiguity of the term natural. By natural theology, Dr. Chalmers and writers of his day would seem to mean the witness for God, in the physical order and in human life, exclusive of Christianity and its new creation in the spirit. The limitation here is obviously artificial. To Paley natural theology amounted to cosmical theology. His true forerunner was a certain W. Derham, Boyle lecturer in 1711, who elaborated a physico-theology and an astro-theology, and whose German disciple, Fabricius, completed his master's work in a hydro-theology and a pyro-theology, which last designation might serve for a good deal of historical theology.[1] The deists opposed the natural to the supernatural, the rational to the mysterious and superstitious. The unaided reason was an idea common to them and their orthodox antagonists. This phase of the intellectual movement reveals strikingly the shallowness of its thinking. Individualism made depth and soundness of insight anywhere impossible. In still another sense the term natural was applied to theology, as theology credible on its own account. Augustine informs us that the Stoic teachers divided theology into three parts: the poetic or mythologic, the civil or political, and the physical or natural.[2] Here again nature is made to include all reality. For Paul " the invisible things " of God are a valid conclusion from " the things that are made." The creation is a path to the " everlasting power and

[1] *Essays and Lectures*, William Wallace, pp. 3–16.
[2] *The City of God*, vi. 5–12.

divinity ; " and again nature means the universal human conscience.[1]

It is but just to recognize under this mode of
thought a wide range of important truth. The
desire was for a faith that should be its own
witness. The feeling was that somehow there
was no incompatibility between reason and religion. The natural was the real, the orderly,
the permanent, the self-evidencing ; and belief
about the ultimate meanings of the universe and
human life must grow up out of that. For some,
Christianity had become hopelessly entangled
in superstition ; for others, it was in its essence
miraculous. The plain, stable reality, both in
the physical order and in the moral reason of
man, was the common resort of thinkers. Nor is
it difficult to see in this way of thinking adum-
brations of still greater things. Natural theology was a confused voice testifying to the fact
that man is the interpretation of the cosmos,
and that religion is the interpretation of man.
In man, the highest product of the cosmos, the
character of the aboriginal force behind the
cosmos is first seen. These writers were thinking of the interrelation between man and the
physical order ; they were feeling after the conclusion, although they did not find it, that since
intelligent man discovers himself in an intelligible world, the source of both must be in

[1] Romans i. 20; ii. 15.

Supreme mind. They believed that thought was the key to the interpretation of the universe, and therefore were forerunners of the endeavor that would show that the finite is intelligible only as it completes itself in the experience of the Absolute.[1] Professor Wallace thinks the phrase stands for " the application of science to religion, the interpretation of faith and worship by the intellectual principle, and in accordance with the results of ascertained knowledge." [2]

The trouble with natural theology is its confusions. It seems to be hopeless to try to clear them away. It would appear to be better to let the whole literature on the subject quietly die, and to begin the work of thought afresh. For the transmigrations of Inder are hardly a parallel to the transformations of the term natural on its romantic way through the world of faith. It means the cosmical, as in Paley, and the ethical, as in Butler. Now it is the rational with the deists, and again it is the irrational in the doctrine of the natural man. In Plato it is the highest of all attributes, the last account of the best order ; in Paul it is frequently the lowest, the mere beginnings of things. Its antitheses might serve as puzzles for a Pyrrhonist. They are not-man and full-man, animal and ethical, incredible and credible, not-real and

[1] Royce, *The Conception of God*, Supplementary Essay.
[2] *Essays and Lectures*, pp. 16, 17.

real, superstition and truth, lowest and highest, and so on *ad infinitum*. There is no denying that it is a wonderful word, and perhaps it is one that must always remain in use. The terms φύσις and νόμος mark a most important contrast in the thought, metaphysical and ethical, of the ancient world. Reality as opposed to convention must always deserve distinction. Nor can clear thinking get on without the fundamental discriminations that are carried by the phrases κατὰ φύσιν and παρὰ φύσιν. The idea of action in harmony with a fixed order or in violation of it is indeed basal. Whether as the translation of φυσικός, ψυχικός or σαρκικός, the word natural covers a mass of meaning that should be carefully conserved. Paul employs the term to denote both the physical order and the moral; and here is the germ that has become the disease of theology. Paul is blameless; for he supplied the correction in his use of the natural as equivalent to the beginning, the rudimentary, the imperfect, as the introduction to the spiritual that supersedes it.[1] Here is a supreme distinction, and it reminds the student of Aristotle's idea of soul. Soul is vegetative, sensitive, and finally rational; and the rational, while in continuity with the others, is their prophet and king. The physical order and the human are continuous; but they are not on the same level.

[1] 1 Cor. ii. 14; xv. 44.

Nor again is it valid thinking to separate the human and the christian or the human and the divine. Theology is indeed divisible into two departments, but it is unreal to describe them as natural and revealed, or to speak of one as the product of the " unassisted reason " and the other as dependent upon the fruits of inspiration. The true position would seem to be that all knowledge is revelation and that all revelation is knowledge. The truth is both an achievement of man and a gift from God. The two sources of the knowledge of the Infinite are the cosmos and humanity, and of the two, humanity is the sovereign.

Still, in relation to man the cosmos has a religious meaning. She presents two aspects to him, one of sympathy and the other of hostility. The cosmos is the basis of human existence, and her healing ministry both to body and mind is marvelous. God is waiting in the open spaces, in the great silences, in the wonder of sunrise and sundown, in the wild winds and the free air. The side of the cosmos sympathetic to man plainly implies an adjustment that has a religious value. And in no small degree this implication goes with the hostile side. Nature even in her fierceness is never a runaway horse; she is always under control. She seldom does more than warn man to keep to his own side of the road. Even in the severest aspects of the

physical order the psalmist could see a religious
meaning : " stormy wind fulfilling his word." [1]
True the cosmos gave man being and she takes
it back finally in every instance ; but while life
lasts her antagonism is mitigated by regard for
human endurance. In a rough way it implies
consideration and pity. The saying of the clown
in Lear, that Dr. Mulford was so fond of quot-
ing, —

> " Here 's a night that pities
> Neither wise men nor fools," —

is not true, for both wise man and fool survived,
which could not have been had not that terrible
night pitied them. The limitation that lies
upon nature's hostility to man is too constant
for chance, and it has, besides, too long a history
for anything short of intelligent consideration.
The proverb that the wind is tempered to the
shorn lamb states the general truth that between
the fierceness of the cosmos and human endurance there is an established relation. Otherwise there would swiftly be an end of all things
human.

It must be further noted that nature's antagonism to man is the condition of much that is
valuable in human life. Physical necessity becomes moral inspiration. The food-problem
originates in the stern necessity of nature. If
he is to eat at all man must do it in the sweat

[1] Psalm cxlviii. 8.

of his brow. The pressure upon the race as a
bread-winner is benign. If we look at the facts
and do not fly away into imaginary worlds, we
shall find that the meagre ready-made provision
which nature offers to man is one source of civilization. The immensely diversified production
and distribution of to-day, and the social combi-
nations that the present industry of the world
necessitates, are an evolution. And that evolution has for its primary inspiration the hostility
of nature. There are enormous evils incident
to the working of the present industrial system ;
still, the general result is an influence for social
unity and good-will beyond calculation. It may
be said that through her meanness nature has
forced men to industrial organization, and this
has led into a new world of social sentiment.

The same remark applies to dress. The
dressless savage is encouraged in his inhumanity by the excessive kindness of nature. Dress
has its origin in physical necessity, but it passes
at once into a teacher of self-reverence. It has
a more incessant and powerful influence upon
character than any other human custom. In
the Bible story sin is made the beginning of
dress, and there is the deepest truth in the
legend. God alone is worthy to look upon
life unclothed. Human beings need protection
against themselves and against one another.
The functions of life are too sacred, and the

feelings proper to such functions are too delicate for anything but the innermost shrine of the holy of holies. Shame is but an aspect of reverence. It is at once the indication of unworthiness in the presence of life, and the confession of the awful beauty inherent in life. Nature's severity is again the friend of man. The pitiless day is but the herald of the gospel of human dignity, the high compulsion that drives the race out of the vulgarity of the brute into the self-reverence of the man.

The dwelling is but the extension of dress into a further protection against nature. And in looking at the long evolution of human habitations, in considering the advancing improvement in successive centuries, in noting the sphere that art has found in beautifying man's dwelling; above all, in estimating how much the word home owes to the place and the structure and the utilities and adornments to which it is attached, it is impossible to think without respect of the sternness of climate to which it is primarily due. In the rich texture of the word home one discovers, woven thread for thread with a father's love and a mother's tenderness, a brother's affection and a sister's sympathy, the green of nature's fields, the blue of her skies, and the fierceness of her storms. The confessor at the domestic shrine should not forget the religious austerity of nature.

Thus far in our discussion nature has meant that section of the cosmos that lies behind animal life, and that is the ground of it. Still, nature as inclusive of all forces and all forms of life below man is a familiar conception. And recently there has been noted with fresh insight the play of feelings within the animal sphere that in their richer development make human society possible. The struggle for life and the struggle for the life of others have gone together from the beginning; and in the nutritive and reproductive functions there has been seen the physical basis for the individualism and the socialism that are features of all forms of life, that eventually appear in man in a more momentous process, and that when they have vindicated the reality of the individual and assured the equal fullness and permanence of public interest shall become an eternally reconciled passion of love. The survey of the animal life below man may well be with sympathy. In that sphere there is a rude prophecy of human society; the eternal builder of man's world is at work there, and in the rising tide of social feeling there is the hint of the fullness of Christ's love upon the cross.[1]

It will be observed that, according to this discussion, the religious value of nature rests upon a recognized adjustment of nature to man.

[1] For extended discussion of the final meaning of nature, see *The Christ of To-day*, pp. 81-93.

Nature as interpreted through man originates in the moral reason of God. What is last in development is first in the intention. Man as the product of nature is the final account of the power behind nature. This is the basis for the larger conclusions already mentioned. Man finds nature intelligible, and the assumption is nearly inevitable, that human intelligence and the intelligible cosmos are unified in Supreme mind. The celebrated " design argument " is at heart but the endeavor to read the history of nature through mind. Both its cosmical and human divisions have no other end. The evidence of mind in man's dual world compels the retreat upon Creative mind. The validity of the process consists in the recognized adjustment between intelligent man and his intelligible environment. In the interesting and thorough discussions of Professor Royce, to which reference has been made, the final meaning of nature is arrived at in this way. Nature becomes at last but a phase of the experience of the Absolute person, and this generalization is founded upon the relation of nature to the limited human person. Pressed by the consciousness of incompleteness, and by the logic of idealism, nature turns out to be but an aspect of the Divine mind. In tracing the interrelation between man and his environment, a new natural theology may be developed, if thinkers will persist in the use of that term. It will have many divisions. The intelligent and the intelligible will be one section, the physical and the moral will be another. To these will be added the interactions between man and nature that have resulted in art and religion. The study of historic man in his cosmic environment must not be overlooked. Upon the basis of the recognized interplay between the cosmical and the human large and luminous conclusions concerning the Creator may be drawn.

But it is time to come to the point of these remarks. They are made mainly as a concession, and to prevent misunderstanding of the position now to be stated. Regarded as something by itself the cosmos has no religious value. The fault with whole libraries of natural theology lies here. The human meaning of nature was not seen, and therefore the divine could not be found. Endless ingenuity is expended by a succession of writers, many of them of great ability, from Paley to Chalmers, in exhibiting special adaptations in the external world, but the position is never reached that the external world derives its whole religious value from its relationship to man. It is another evidence of the genius of Bushnell that he saw this relationship. To him nature had a divine because it had a human meaning. The full title of his greatest book marks the position for which I contend, and it indicates an enormous advance over the Bridgewater treatises : " Nature and the Supernatural as together constituting the one System of God." What was imaginative insight with Bushnell, an idealistic philosophy has rendered in the forms of reasoned thought. And one of the signal achievements of idealism is the demonstration of the human meaning of nature. By herself she is no longer anything. As the partner of man's life she lives and moves and has her being. Her colors, sounds, flavors, and odors ; her softness and hardness, her space and time, are what they are in and through human intelligence. Even her universal and persistent force becomes intelligible only through man's will.[1]

---

[1] During the last twenty years many able and admirable books on theism have appeared, among the more important of which are Flint's *Theism*, Janet's *Final Causes*, Harris's *Philosophical Basis of Theism*, Diman's *Theistic Argument*, Fisher's *The Grounds of Theistic and Christian Belief*, Knight's *Aspects of Theism*, an unsatisfactory discussion but highly suggestive, and Professor Fraser's *Philosophy of Theism*. What may be termed the older theism receives an expression in Professor Fraser's volumes that leaves hardly anything to be desired. Still, one longs for, if not a new, a more explicit point of departure. Theism is essentially the human interpretation of the universe ; it is the result of the personal spirit of man used as the key to the meaning of all existence. From the explicit admission of this as foundation, and from fidelity to it, a new theism may be evolved. It need not be less thorough philosophically, and it would be better founded, richer, more human and greater in reality.

Those who first take the humanity out of her, and then proceed to commune with God through nature, are simply nourishment for humor. Thus conceived the religion of nature is a sham. Without man's mastery what will nature do for him? She will supply him with air and water, both badly adulterated, in all likelihood, and with acorns and sour apples. She will roast him in summer and freeze him in winter. She will not hunt or fish or cook for him. She will not build even a log-cabin to shelter his children. To watch by him in sickness, and to change his whole environment that he may get well is far from her thoughts. Only man can thus serve man. And yet, because nature is an æsthetic wonder and inspiration, because in relation to the human spirit she has this magnificent charm, and through her adjustment to man's sensibility and insight she takes on the character of source and cause of great moods, certain writers, forgetting that society owes almost all its comforts and graces to the mediation of persons, go about vaporing over the glories of the cosmos, as if in these, considered by themselves, there lived eternal regard and profusion for social welfare, instead of eternal stinginess and indifference. Nature becomes all that she is for man through man. In this association of nature with man, in the large place that is hers in his education, as field and oppor-

tunity, primal sympathy and benign hostility, as
intelligible world to his thought and aspect of
the ordered experience of the Absolute Spirit,
and finally as the force that upon touching him
becomes life and fire and victory, a light can be
seen in her face truly divine. She is the organ
behind the choir. Her form, pipes, stops, order,
and compass bear witness to the creative spirit
of man. She is something in herself no doubt,
but her elemental energies have taken this grand
musical shape largely in response to the genius
of humanity. Even when nature has been built
into this great supporting instrument, she is
dumb without the magic touch of the human
musician. The world of laws and harmonies, in
which are set the voices of human endeavor and
hope, is a world called out of nature by the play
of man's thought. Without man, nature is but
crude possibility ; with man, she attains to order
and definite reality; and all that she is for
humanity she has become through humanity.
A religion of nature is, therefore, a religion of
an inferior kind. It is the consecration of the
basis of physical existence, the apotheosis of the
cosmic environment abstracted from the mighty
race set in its heart. Indeed, for a moral being,
the religion of nature is no religion at all. And
this would seem to be the conclusion toward
which wise men are more and more tending.
The poverty of the conventional theism is seen

in Mill's examination of it![1] It is amazing that
a thinker of Mill's honesty and capacity should
not see that the cosmos was but the smaller part
of man's world, and that man himself is an
immeasurably stronger argument for God than
the physical order. Somehow the "unassisted
reason" of the orthodox thinkers developed into
a self-sufficing humanity that, for writers like
Mill, could bear witness to nothing but itself.
Something like this must be the explanation of
French atheism in the eighteenth century. The
new insight into the perfectibility of man, the
unmeasured capacity in the individual for self-
improvement, and the irresistible force by which
society advances, come to nothing for theism.
In the more eminent of the Encyclopædists there
was a faith in man that should have led to a
new faith in God. As it was, they never went
beyond a half truth; and this half truth Mill
inherited. The perfectible race became the self-
sufficient race, and this conclusion was justified
by the habit of thought that regarded all human
achievements outside those belonging to the re-
generate life as products of the "unassisted
reason." Happily this entire mood is now part
of the former things that have passed away.
Cosmic theism is a secondary, even a slender
affair. This does not ignore the presence of
mind in nature; it simply subordinates it to the

[1] J. S. Mill, *Essays on Religion.*

mind in man. It is true that "man discovers his own intelligence in making nature intelligible," and that "man develops and disciplines his own personality in the struggle with what appears a hostile nature, and so nature, even in its opposition, becomes a minister of spirit;"[1] at the same time, this contention is a confession of nature's subordination to man, at least for theistic purposes, as its author meant it to be. Nor is there here intended any discrediting of the principle of cause and effect. As an inference from a dependent world to an independent the old theism is valid; the trouble is with the meagreness of its dependent world. The new theism insists that there is a humanity to be accounted for. In the world of events there is Christ; there is, besides, the new humanity in his spirit. The inferential procedure of theism is as old as the human mind and as wide as the presence of reason in life; but the fact upon which its august conclusion is based has become new.

This reach and richness of the fact upon which belief in God depends is what Schelling refers to in one of his lectures: "That is no real knowledge of God where he is merely object; either God is not known at all, or he is at once subject and object of knowledge. He must be at once our very self, our heart of hearts, and yet

[1] *The Ritschlian Theology*, p. 59. A. E. Garvie.

comprehending all hearts far beyond us." [1] It is acknowledged that the highest meaning of the universe can be known only through man, its highest product. All true religion must be, therefore, a religion of humanity. Man as the interpreter of nature and the revealer of God, gives his own name to the product; and for a natural theology he substitutes a human theology, which, in its highest form, becomes Christian theology.

II

In a stall carving in Winchester Cathedral a pig is represented playing upon a whistle, the companion carving to which is a pig playing upon a violin, in accompaniment to which another pig appears to be singing. It must be remarked that these musical pigs in a great Christian church are still nothing but pigs, and the meaning of the stately edifice in which they live is not for them. Enthusiasms directed upon pigs may be useful, but they do not prepare the mind for the highest interpretation of the character of the universe. Pigs may be kept in clover, but they are not at home in churches. It was a true religious instinct in the Hebrew that early and lastingly divorced these two incompatible objects. And yet it must be confessed that the musical pigs in the Christian temple

[1] Quoted by W. Wallace: *Essays and Lectures*, pp. 58, 59.

have a symbolic meaning of high importance for students of religion. Here in parable is the source of human failure to understand Christianity. The pig has somehow been the standard of judgment, — a refined pig, a gifted pig, an accomplished pig, a musical pig, indeed, but still a pig. This is the mood that in the world and in the church has made the high appeal of the religion of the cross, in a true and in a large sense, as good as wasted. Pig philosophy cannot understand Christian philosophy. The thing is sheer impossibility. In such centuries Christianity must work silently and unconsciously as evolving force, changing the pig into the man.

It would be rash to say that this has been satisfactorily accomplished. Still, considerable progress has been made in the right direction. The best wisdom and spirit in the world have not been wholly without effect. More and more since Socrates turned from the study of nature to man, the successive centuries have given a deeper if often a sadder sense of human supremacy. For the dominant mood at the close of the nineteenth century a new symbol must be found. Let it, too, be found in the Christian church. Let it be remembered that in the Strasburg Cathedral there is a clock that represents the order and movement of the solar system. The position of the planets in relation to one another and to the sun is truly indicated, and the hours as they are rung out repeat the goings and register the doings of this great section of the heavens. But high over the clock and its solar arrangement appear Christ and his apostles. The hours as they are rung out show these apostles revolving round their Master. They hint that the Divine man is above all things, and that the order and movement of the physical universe have their full meaning only in the light of human history. They declare that nature is for humanity and that humanity comes to the complete sense of itself only in Christianity. This is the symbol for to-day; this is the mood which Christianity has created and to which it makes with new hope its ancient appeal. The passion for humanity, as will be seen at once, is the best sort of preparation for a new appreciation of Christianity.

Christianity is not a religion of nature. It has no quarrel with nature. The cosmos and the play of life there are the great sensuous analogue of the spiritual world, the vast mirror in which man may behold his own face. Hence the parables of Jesus, where nature appears, not as in the hands of the teacher of science, but as poetic symbol, as large and free form for ideas that belong essentially to the human sphere. The relation of nature to man has indeed become a new subject. The progress of knowledge and the presence of a sounder philosophy make pos-

sible a deeper insight into that relation. The
Christian miracle is sure to emerge for fresh
discussion. The comparative silence that has
overtaken the miraculous in the gospels marks
indeed, like nightfall, the end of one stage in
the toil of the Christian intellect; but after a
period of repose one may anticipate a new day
for this whole subject. Nothing that has reality
in it can be banished as illusion. And the
miraculous has too vast an association with man
to mean nothing; it has too intimate and deep
an association with Christ not to signify something great. Still, it must be borne in mind
that Christianity works not through nature but
through man. The forerunner of Christianity
is a man : "There was a man sent from God
whose name was John." [1] The origin of Christianity is set forth by its philosophical apostle,
not in terms of nature but of humanity : "When
the fullness of the time came, God sent forth his
Son, born of a woman." [2] Christ puts man in
contrast to nature as a value for God : "Are not
ye of much more value than they?" [3] According to Christ nature is indeed a teacher of the
divine economy, but in a manner quite insignificant when put into comparison with human
history. The central idea of the gospel is that
man is essential to any expression of the moral
character of the Infinite, and that man at his

[1] John i. 6.   [2] Gal. iv. 4.   [3] Matt. vi. 26.

best gives God at his best. This is the heart of the Christian doctrine of the Incarnation. It is the exaltation of man in the person of the Supreme man, as the organ of the Eternal righteousness. The current teaching concerning the dignity of man indicates the sympathy that exists between the characteristic mood of the time and the central message of the gospel. The age that has come, in a deep and serious way, to think well of mankind, is in a promising condition of mind toward the religion that claims its disciples as an elect race to show forth the excellencies of the electing will, that looks upon the nations as ordained to become the habitation of God through the Spirit.[1]

The fundamental idea of the gospel may be stated in a sentence. The glad tidings consist in an ideal incarnation of God in the interest of a universal incarnation. The Eternal wisdom was made flesh in Jesus Christ. Reversing a phrase of a German theologian, it may be said that God has for men the value of Christ. He is the perfect human utterance of the moral being of the Infinite. According to Christian teaching Jesus is the utmost that God can do for mankind. That this was Christ's conception of himself is seen in the parable of the vineyard: " He had yet one, a beloved son: he sent him last unto them, saying, They will reverence my

[1] Peter ii. 9; Eph. ii. 22.

son." [1] Jesus here represents himself as being the last and best that God can do, his supreme single achievement. He becomes, therefore, the standard of all human life, the model for mankind. This uniqueness for the sake of universality Jesus is continually setting forth. " No one knoweth the Son, save the Father ; neither doth any know the Father, save the Son, and he to whomsoever the Son willeth to reveal him." [2] In this remarkable passage it is claimed that perfect fatherhood alone knows perfect sonhood, that the ideal filial consciousness alone can fathom the paternal mind, and that this perfect filial spirit is the only sufficient mediator to mankind of the true knowledge of God. The expression " Son of man " would seem to have several meanings upon the lips of Jesus ; still, its highest significance is clear. It is the announcement that Jesus is the standard man, the measure of use and worth, the σπουδαιος ἄνηρ of Aristotle, the Lord even of the Sabbath. It asserts that Jesus is unprivileged, that he is full of sympathy, that dominion is in store for him, as Professor Bruce says, and it doubtless serves, according to the same writer, as an incognito.[3] But it runs up into the assertion of the pure and sovereign humanity of Jesus. The designation, Son of God, serves the same double purpose. It

[1] Mark xii. 6.   [2] Matt. xi. 27.
[3] *Kingdom of God*, pp. 172–177.

asserts the unique for the sake of the common.
" He that hath seen me hath seen the Father; "
" I and the Father are one." [1] These passages
express what in the consciousness of Jesus is
without parallel, and at the same time the con-
text in each case makes it plain that the aim of
Jesus is to establish a kind of parallel to himself
in his disciples. The first words of the Lord's
Prayer, " Our Father which art in heaven," are
a classic revelation of the mind of Jesus. He
and his disciples, and, by implication, all men,
are sons of God; and yet it is clear that the
Master, whose stamp is upon the great prayer,
is Son of God in a special way. He proves his
unique filial consciousness by finding and au-
thenticating a voice for the common filial consciousness. Jesus calls himself " the bread of
life," [2] with the evident purpose of claiming for
himself manhood pure and complete in its substance, carried to its best by divine education,
and as divine result offered to the hunger of the
world. The metaphor is essential to the idea.
The meal is the best, the baking is the best, the
loaf is the best. In endowment, in training, and
in resulting character Christ is unique; and yet
this uniqueness is in the interest of the universal
human capacity. Other self-characterizations of
Jesus are equally remarkable. He is the centre
of rest: " Come unto me all ye that labor and

[1] John xiv. 9; x. 30.   [2] John vi. 35.

are heavy laden and I will give you rest." His humanity is the judgment of the nations : " Inasmuch as ye did it unto one of these my brethren, even these least, ye did it unto me." He is the source of the life which he shares with his disciples : " I am the vine and ye are the branches." He is the suffering love by which his people are saved : " The good shepherd giveth his life for the sheep." He is the meeting place between the living truth and the human heart : " The sower went forth to sow." He is the life that cannot die, that in itself is resurgent, and that in its resurgence sets forth the divine law : " I am the resurrection and the life." [1] Here is a sample of the testimony of Jesus to himself. The nature of it seems to me to be plain. It is everywhere the assertion of the unique for the sake of the common. Ideal would appear to be the fittest modern expression for the consciousness of Jesus. The ideal is always the unique and it is always universal. If it were not absolutely distinct in its perfection it would have no right to become the possession and rapture of all good men. Nothing but the ideal can be the ideal ; no one can be Christ but Christ. What other men ought to become he is.[2] His uniqueness is assured by his place in history, his individual-

---

[1] Matt. xi. 28 ; xxv. 40 ; John xv. 5 ; x. 14 ; Matt. xiii. 3 ; John xi. 25.

[2] Wendt, *Teaching of Jesus*, p. 386.

ity, his distinct contribution to the highest culture of the human spirit. There is a yet deeper assurance. It goes with the note of perfection in his character, it lies in the fact that he is the standard man. Christianity does not deal in abstractions. Its ideal is personal life. It calls upon men to fashion their spirit and behavior, not in the presence of a heavenly conception, but a divine man. For the gospel there is no God, no moral government, no moral reality except in and through human society. And the perfect man gives at once the real life of God and the ideal life for man.

This ideal incarnation of God in Jesus Christ the New Testament writers are very careful to maintain.[1] One says, "God was in Christ reconciling the world unto himself;" another declares that he is "the very image" of God's substance; another that he is the manifestation of the Eternal Life, and that in consequence he is the standard of all moral excellence for the disciple; and another that he is the inspirer of belief in God in the Christian society.[1] A typical statement of the special for the general is the declaration: "Because ye are sons, God sent forth the Spirit of his Son into our hearts crying, Abba, Father."[2] Here there is the recognition of universal human sonship in the light and under the

[1] 2 Cor. v. 19; Heb. i. 3; 1 John i. 1–3; 1 Peter i. 21.
[2] Gal. iv. 6.

inspiration of the unique sonship of Christ.
This mode of thought pervades the New Testament. It is part of the substance of the whole
thought of Christ; it is a permanent and discernible element in his consciousness. He is
first of all something for himself, something in
himself, something distinct and transcendent in
his relation to God. And because he is this in
and for himself, he is a possession for mankind.
He calls himself "the light of the world;"[1]
there is the note of his eternal distinction. He
tells his disciples that they are "the light of
the world;"[2] there is the sign of his significance for all men, the token of the standard and
inspiration that his revelation of God becomes
to them in theirs.

To-day the insight of religious men is weakest
at the point of the ideal incarnation. It is
nearly impossible for the serious student of the
New Testament not to see that it is part of the
consciousness of Jesus. But it is for most men
so difficult to understand that it is allowed to
drop out of faith, and the universal incarnation
is seized upon and made to do duty for the whole
truth. This substitution of the second for the
first, the derivative for the original, the universal for the archetypal, is in the face of the entire
teaching of the New Testament. This strange
procedure is not from irreverence; its source is

[1] John viii. 12.   [2] Matt. v. 14.

rather in the honestly confessed failure to see
the reality or the utility of the unique in Christ.
Because it is the result of a limitation in insight
it is sure to pass away. It is to be forgiven if
the father in the joy of his first-born for a moment forgets the mother. The dear possession
that temporarily limits his vision is sure to ex-
pand it wider than ever. The love of the child,
while it may be, for a brief space, exclusive,
must finally lead to a new appreciation and veneration of the suffering life through which it
was made possible. The fondness of the father
for the child is the certain promise that the
mother cannot be permanently forgotten. Unitarianism especially is in this mood. She is in
rapture over the child. The question of origin
is forgotten in the joy of possession. The derivative truth is so precious that the original
has been allowed to pass out of sight. But this
dandling of the baby at the expense of the homage that belongs to the mother cannot last. The
incarnation, of which all men are the subjects,
will lift and extend the happy vision to the
ideal incarnation in Jesus Christ. The child
and the mother belong together, and the truth
of the utterance of God through all good men,
which wields over many noble thinkers to-day
an exclusive fascination, must sooner or later
cry out for the renewal of vigor that can come
only through the great mother truth of God's
unique utterance through Christ.

Upon this subject the critical spirit must become the sympathetic and understanding spirit. There is a fact to be studied, and, if possible, understood.[1] The fact lives in the gospels, although not exclusively there. The fact is the value which Jesus seemed to possess according to the supreme judges, himself and those who best knew him. For this part of the fact the source is the New Testament. For the value of Jesus to the life of Christendom, history is the source. The evangelical source especially calls for a deeper and a more discerning study. Fact yielding up its meaning to insight is alone decisive. Putting situations and sayings and doings together, one may come to frame a picture of the apocalypse of Jesus. In this way of deference and patience, as the only way to master the results of scientific investigation, in the mood that assumes that the object of study is a transcendent one, in the manner of sympathy and love, it is still possible to see the Lord. Let it be understood that criticism of the sources is but the beginning of thought. Let the material

[1] "In this study of the Person of Christ, the stress of thought and inquiry has been laid upon his moral character, his human insight and sympathy, his spiritual elevation; and above all his consciousness of entire and perfect union with the Father, yet with no sense of guilt or confession of sin or cry for forgiveness — characteristics making his career unique in the religious history of man." Professor A. V. G. Allen, *Christian Interpretations*, p. 383.

be thoroughly and honestly considered. It is already evident that from scientific criticism as basis for spiritual insight faith has nothing to fear.[1] Still, vision is the final thing. One must see the Lord. What one does not see one must not pretend to see. But again positive discoveries should be honestly reported. That Jesus thought of himself as having a unique relation to God, and on that account as having a universal mission to men, seems to me beyond doubt. That Jesus encouraged his disciples to think about him in this way, likewise appears to me plain.

This manner of thought upon the part of the Master and his disciples may be all wrong. On the other hand it may be the truth. The presumption of truth would seem to be in favor of the New Testament rather than the destructive critic. The reality in question is confessedly so high and serious that it would seem to be less likely to overestimate or misunderstand itself than the most accomplished outsider. Upon this question of a unique incarnation of God in

[1] " The idea that the severely critical consideration of the gospels . . . would render problematical the historical figure of Jesus, or at all events derogate from the ideal loftiness and purity of his life and teaching, we must at this day pronounce as simply obsolete. Critical inquiry has led, though not immediately in its first attempts, yet gradually and in course of time, to results, whereby the historical picture of Jesus has lost nothing, but only gained." Wendt, vol. ii. p. 400.

Christ, the appeal must be taken, first of all to the fact ; and if the fact appears to be unmanageable, and to stand in the way of a just philosophy, the presumption is that the fact is right and that the philosophy is wrong.

It has always appeared to me an impenetrable mystery why a special incarnation should be superseded by a universal. I have thus far been unable to find any argument against the reality of the two, and their due relation to each other as ideal and actual, as perfect and imperfect, more convincing than prejudice or more reasonable than one-sidedness. There is, as Professor James has told us, the will to believe; and there is the will not to believe. Candor is the monopoly of no sect. Unwarrantable assumption, like the guest without the wedding garment, forces its way into strange places. To say that a special incarnation cannot be, is to affirm that God cannot make a perfect man. To hold that a special incarnation is not needed, is to declare that the wisdom and love of the perfect man are not needed. To contend that Jesus was not perfect in relation to his Father's will, is to abandon philosophy for history ; it is to admit, by carrying the issue into another field, that there is nothing against it in this. To confess that Jesus was perfect, and to attempt to render null and void this confession by the proposition that he is but one instance of that perfection toward the full possession of which all good men are on the way, is futile.[1] For the appearance of a perfect man in the first century of the Christian era is a very different phenomenon from the appearance of a perfect man in the final century. In the first instance the influence of inheritance and environment is against the fact; in the final it is wholly favorable. The one case is an exception to the rule, the singular character that contradicts the law in the universal experience of the time; in the other the special instance gives the rule, it does but illustrate the common human condition. Jesus is thus an interjected perfection that demands an explanation deeper than that perfection which results from the long sequences of Christian history. That interjection marks the uniqueness of his position both in relation to God and to man. It is something that cannot be repeated. It has a distinction that is eternal; and this distinction is expressed by the statement that Jesus is singular in his relation to God that he may be universal in his meaning and service for man. The issue may be reduced within narrow limits. If Jesus was perfect, spe-

[1] "As Son of God Jesus stands in a unique relation to the Father. The title involves his ethical perfection. Now we cannot simply stop short with these assertions; to do so is to decline the problem to which the uniqueness gives rise. Why was Jesus the only sinless man?" *The Theology of the New Testament*, pp. 63, 64. Professor G. B. Stevens.

cial incarnation is admitted; if the claim is that
Jesus was not perfect, the philosophical objection to special incarnation is abandoned for the
historical; if the contention is that Jesus is but
a typical instance of that perfection to which all
good men will ultimately attain, it is to be noted
that interjected perfection is not the same thing
as the perfection which is the final issue of
eonian discipline; if it is held that the cases of
perfection are numerous, it must be said in reply
that this position has not yet been made good.
The story is that Bronson Alcott said to Carlyle that he could use the words of Jesus, "I
and the Father are one," in the full sense in
which Jesus used them. Carlyle's reply is significant, Jesus got the world to believe him;
Bronson Alcott has failed at this point. The
world goes with Jesus; it feels that he is worth
taking at his word.[1]

When one comes to the universal bearing of
the incarnation in Jesus Christ one becomes
aware of the presence of a sympathetic habit of
thought. It is generally accepted that man is
the highest known form of life. It seems reasonable that the ultimate character of the universe should be judged by its highest product.

[1] *The Christ of To-day*, pp. 112–136. The discussion here is
only supplementary since the uniqueness of Christ emerges
but incidentally. Reference is here given, therefore, to the
more extended treatment in the earlier work.

The final standard of judgment is therefore man. Man at his best gives the universe at its best. He, above all else known to human intelligence, is the organ of the Infinite. If Plato's wise men were right in their agreement that "mind is for us king of heaven and earth," [1] the human mind is the highest known mediator of it. If there is an eternal power not ourselves that makes for righteousness, the human conscience and the course of human society can alone declare it. If it is true that there is at the heart of all things Infinite pity, the soul of man is its highest organ. The ultimate character of the universe is to be judged, not from its first but from its final product. That which made man, brought him on his way, inspired his creative moods, became the fountain of his social order, ideal, and hope, and lifted him slowly but steadily into higher character, is the divinest force known to the human mind. In reference to the Supreme being human thought and love and character are mediatorial. Eternal wisdom, Transcendent love, Infinite power are not denied ; they are objects of faith. Only as they are mediated by men to men do they become part of the spiritual life of the race. That the Divine thought should come into human society in any other way than through thought is inconceivable. The love of God has for its exclusive

[1] Philebus, 28 c.

channel the love of man. The moral government of the world has but one way of declaring its reality, and that is through the process of human society. The tree of life is for all forms of existence; the fruits of the tree of life man alone can reach; they fall only at the touch of his hand.

The prophethood of Jesus is not generally recognized as it should be. The perfection of his utterance of the wisdom of God, the supremacy of his mind upon the ultimate concerns of faith, does not receive the unreserved recognition which is its due. The uniqueness of the prophethood of Jesus is the first great note of the uniqueness of his incarnation; and here again the thought of the time that runs so strongly toward identities is comparatively unresponsive. But while unable to see the unique in the prophethood of Jesus, it does confess in him the highest example of the office of the spiritual mind. A large and very noble literature has grown up in the attempt to expound the teaching of Jesus. A book like Wendt's is not only a critical study; it is also an appreciation of the supreme prophet. The works of A. B. Bruce, particularly his "Training of the Twelve," "The Parabolic Teaching of Christ," and "The Kingdom of God," have given a new sense of the richness and depth and beauty of Christ's mind. Leading scholars for a generation have been engaged in the task of exhibiting a valid historical picture of the teaching of the Master. The result is that it is seen with special clearness that "it was through his personality, his life, and his doctrine as a teacher that his own spirit entered into human lives, as an inspiring, purifying force."[1] The further consequence is that the prophethood of the race is admitted to be conspicuously exemplified in him. If the office of prophet in its full application to Christ is but imperfectly apprehended, in the case of the disciple of Christ it is understood as never before. If the final revelation in the Master is not always acknowledged, the continuous revelation through the servant is one of the great convictions of the time.

Humanity is the prophet of the Most High; such in unexampled vigor is the religious belief of to-day. The thought of God is to be translated into human conditions, articulated in the conscious insight of society, revealed in the rational strength of mankind. One man dies and another is born, one generation goes and another comes, centuries fade and other centuries appear, but the one great process of the continuous and increasing revelation of the Eternal thought behind history remains unbroken. This is the true apostolical succession. The generations of the believing and faithful follow

[1] Professor A. V. G. Allen, *Christian Institutions*, p. 385.

one another at the great task. The vocation of man is the discovery of God. Single prophets may have their singular mission and they may deserve singular honor; but the universal movement does not exist for them, they exist for it. Science is in duty bound to find the fact and to carry it to the proper tribunal for judgment; art is under orders to remember that ultimately her vision of beauty is the beauty of the Lord our God; industry is reminded by a whole army of secular preachers that she is a form of human brotherhood, a brotherhood which reflects in itself the highest in the universe; philosophy is recalled by her strenuous apostles from individualistic views and enjoined to seek for the thought of the Absolute as it returns through social experience to itself. And science and art and industry and philosophy come to religion to be baptized into the one universal vocation. They represent the factual, the imaginative, the practical, and the purely rational aspects of that human mind which in its totality is held by faith as the prophet of the Lord.

The conviction still lives that God speaks, but it lives with this limitation, that God speaks to man only through man. The faith still survives that God educates, but with the modification that this divine education is carried on through human education. The light of God is available for the multitude only through their leaders.

The sources of wisdom are in the infinite mind, but they are open sources only when human minds are at work upon one another. The mind of God is doubtless transcendent, but its immanence, actual and possible, alone concerns human experience and hope. The public school, the college, the university, the mission to the heathen at home and the heathen abroad lie in the light of a new necessity. There is no enlightenment upon things human or divine for man except through his brother. The function of the teacher has become divine. The word of God waits upon the utterance of man. The prophetic capacity of the individual man is the channel which God has ordained for the expression of his truth, and the individual man comes to himself through the influence of the social man. Wisdom is thus from God for men through men.

Here is a new and most important appreciation of one great aspect of the truth of the Incarnation. Christianity can wait for just discriminations and adequate proportions. The Master, who counted those who were not against him as on his side, must look with approval upon the vast and vital, although partial, apprehension of his message. It is not the whole truth to say that the Incarnation is repeated in the life of every genuine disciple; but it is an essential part of the truth. The world depends upon the succes-

sion of the prophets of Jesus Christ. Without
that succession his work could not endure. The
brotherhood of teachers is the continuance of
Christ's mind among men; and it is a melancholy
reflection that the mind of Christ has been so
poorly represented. We shall have more of the
consciousness of Christ to draw upon, and a
larger and nobler total of Christ's truth in use
when the leading representatives of the prophethood of believers become less inadequate.
Language is but a symbol, the records of Christ
in the New Testament are but symbols; and the
construction of these according to the Lexicon
and the Grammar, although for that much one
would be thankful, is only the beginning of
study. Nothing but rational insight is of any
avail in dealing with symbols, and when the
world behind the letter is missed, everything
is missed. Meanwhile the note of joy must be
struck. Among serious men there is a new
appreciation of Christ's way of making the wisdom of God available for human life. The
Christian intellect is to-day confronted by an
opportunity and spurred by a necessity such as
no words can describe. It is felt that where
there is no vision the people perish; a relation
of recipiency to the Eternal mind is confessedly
essential to the sanity and fruitfulness of the
mind of man. It is seen that the vision grows
as it is carried by prophetic soul to prophetic

soul. The words of Jesus that commission his disciples as the teachers of the wisdom of God to men touch the mood of the time with singular power. To-day the true statue of Memnon is the Christian prophet who answers the earliest greeting of the light with the music of insight and inspired activities, and round whom men still gather that they may hear the voice of God in the voice of man.

The priesthood of Christ, the cost at which he did his work, the expense at which he uttered his message, the suffering love that carried him through ever-increasing hostility and through death itself to his great goal, is again missed in its special character; but as an illustration of the law of the spirit of life, it has taken hold of the intelligence and heart of no generation as it has of the present. What is called the atonement is little understood. The revelation which is given once for all, in the suffering love of Christ, of the eternal sacrifice in the Godhead; the discovery in the cross of the Master of the ground in the Infinite of all righteousness, all pity, all reconciliation and hope; the vision that the redeeming passion of the Lord originates in his perfection, and the assurance therein given to the world that the moral character of God is the ultimate source of that grace which everywhere makes peace, receives to-day but slight attention. The unique significance of the priesthood of Christ is not widely seen. That it is so is indeed melancholy. The world cannot afford to lose the vision of what was done by Jesus Christ to discover the eternal basis of union between man and man, and between man and God. It was a transaction wrought not only through an agony and a bloody sweat, a cross and a passion, but also through his whole divine endowment in wisdom and love. Christ was no bringer of the light that he did not see, like so many of the world's heroes. His was the comprehending mind, and the path of sorrow and death was foreseen to lead up to the love that reconciles the world unto itself. One must pity the religious man who sees nothing in the sacrifice of Christ that he does not see in the sacrifice of Socrates or Stephen or Huss or Lincoln. The magnitude of Christ and his utter holiness should make that failure impossible; and the relation of mediator of the Infinite pity which he has borne to every disciple who has been worthy of his name attests his uniqueness here. Windows let in the light, whether they are large or small, and where light is allowed access, however narrow it may be, thankfulness is a duty. But when the midnight sky is to be surveyed and studied, a window here and there, and mostly in the wrong place, will not do. The demand is then for the open heaven. And when one comes to the mediation of the pity of

God the same principle holds. Gratitude for every large mind and true heart through which the Eternal tenderness has found its way, oftenest by reflection, cannot suffice when the opportunity is given to look up through the divine transparency of Jesus into the heights of the Infinite splendor and peace. Christ is our peace in a way in which it is true of no other man. The atonement of Christ still shines through his priesthood; it is part of Christian truth and history and cannot pass away.

The neglect into which it has fallen is due largely to the blindness of its teachers. The subject of the atonement has come down to this generation burdened with mountains of immemorial misunderstandings. It has been turned by an unmeasured accumulation of unmeaning or irrelevant jargon into the superlative unreality. It has been divorced from rational insight, from the principles of moral obligation, and made to do duty as a Christian truth in servitude to pagan notions, and as a satisfaction to pagan sentiments and superstitions. What has been held to be the orthodox doctrine of the atonement is the fabrication of incompetent intelligence; that is, of intelligence that has never really seen the evangelical fact. It is a caricature upon Christianity where Christianity is most divine; a conformation of the gospel to earthly standards of judgment, habits of thought, and modes of feeling where the gospel presents its sublimest contrast to the world. In this infatuation the church has persisted, deposing a McLeod Campbell, hemming in with the battalions of hostile opinion a Bushnell, conspiring to ignore a Maurice, and regarding as heretics the few men to whom God gave a really profound and valid insight into the sacrifice of Christ. The consequence is the widespread loss of the sense of the unique priesthood of the Lord.

Still, serious men have not allowed themselves to be cheated wholly out of the truth. They have been able to see behind a suffering Master a suffering God. They have become convinced that the suffering love that educates the world in whatever righteousness it has is an expression of the suffering love of the Most High. And among many who have broken loose from all theological faith, and from all religion save the religion of service, there is an apprehension of an impressive kind, of the reality of the sacrifice in human character and effort by which the world is carried from the more to the less deplorable. The sympathy that finds its great organ in motherhood, the law of struggle for others that shines in the conduct of genuine fatherhood, the love that is the indispensable qualification of the teacher, that makes for itself conspicuous examples in all disinterested public

servants, that becomes a contagion in the reformer and saint, that softens the hard relations
of capital and labor, that introduces dignity and
sweetness into the frivolousness and bitterness
of the social fellowship, that is the fountain of
all the release from brutality that civilized man
enjoys, the source of all the frictionless life and
positive righteousness which he possesses, the
spring of human hope as it dreams of the coming
brotherhood, is beheld to-day as never before,
as the ultimate necessity of society. The feeling of kindness is essential to human life. Man
cannot get along without his brother; and his
brother must treat him like a brother. Sympathy is the climate in which society grows; and
respect, consideration, compassion, are indispensable to human progress and comfort. Many
doubt if there be any pity for man outside of
man. They look with a hopeless eye upon the
universe, but they turn toward one another with
a consoling assurance. The sympathy, the tenderness, the respect and love, without which life
becomes unendurable, it is in man's heart to
give to his brother. It is like Niobe and her
children; in the pitilessness of the universe the
human soul clings the closer to its kind.

This is nothing but the priesthood of humanity sadly conceived. It is the second great opportunity of Christianity. Christianity is the
religion that claims the heart of the disciple of

Christ as the organ of the pity of God. There is no divine pity, no sympathy, no love in human society, according to the gospel, save as it is mediated by human hearts. A pitiless race would exclude God in the form of compassion from the world. This is as sure as the divine decree. We attain to the consciousness of the Eternal sympathy through the sympathy of good men. And the priesthood of the disciples of Christ is a necessity both for man and for God. God has ordained this method for himself; and upon it, for all that he may know of the love of God, man is dependent. One may as well expect pity from a wild beast as to look for it from the universe apart from one's own heart and the heart of one's brother. The Infinite tenderness comes in but one way, through man to man. This is the terribleness in the heart of a savage, a barbarian, a Turk, a brutal man anywhere, that it shuts God out of the human world. Why does not God stop the atrocities of the race? Why has he allowed men to drench the earth in the blood of their fellowmen? The answer is that God removes the scourge by removing the cause under the penal action of his government, and that beyond this he has ordained that his pity shall be mediated by man to his brother. If there is no pitiful man the pitiful God cannot interpose except by the action of retributive law. The pitilessness of the world is the great barrier to the coming of the Infinite pity. The priesthood of man to man is denied, and to this extent destitution of divine help follows. If the disciples of Christ did but see this mood of the time, they would surely feel the greatness of their opportunity and their obligation. Nothing is too great in the way of hope from the mood of a generation that looks with the utmost seriousness to the people of God to reveal the love of God. The new faith in God is to come in this way. The community of believers, swayed and purified by the passion of love, repeating the sacrifice of Christ, reproducing the spirit that spoke through his cross, and in their devotion to the highest good of their kind filling up what is lacking in his sufferings, will assuredly lead men to look for the source of this new creation. It will not take them long to date this movement of kindness and pure service from the Infinite. They will find God, as the heathen did in the first generation of Christians, through the church. The priesthood of Christians is the highest accessible assurance of the love of God. The atheism of the modern world is to be laid at the door of the church. Instead of being the continuous high-priest of God, through the life of her ministers and her members, she has been so only fitfully and here and there, and for long periods and in many sections she has become the priest of Moloch. To-day the church should awake to the vision of the Macedonian man. The ripeness of Europe for the gospel was felt by the apostle while he was in Asia. Europe did not know that her previous discipline had issued in a mood hospitable toward Christianity. The world at large is unconscious of the fact that much in its prevailing habits of thought constitutes a preparation and an opportunity for the gospel. Toward the universal bearings both of the prophethood and the priesthood of Christ the serious mind of the time is full of unconscious sympathy and appeal.

The same is true of the kinghood of Christ. The moral government of the world is a government in human society, and the perspective of human history is essential to the best view of it. But this is only another way of stating the fact that the moral will of God is disclosed through the moral experience of man. The moral experience of Judas and the moral experience of Jesus are the two extremes of the manifestation; the one discovers the ethical order of God through a ruined character, the other through the supremely good and powerful life. If there is any ultimate law of moral failure and success, any final order according to which as they are disposed toward it, men either fall or rise; if there is in God the authority that overwhelms iniquity and establishes righteousness, it can appear only through human character and experience. The Hebrew idea of theocracy is the deepest upon the subject of the moral government of the world that has ever appeared, and the most philosophical. The righteous God works through the righteous King. The supreme ruler is the supreme servant of God. The moral will of the Eternal gains expression and enforcement through the moral will of his kingly representative. The power by which God puts down the proud and exalts the humble is a power delivered through good men, delivered through the best man who stands at the head of the national order. When this theory would not work, — when a Saul, a Solomon, an Ahab ruled, — the theocratic hope did not die ; it created for itself an ideal king waiting somewhere in the future ; and the power of God by which the false king was dethroned was a power wielded by the people of God. The human mediator of the divine government of the world was still recognized as supreme. The Messianic hope was the expectation that God would appear as king through the authority of the ideal man.

It is another proof of the insight of Maurice that he saw that the basis of Carlyle's mind was this theocratic idea. The man who wrote " Heroes and Hero-worship," " Oliver Cromwell," and " Frederick the Great," believed profoundly in the authority of righteousness ; and now with good success, and again with poor, he was trying to trace the history of that authority in the effective lives of strong men. It was his belief that the hope of the nations lies in great rulers, and that only thus can the saving strength of the moral order pass into the life of mankind. The king should be the best man ; the person in whose hands is vested the supreme power should be supremely moral. Then his ruling character becomes an organ for the authority of the Infinite righteousness. Carlyle's religion was Hebrew moralism as humanized in Hebrew theocracy. His creed was the reign of the eternal righteousness through the reign of great men. His defect was that he found evidence for the reality of his theocratic conception only in the past, that he bound it up with the forms of political government, that he did not recognize the higher characters behind the thrones of the world, and that he failed to appreciate in any degree the Supreme historic character that has been slowly but steadily conforming society to itself. It is in accordance with the irony of truth that Carlyle was essentially a representative of the race for which he had the deepest contempt ; he was not a Christian, he was a Hebrew.

The popular interest in political authority has been greater in the nineteenth century than in any one of its predecessors. The character of the supreme ruler has become the object of intense and widespread concern. Opinions differ as to the best way of discovering the fittest man. The hereditary path is still adhered to by the majority of nations; but even among them a distinction is drawn between the nominal ruler and the real, between the figurehead upon the ship and the veritable force that cuts the waves. That this real ruler shall be competent in the highest degree is the new passion of serious politics. It is the form peculiar to the time of the theocratic idea. The moral government of God can become the highest good to society only through the moral government of man. The universe often takes the place of God, but under both words the meaning is the same. The holiest power outside of nations can become the servant of nations only through the government of the nations. Amid the fearful corruptions of political managers the world over, and the equally fearful mistakes of the people; in the heart of all the contradiction of the highest ideals of government, and the desperate disappointment that waits upon every lover of a pure and competent civil service, this new popular concern about the character of the supreme ruler is a fountain of hope. The people still look for the moral power of the universe through the moral will of the best man.

Here is another new appreciation of Christianity. That Christ proved stronger than the chief priests and Pharisees, and the Roman corruption through which he died, mightier than the total hostility that stood out against him, and that crowded him out of the world, is universally seen. The order that fought against him, and that temporarily prevailed, passed, and the order that he represented held the field. History has nothing but an amen to repeat after the assertion that his kingdom is an everlasting kingdom. The strongest character in the world is the character of Jesus Christ. Behind the moral customs of society he stands, back of its low habits and practices, wielding upon them his resistless power. It is impossible to read the record of social progress without the recognition of his shaping strength. His moral will is forcing the civilized world out of its injustice and inhumanity. His sublime spirit is in the evangelical record, it is in the history of Christendom, it is in the present struggle and hope of society.

The authority of Christ in the authority of the genuine people of Christ is a fact. In his book, " The Coming People," Charles F. Dole has given striking expression to this fact. The first chapter of that book is an appeal to the moral life and the moral order. The strong race is shown to be the race that accepted the law of moral amendment. The race that is to remain the ruler of the earth is the race that shall repreresent in its character Christian righteousness. This fact is the basis upon which the moral view of the world is built. In the long range history is the great theodicy. Finally the fact emerges that the people of God are the masters of the earth. Behind the prophethood of humanity is the Eternal wisdom, behind the priesthood of humanity is the Infinite pity, behind the king-hood of humanity is the Absolute righteousness. In its highest endeavor the race is backed by eternal intelligence, passion, and power. This is not the whole of the religion of Jesus Christ ; still it represents at once its greatest achieve-ment and its largest opportunity.

In the briefest outline of things fundamental in the gospel of Christ, to those already men-tioned, there must be added the sacramental idea. The main purpose in this chapter has been to indicate a new, although an incomplete, appreciation of Christianity. The line of sym-pathy between the message of the New Testa-ment and the mood of the time has been here the chief concern. Criticism upon this mood has been incidental; exposition of its signifi-cance for believers has been the burden of the writer's purpose. The sacramental idea is ap-proached in the same spirit. Its special mean-ing in the life of the Lord, the spirit of the age is slow to see, its special value to the church it is still slower to grasp. Nevertheless, it must be said that at this point of contact with Christianity, the age in its serious representatives is at its best. It may miss from first to last the adequate vision of the uniqueness of Christ. In the sacramental conception this failure is of slight consequence in comparison with a just appreciation of its value for the total of human life. And this the church has notoriously missed, and in missing this, the divine source of the idea in the Lord has not been understood.

Jesus instituted two sacraments, one for the beginning of the Christian life, the other to mark the law of its growth. The two together indicate that for the Christian the whole human life is sacred ; together they signify that man's true world lies in the realm of the spirit, that it carries in it infinite values, and that for these values between spiritual men and the Eternal spirit there are these two special signs, baptism and the Lord's Supper. Baptism is the sign that the believing spirit has entered the divine world, that it has renounced the world of its own lust and shame, that it has found in sorrow and tears, and in unutterable joy, the Infinite Father of men, that it has seen in Christ the Perfect Son, and that it has accepted as its own the life made possible for the sons of God. This entrance into a world that lies in the region of the spirit, that is wholly hidden save from the vision of God, and that possesses in its silence and mystery infinite values, it is altogether just and meet to indicate by a special sign. This special sign is baptism. When it is administered to children it is done upon the faith of their parents that these children belong to God ; upon the confession that the end of family education will be to ground them in the consciousness that they are sons of God; upon the expressed purpose to hold them in the divine world into which they were born. The faith that the children of men are the children of God, that there need be no lapse from the level of true life, that education may be so wise and inspired as to keep them in alienation from the spirit of evil, and in ever deeper association with the spirit of Christ, is great enough to be indicated by the holy sign of baptism. For the preservation of this valid and beautiful idea of the Christian faith all believers are under the deepest obligations to the thinkers of the Broad School in the Protestant Episcopal Church.

The Lord's Supper stands for the entire Christian life. It indicates, again, the divine world in which it is the believer's aim to live and move and have his being. The omnipresent reality of God the Father, the unseen but ever-present Christ as the revelation of the Father, the Holy Spirit as the love of the Father, the spirits of just men made perfect, the communion

of believers on earth, the law of the spirit of
life in Christ Jesus, the ends of the church in
time and beyond, the progress of history toward
its divine goal, the union of the worlds visible
and invisible in the purposes of the Eternal and
the fellowship of life, — these are the sublime
and blessed realities indicated by the sacrament
of the Lord's Supper. Again, it is a world of
infinite values. It lies in the region that is
deeper than all utterance; it gives to all utterance its significance; it is fitting that it should
be covered with the grace of the tenderest and
noblest of all signs. It is in its widest and deepest meaning the sacrament of a divine universe.

This great and beautiful conception accords
profoundly with the best insight of the time.
The senses are sacraments between the human
reason and the Infinite. This idea for which
philosophy is indebted to the genius of Berkeley
is an acknowledged truth of science. The world
of color, by virtue of an association earlier than
distinct consciousness, and older than abiding
memory, is a basis upon which the mind passes
to the world of touch. The intellectual values
covered by the sacrament of color are elaborated
in the Dialogues of Berkeley with classic beauty
and strength. Sound is equally sacramental;
the judgment passes to decisions every hour,
and often every moment, upon the basis of this
sense. The booming of cannon off the English

coast June 3, 1665, was translated by the Londoners of that day into a great battle between the navies of Holland and of their own country; the striking of the clock upon Westminster is a sign never lost upon the workman under it. One sort of sound means the boatswain's whistle, another the trumpet, and yet another the foghorn. At sea the comfort of an even incessant noise is seen by the judgment of alarm to which the mind flashes upon the cessation of it. The tumult of the storm is a solace compared with the terrible peace that means the stopping and perhaps the crippled condition of the ship. Sounds are of great compass in their significance; childhood, youth, manhood, womanhood, and old age reveal themselves to the judgment through the ear. The voice of man is understood in the night. Social happiness and misery clothe themselves in the sacrament of sound. There is Lohengrin's "Wedding March" and there is the "Dead March in Saul." Bridal joy and the sorrow of death seek sacramental voices. The family, the business community, the social fellowship, the law court, the senate, and the church could not exist without the sacrament of sound. The notes of the bird, the audible sweep of the river, the whisper of the wind in the trees, the roar of the tempest, the tumultuous anthem of the sea, the varied and multitudinous voices of nature become meanings, judgments, worlds for reason through the sense of hearing. Through the sense of smell the mind construes the air polluted by the presence of the gas reservoir and that blowing fresh from the hills into the world of sickness and the world of health. For the normal man taste is every day fulfilling the same end. It is a basis upon which the judgment passes to conclusions. The instinctive action of the judgment when one is walking is symbolic. The constant sensation of the solid, resisting substance under the feet is, in a seemingly unconscious way, understood to mean security, but the moment that the sensation of solid resistance gives place to that of softness and sinking the mind takes alarm. Thus the senses are a system of signs between man and man, and between man and the universe. They are the universal sacrament without which the reason could not understand nature or convey its meanings to the reason of others. For the philosophical believer in God this universal sacrament of sense is the bow in the cloud. The arch of ineffable color that the prophet translates into the spiritual beauty of a divine promise and a human hope is the parable of that vaster translation of the signs of earth and sky into sure words from the Supreme being in which all men are forever engaged. The universal and inevitable sacrament is the sacrament of the senses.

The fine arts are sacraments, and they are founded upon the senses. Color serves the painter, sound the musician, form the sculptor and builder, articulate speech the poet. The Sistine Madonna, the Fifth Symphony of Beethoven, the Venus of Milo, the Milan Cathedral, the Odyssey, the Divine Comedy, and King Lear are truly sacramental. The senses are touched, the materials of sense are used for the purposes of high creative genius. The worlds of color and sound and form and articulate speech are shaped into sacraments of the worlds of truth and beauty and goodness. Art is not art unless it is the utterance of the ideal. Immoral art is a contradiction; that which is low, and which calls itself by the holy name of art, is excommunicated by philosophic criticism. It is false to the best meaning of life; and with the best meaning of life art lives and dies. There is therefore a great gulf fixed between true art and its counterfeit, between the spirit that uses color or sound or form or articulate speech to embody the best meanings of existence, and the spirit of lust and lies that makes for itself a sacrament of shame. The pictures, the sculpture, the buildings, the books that have won their places among the supreme expressions of the best meanings of human life, may be most suitably regarded as sacramental. They are created by life at its highest, and they remain its imperishable monuments. When one remembers its profound relation to suffering and love, and notes in it the answer to the elemental passions and faiths of the soul, to think of the highest in literature as other than sacramental is impossible. The Book of Job is the sacrament of sorrow; the Gospel of John is the sacrament of the Divine life. To translate great literature back into great life is the only true way to read it. Imagination must ascertain its living sources, appreciate its values in the silent worlds of suffering and faith, and weigh its merits in the scales of flesh and blood. There are many who can translate from one tongue into another, who are yet incompetent for the far more important task of translating literature into human experience. Whoever has learned this art can never think of literature as other than one great aspect of the universal sacrament.

The Roman Church was right in its insistence upon the sacramental meaning of marriage; the mischief of the habit of thought associated with this act lay in the general misconception of the idea of the sacrament, and in excluding from the domain of the holy, by inference or inadvertence, other sections of human existence. The New Testament method is philosophical; there is one sacrament for the entrance upon the divine life, and there is one for the total of that life in this world. Still, the Roman Church even in its blindness bore witness to a fundamental truth. If the words of love unto death at the marriage altar are not sacramental nothing is. The worlds of honor and faith that meet in true marriage have values that are infinite, and the association of the outward lives which is their symbol cannot be held in too great reverence. For the men and women who have been at all fortunate, the greatest words in the language are father and mother, husband and wife. Home is nothing less than the sacrament of humanity. The word represents higher values than the largest intelligence can conceive; it is a word for a world of love and sorrow and faith that is ineffable. Even when it has become a memory it is a world whose sun goes not down and whose moon does not withdraw itself. It is the shelter, the solace, and the hope of man; it is a world whose tears are transfigured by love, rolling in the faith that wipes all tears away. When it has vanished like the guest that tarries but for a night, " the remembrance of it is like music." That it should be covered with the holiest symbol is indeed fitting.

The words that pass between friends, that are the signs of social interest and sympathy, that express the honor of the business man and the obligation of the citizen, are not unworthy of the same high interpretation. When the kiss is the kiss of the betrayer, and the social greet-

ing covers an empty or a venomous heart; when
the financial promise is made to the ear and
broken in fact, and the covenant of devotion to
the state is kept in profession and denied in
practice, one sees in the fraternal, the social, the
industrial, and the political abuses how truly
sacramental in intent words are. They are false
only when they are made to mean nothing, or
when their plain meaning is perverted. Judas
with his kiss, Herodias in her dance, Ananias
and his money, and Felix and his hunger for
bribes remind one of the immemorial outrage
that has been committed upon friendship, social fellowship, industrial brotherhood, and the
communion of men in the nation. Nothing but
sacrilege is strong enough to mark the abuse,
nothing but sacrament is holy enough to serve as
the name for the righteous use of words in these
great human relationships. The sign-language
of the race, whether of honor, like the salute of
a fleet of battleships for their commander, or
of solemn warning, like the lights which the
great steamers hang out when they pass in the
night, or of compact, when the flagship sets her
signals and the others respond, or of widest
obligation, as when a navy goes forth under sealed
orders, is the assurance of truth between man
and man. To pervert it is the sin against the
Holy Ghost; to honor it from slightest detail to
widest scope and from first to last is to keep

faith with mankind, and to walk in truth before God.

Here in the sacramental view of life is another vast opportunity for Christianity. The world of divine meanings is the burden of the gospel. Its ultimate aim is to make the sign-language, the entire self-expression of man, rich with the highest meaning. Its purpose is to put into the total of existence a vaster and a nobler content; to place behind the sacraments of the family, of the social fellowship, of the community of trade, of the brotherhood in art, in science, in thought, and in citizenship the whole divine truth. The practical side of its doctrine of the Holy Spirit means that ultimately Christianity claims humanity as the sacrament of Deity. Here is an opportunity of which the foolish ecclesiastic and the vain ritualist and the blind dogmatist never dream. They see only the world's indifference toward the church, its contempt of ceremonial, its rejection of dogma. They walk in the vain show of their hysterical sorrow and their unreal and unavailing pietism. They can read the great world's indifference to the trivial aspects and traditional accidents of the sublime institute of Christian faith; they cannot read the deeper signs of the times, the slow-gathering and the wide-extending consciousness that the vocation of man is in becoming the sacrament of God. The meaning of redness in the evening and

morning sky was never better understood than
now; the prophets of the mere weather of human life afflict one with their multitude; but
the discoverer of the true signs of the times, the
seer of the forces that are working in society,
and of the steady answer of society to the ever-
increasing appeal of the Eternal spirit, is still
an infrequent presence in the administration of
the great trust of the gospel.

III

The central truth of Christianity is the manifestation of God in Jesus Christ. The gospel
is essentially the gospel of the Incarnation. It
has been asserted that the Incarnation expresses
itself in the prophethood, the priesthood, the
kinghood, and the sacramental character of
Christ. He is for men the wisdom of God, the
love of God, the moral authority of God, the
sacrament of God. So far as Christ is unique
in these high offices, the time is not one of insight; but upon the vocation of man in them
under the leadership of Christ the age has laid
hold with unexampled strength. Never have
the universal bearings of Christianity been acknowledged as they are to-day; and every criticism upon the religious limitations of the age
should be set in the light of this fact. The
insight that discovers in the gospel the religion
of humanity, that sees in it the revelation of the

final meaning of humanity, and that discerns in it the grounds for the prophethood, the priesthood, the kinghood, and the sacramental office of humanity, may be an incomplete, but it is still a very great appreciation. There is reason in it for the largest and best hope that the church has ever cherished. Like Wellington's centre at Waterloo, this is the force that controls the field. Defeat at other points may be inevitable ; but to miss the advantage and the assurance at the heart of things would be deplorable. Losses should be computed in the presence of gains, and among the gains should be reckoned the new opportunity. Among the teachers of Christianity nothing is more needed to-day than a just perspective. In the mental picture, objects should be graded as they are in fact, the flats and the foothills where the enemy is strongest should be commanded by the great mountain fortresses of truth, and these should stand supported by the Infinite. It may be said that optimism and pessimism in regard to Christianity reduce themselves to-day to a question of perspective. The losses are facts, and if they are the only facts, and, further, if they are as serious as to some minds they seem to be, the picture must be one of despair. On the other hand, if the losses are providential, like the Federal defeat at Bull Run, if the gains are unspeakably great, if the opportunity of the new time is a veritable day of the Lord, however shadowed here and there, the picture must be one of hope.

It is true that all things are changing in the intellectual form of Christianity. There are indeed signs that among thinkers the higher criticism of the Bible has nearly exhausted its interest. Still, it has done its work. Among intelligent people the Bible can never again be what it has been, the complete and infallible authority, from its first page to its last, upon faith and practice. This means loss. Literal security for faith is no longer found in the indiscriminate use of the Bible. It can no longer coerce the reason or override the conscience. As an unquestionable authority for the support of questionable opinions it is no more. Never again can it be deemed conclusive proof of the truth of a belief that a text from the Bible may be quoted in its favor. It has been shown that the office of the Bible is not as a substitute for moral insight, or as a check upon it. For the literalist the loss is absolute. The letter that killeth is itself killed ; but this itself surely is an immense gain. The Bible has become the monumental witness in history to the spirit in man and the Spirit of God. It has been reduced from the position of master to that of servant ; and this reduction from a false eminence is in the interest of its permanent influence. Its whole ultimate value has been shown to consist in the witness it bears to God, to Christ, to the divine life, and the moral order of the world. These are distinct from it; these are greater than it. In the service of these, it is often above all praise, more potent than ever because of the deeper insight to which it speaks; and again, in many parts of it, it is seen to fall distinctly below the mood of an honest Christian man. For work, the Bible is mightier than ever; but as an idol it is among intelligent people no more. Here is a fact, a blank defeat, which may mean nothing for the Napoleons of destructive criticism, but which for the soldiers of faith may be providential, directing closer attention to the centre and opening up new vistas of victory. The higher criticism of the Bible is simply the supreme instance of the severe but gracious process whereby believers to-day are passing from idolatry of the letter to the worship of the spirit. Only the consciousness of an inexpressible gain in faith can explain the audacity of Paul's words: " Wherefore we henceforth know no man after the flesh: even though we have known Christ after the flesh, yet now we know him so no more." [1] The escape from the flesh is the escape to the true and divine Christ, from the Christ of Pilate and the Pharisees, the mocking soldiers and the uncomprehending disciples to the Christ of Pentecost, the missionary journeys of Paul

[1] 2 Cor. v. 16.

and the holy and happy life of the church. The transition from the letter of the Bible to the spirit of the Bible is an exodus from bondage into freedom.

Orthodoxies are breaking down. A quotation from the Fathers carries with it the authority of its good sense and no more. The schemes of Augustine and Calvin and Edwards, and their descendants, lineal and collateral, are no longer adequate for any one who thinks with the facts before him. These men themselves are strong and worthy of everlasting remembrance, and many of their thoughts are as abiding as human life; but their schemes will not work, their plan of salvation has become like an antiquated map. Since then the world has been navigated anew, fresh continents have been discovered, the old realities are absorbed in larger relations, and the eternal fact has become infinitely richer and greater. To say this is not to insult these old thinkers; to say less would be an outrage upon truth.

Here is another change in the field of battle between belief and unbelief. Those who try to defend dogmatic Christianity in its unmodified and unreconstructed form are beaten. It is the Prussian endeavor to arrest the French Emperor at Ligny. To every one who sees and understands the situation it is plain that it cannot be done. If this fact of defeat upon the old dogmatic ground is taken by itself, as it is by many persons, and regarded as an irremediable disaster, the future of the gospel must seem dark. If, on the other hand, the defeat be viewed as a step to an essential victory a new face is put upon the event. How is progress possible in the philosophical interpretation of Christianity, and in the philosophical interpretation of the universe in the spirit of Christianity, unless free criticism is let in upon doctrine? The exclusion of all but fruitless and unavailing criticism means the arrest of theological thought. Philosophy is growth through the freest play of criticism into ampler, saner, and more adequate interpretations of man and his world. Exclude the criticism and progress in philosophy is at an end. And unless believers are content to keep theology in the immaturity of youth while philosophy goes on into full manhood, criticism must seem indispensable. The dogmatic defeat means the presence in belief of the divinely commissioned critical spirit. The more serious and fundamental the criticism is, the more obviously is it the product of the Spirit of God. It is a happy intimation that theology is about to break free from its arrest; that it is about to take a new journey in God's world, attain a vaster vision, and put on a maturer and more influential mind.

Heterodoxies are changing their character.

A large portion of the truth which was the noble message of New England Unitarianism has been absorbed by the enlightened of other denominations. This truth has been won, in most cases, from sources other than Unitarian, none the less is it on that account the same truth. This quiet cultivation under the sanction of orthodoxy of territory only recently mined by the explosives of heterodoxy strikes one as strange. Meanwhile Unitarianism is beginning to question about its own life. Its old antagonist has vanished; its new antagonist is in possession of much of its effective truth. Is it to become prey for organisms that seem to have an assimilative and creative power greater than its own? Those who defend Unitarianism on the old lines are doomed to the same disaster that is overtaking their ancient antagonists. There is no hope for either party upon that field. Old things have passed away for both warriors; all things have become new.

The creative mood is to-day essential to the denomination that is to live. Christianity is other than the old orthodoxy and the old Unitarianism conceived it to be, and it is infinitely greater. The vice of orthodoxy was its conceit in its own construction of Christianity; the vice of Unitarianism was its high and mighty spirit of patronage. The one magnified itself immensely, and the other looked with infinite blandness upon the simple gospel. Everlasting sterility has overtaken both moods. Out of the mood that regards opinions as perfect, out of the pride that looks with compassion upon the inconsiderableness of the subjects of opinions, nothing great can come. In new times, and greatly altered circumstances, Christian thinkers of every name are confronted with the sublime reality of the gospel. It is forever secure because the universe is its keeper. But they can remain only as they pass through the creative mood into a new and more reverential consciousness of the immeasurable greatness of that with which they are dealing.

Sects are to-day undergoing judgment at the great world's tribunal. The authority of the church has become the authority of the churches, and this turns out to mean the authority of the good sense, the just reasons, the valid conceptions, and the exalted life which these bodies of men possess. Ecclesiasticism, whether Roman or Anglican, Presbyterian or Congregational, upon the old basis is an impossible interest for a reasonable man. No intelligent person cares for a Papal encyclical as such, or an Episcopal letter, or a Presbyterian decree, or a Congregation council. When the utterances from these sources are great with wisdom they are indeed widely recognized as authoritative; but their official and ecclesiastical character is no longer

a help. It is a hindrance. No one now fears
excommunication; it is in fact coveted by the
sensational as an express to fame. The contro-
versies in which John Henry Newman figured
are about the poorest that the nineteenth century contains; and the various ecclesiasticisms
that have descended from them by extraordinary
generations would seem to be among the vainest
of human interests.[1] Continuity in dogmatic
belief, in ritual, and in institutional form can
give the church authority over no reasonable person; continuity of life is the note of the church
catholic and universal, the life that becomes as
the centuries pass a larger wisdom, a purer
heart, a nobler will, a vaster witness of the Holy
Ghost. And if any Newmanite, Roman, Anglican, or Congregationalist shall contend that a
given ecclesiastical order is the assurance of the
availing type of life, the answer shall be that
the syllogism that supports his contention is
constructed out of two propositions, ignorance of
history and human credulity. The church that
has the amplest and soundest intellect, the deepest and devoutest heart, the bravest and strongest will for righteousness, is the best organized
expression of Christianity. The idea of the

[1] Dr. Fairbairn's masterly exposure of Newmanism is some
consolation for a half century of ecclesiastical imposture; yet
one must lament the devotion of such learning and ability to
the exposure of what must seem, to a normal mind, axiomatic
nonsense.

church in the books of the wisest thinkers is profoundly attractive ; what one wants is an answer in fact to this heavenly vision, some institutional servant of Christ near enough to its ideal to keep from unseemly mirth the reasonable student of it. The truth is ecclesiasticism of the old type is discredited, and from every point of view the defender of it is a child of darkness. He is degrading the sublimest interests into an identification with the pettiest.

Like the student of the Bible and the inheritor of orthodox or heterodox opinions, the new churchman must move upon his subject in the strength of a creative mood. His passion should be to make his church great in intelligence, in love, in righteous strength. He should scorn all extraneous and mean claims for his ecclesiasticism. That any method should have any worth other than that disclosed in the service of life, he should be the first to disavow. That different methods of serving life should meet as methods upon equal terms he should be foremost to aver. That machinery should ever count for more than machinery, that wheels should ever be other than wheels even when the spirit is in them, should be for him impossible. When the world has gone mad the genuine churchman remains sound. He sees that more and more society is commanded by the reason that is wisdom and love and righteousness. The church that best represents this ultimate commander will absorb all others. Finally it will have the field of the world to itself. Increased rivalry along this line would be a precious ecclesiastical novelty.

Christianity perpetuates itself by the power of the Holy Spirit. More and more it is becoming the religion of the Holy Spirit. The church has always held this faith, yet it has seldom believed in it with all its heart. Few are the instances in which the leaders of the church have stood in the vision and repose of this fundamental belief. It is, however, the faith to which conservative and progressive thinkers alike must come, if they are to continue living forces in society. Those who look upon the age as a time of apostacy, and those who regard it as the widest and most inspiring opportunity that has ever confronted the church, need equally the baptism of the same Spirit. The salvation of the pessimist is here. The truth that has been lost, the love that has disappeared, the righteousness that has vanished, and the power that has departed can be restored under the discipline of the Holy Spirit. He is the source of the Christian intelligence and heart and will. The reason is renewed through him, its lost insight recovered, its dead appreciations brought back to life. The believer who is despondent over the signs of the times must remember that the Christian truth of the Holy Spirit is a truth for the intellect no less than the heart. It is the assurance, the only ultimate assurance that nothing essential to the gospel shall fall permanently out of the faith of believers. It is the ground of all hope for the recovery of what is lost no less than the basis of all confidence for the realization of what is simply alluring opportunity. Ships that wait for the tide do not wait in vain; when the deep returns to the flood they come with it. For believers of both the despondent and hopeful mood this is to an important extent the condition of faith. Truths are anchored off shore; the shallows do not allow them to come in. A new use of the grace of the Spirit, a fresh experience under him, is essential to the incoming of these excluded truths. The flood tide of the Spirit is the only hope of the believer, conservative or radical; for the conservative it is the ground of recovery, for the radical it is the basis of new conquest.

The parallel between the world in the first century and in the nineteenth has often been noted. Paul was the great Christian optimist of the first century. The world was far enough from being according to his mind. No one had so clear a sense as he of the distance at which it stood beneath the true level of human life. No one comprehended so well as Paul the contradiction which the Roman Empire presented in thought, in character, and in custom to the law of love in the Kingdom of God. To the apostle

the world was a world to be redeemed. The
points of antipathy to his message were fundamental, and they had always their full reflection
in his intelligence. But the forces in the imperial environment which were sympathetic to
Paul's gospel were even more important. The
Holy Spirit had gone before him; in the human
issues of a great preceding discipline he was
waiting for the Christian preacher. When the
apostle spoke in the demonstration of the Spirit,
there were many who had been prepared to hear
in the Spirit. The apostle made use of the
means of travel, of the chief centres of intelligence and trade, of the protection of Roman
law, and of the support of Greek poets. Everywhere, as at Athens, he began with the devout-
ness and the faith already in existence, and the
altar to the unknown god was the shrine upon
which he unveiled the God and Father of Christ.
Heathenism had a vast range of sympathy toward
the new teacher, and invasion took place at this
point. The invasion and the conquest that mark
the career of this great man owe their existence
to the fact that by the power of the Spirit he
laid a master's hand upon the side of the world
sympathetic toward his purpose.

Parallels to this unconquerable optimist are
the necessity of the time. It is useless to dwell
on the contradiction that the world presents to
the Christian ideal. Let that be assumed. The

world needs to be brought back to itself. Man needs to be redeemed from the ascendency of the animal to the sovereignty of the filial spirit. Let the energy of the prophets of this new day be turned upon the sympathies which society presents to the burden of the Lord that they are sent to deliver. The serious belief that man is God's best work, the high conviction that not nature but humanity is the final organ of the Infinite, the implicit faith that there is for mankind a vocation as prophets and priests and kings of the Eternal, and the dim surmise that the final function of the human is to become the sacrament of the Divine, are opportunities for the religion of the Holy Spirit that no imagination can exaggerate. Only in the strength of the religion that renews the reason, turns its dreams into visions, and its surmises into certain insight; only in the power of the faith that makes the heart aware of its depth and range, and that builds the moral will into victorious might, can the vast invasion and conquest be accomplished which a world in deepest need, through the impressive appeal of its appreciations, makes possible for the Christian church.

CHAPTER IV

THE DISCIPLINE OF DOUBT

I

DOUBT upon religious or theological subjects still receives heroic treatment, not only from the conventional person but also from the average teacher of Christianity. To many believers the doubts of other men appear as a menace to faith, and as something to be put down, not by force of reason but by sheer might. Their method with doubt recalls the speech of the old English commander at Cadiz: " What a shame it will be, you Englishmen that feed upon good beef and brewis, to let those rascally Spaniards beat you that eat nothing but oranges and lemons." [1] In the battle with doubt the honor of the beef and brewis of the dogmatist is at stake as against the presumption of the oranges and lemons of the skeptic. That an unbeliever should sometimes be able to teach a believer, that a heathen doubter should occasionally be in a position to enlighten a Christian, is a supposition that, among minds of a certain type, is not for a

[1] Selden's *Table Talk*, p. 129.

moment to be entertained. The thing would be an infinite disgrace, and it must be averted by the annihilating polemics of assertion.

In other moods with the same class of persons doubt appears as a form of dishonesty. That Lucian or Celsus or Lucretius or Montaigne or Hume should be sincere in their negations is felt to be nearly incredible. It is believed that if the whole truth were known about these great doubters they would prove to be great rascals. Rumor is busy about their agonies in solitude, and there are widely circulated reports of their death-bed horrors. The testimony of a certain lady in black in a stage-coach to her fellow-passengers, who had been discussing Hume's last hours, illustrates the stuff that continues to be meat and drink to multitudes : "Gentlemen, I attended Mr. Hume on his deathbed, but I can assure you, I hope never again to attend the deathbed of a philosopher." [1] It could not possibly occur to this silly person or to the thousands whom she represents that the indirect service that David Hume has rendered to the rational interpretation of the universe, and therefore to faith, is simply too great to be measured. But for conventional believers negative service is worse than no service. The reply of Horne Tooke, when George III. asked him if he could play cards, that he could not tell a king from a knave, covers the

[1] McCosh, *The Scottish Philosophy*, p. 132.

case in hand. The mere traditionalist cannot tell doubt from knavery. His mood reminds one of the picture of the honest lawyer, the representation being a man with his own head in his hands. Nothing but decapitation can make an honest skeptic.

In another mood to the same variety of believers doubt figures as a kind of mean logical strategy. It is a method of evasion, an intellectual trick by which the fox escapes when by all laws of the game he belongs to the hounds. When the skeptic has been reasoned out of every position, forced back from every assumption, when the conflict has ended in a retreat that is a run, nothing can save him from capture at the hands of belief but the warren of agnosticism. Doubt thus appears as an unfair advantage which the game possesses over the sportsman. Plato has drawn the picture of the two in Thrasymachus and Socrates. To the declamatory and uncritical sophist Socrates seemed to be a miserable trifler. His contention that he had no opinions or convictions of his own appeared mere pretense, the mask of hypocrisy, the logical artifice by which he was able to put to confusion stronger and richer minds than his own. The reformer of philosophic thought came to be widely regarded in this way. The critical power by which the current views were shown up as full of contradiction stimulated the conventional

teacher of that day to make a counter-attack;
and when it was found that Socrates professed
to know nothing, the campaign had to be given
up, and the volume of polemical passion sought
vent in descriptive phrases: "How characteristic of Socrates! he replied with a bitter laugh;
that's your ironical style! Did I not foresee —
have I not already told you that whatever he
was asked he would refuse to answer and try
irony or any other shuffle, in order that he might
avoid answering?"[1]   The reformer of thought
in his purely negative service still receives the
same sort of homage.   His doubt is a mean logical trick, and is comparable to the strategy that
named a public house at Norwich, England,
"Nowhere," to aid the belated and overstimu-
lated husband upon his return home to answer
all imperious and troublesome questions with at
least a nominal respect for truth.

To practical persons doubt upon religious subjects is an indication of imbecility; and unques-
tionably the mood may amount to disease.   Upon
the Fichtean ground that the moral will is the
guide to truth, upon the Christian ground that
obedience is the path to knowledge, the exclusive
employment of the intellect in the region of ultimate reality stands condemned.   One can see
that the monstrous productions of the metaphysical imagination in the East, the grotesque and

[1] *Republic*, 337. Benjamin Jowett, A. M.

endless forms of Hindu Pantheism originate in
the riot of the intellect divorced from moral will.
Moral inertia is a universal infirmity, and among
the Indian peoples it is a calamity.   Indecision,
while it may account for excessive habitual
doubting, is no explanation of the intellectual
discontent which is the condition of progress.
If the elimination of the will injures the intellect, the undue prominence of that power is
equally fatal to the discovery of truth.   Between
a willess intelligence and a willful, between
chronic indecision and chronic prejudice, there
is no choice.   The point here made is against
the justice of the sentence that doubt upon the
things of the spirit is necessarily a sign of special weakness.   Intellectual integrity is the rar-
est of all virtues.   A wider and more careful
knowledge of men seems to necessitate the conclusion that the number of those whose judgments are held in strict accountability to fact is
not large.   Candor is far from common, and it
has never been a popular excellence.   Courage
counts its admirers by the thousand, while the
far higher excellence of candor is unable to make
out that it has one.   Candor necessarily assumes
the form of indecision, and on this account it is
popularly branded as weakness.   The judicial
mood is not a natural, it is an acquired virtue.
The hesitation that is necessitated by the evidence is surely praiseworthy ; yet one not infre-

quently sees it represented as a starving donkey equidistant between two bundles of hay. The predicament in which it is placed is meant as a disclosure of its weakness and of the general contempt in which it is held. It is the narrowness and passion connected with this mood that Burns has impaled in his famous description : —

> " Damn a' parties but your ain,
> An' you 'll be a staunch believer."

In his address as Lord Rector of St. Andrews University, John S. Mill told the students that in his judgment the liberal minister had a better right to be in the church than the conservative. From his point of view he was right. He assumed that institutions exist for the people, for the nation ; and those who endeavor to keep the church in sympathy with the intellectual and moral progress of the community, he justly considered the wisest administrators of the trust placed in their hands. The conservative opinion seems to be that institutions exist primarily for the dead, and that they who keep the church as far as possible from all sympathy with the progress of the time are its best servants. Mill's judgment at this point is inherently sound, and contrasts favorably with the reckless and worthless opinion of Carlyle upon the same subject. Of the Church of England he said : " Your rusty kettle will continue to boil your water for

you if you don't try to mend it. Begin tinker-
ing and there is an end of your kettle." Mr.
Froude adds that Carlyle disliked the liberal
clergy ; and, still speaking for his author, he
goes on to say : "Let it once be supposed that
the clergy generally were teaching what they
did not believe themselves, and the whole thing
would become a hideous hypocrisy." [1] To be
sure it would ; meanwhile the alternatives presented are indicative of hideous blindness, and
the description given of the liberal spirit in the
church is a hideous caricature. Popular want
of insight into the character and purpose of serious religious doubt, and the negative mood in
which all reformations both of belief and of institutions partially originate, is exonerated in the
presence of the unmitigated nonsense of genius
vainly paraded by the unhappiest of biographers.

Doubt is essentially distrust. It may be distrust of an inherited creed, or of current conceptions of the ultimate meaning of existence, or of
the highest mood of the human spirit as the key
to the character of the Infinite. While the believer may see plainly that doubt of this description is wholly blameless, that it is temporarily a
necessity, and that it is indeed essential to the
education of man, he should be willing to admit
that it is a fall. For such it is. It is a falling
away from conceptions that hitherto have held

[1] *Carlyle's Life*, vol. iv. p. 385.

him or his fellow-men ; it is a lapse from faith
in the highest mood as the surest guide to ultimate truth.   That mood Plato calls the wing of
the soul ; when the mood is discredited the wing
is broken, and the soul falls to earth.   A different experience follows, and a widely contrasted
construction of the meaning of the universe is
the inevitable result.   This at least is the nature
of the doubt characteristic of the nineteenth century.   For many minds and from various considerations inherited theological conceptions are
discredited.   These conceptions have appeared
to some as inconsistent with the fundamental
assumption of Christian faith in the absolute
rectitude of God ; to others they have seemed
not unworthy in themselves, but as contradicted
by fact; while another class of thinkers have
come to distrust the high moods out of which
optimistic interpretations of the character of the
universe spring.   This last is the deepest, the
most desperate, and perhaps the most characteristic doubt of the age.   To question the adequacy
of an inherited creed may do no more than lead
to its reconstruction ; to set faith and fact in
dead antithesis may result in a profounder reconciliation ; but what save universal pessimism can
issue from the mind of a generation that discred-
its its best mood as reflective of the ultimate
character of the universe ?   This distrust of love
as guide, this lapse from the assurance of the

spirit at its best, this descent from the highest level of humanity in the quest for ultimate truth, is the most important aspect of the phenomenon now under consideration. Upon the character of God and the nature and meaning of existence Christianity is the supreme mood of mankind. To discredit that, not in itself, not as a mood for the individual or for the race, but as a valid reflection of the final truth of things; to regard it as indeed good for man, but too good to be true for the universe, is the last and most painful extreme of doubt. In doubt of this kind man departs from himself; the departure, however, although upon a path of tears, is but going to school. Man needs to learn that the standards of interpretation which he adopts from the life foreign to his own will not serve him, that valid measures of existence and lasting certainties are not to be found in these alien regions, that for the best insight into the Infinite and the surest conviction he must return to himself. There is such a thing as the discipline of doubt, and it is natural to conclude that what reason demands and education necessitates, time will bring to new issues of faith.

II

Under one form or another religious doubt has prevailed ever since man began to think. Under Puritanism, the uncertainty that tor-

mented the best minds was uncertainty of their
election. The world was a lost world. There
was hope for any soul only as God's purpose
elected that soul to eternal life. The will of
God was supreme, it was the foundation of all
human hope of righteousness and happiness. It
was not a will inclusive of mankind, it was for
some and against some, and therein lay the distress. One could never be sure on which side
one would finally discover that one was classed.
Cowper went through life haunted by the horror
that the Divine decree was against his righteousness and peace; and under the midnight of that
horror he died. The sensitive poet is typical of
the spiritual distress of the age to which he
belonged. As men drew near to death they
became more and more serious in the review of
the evidences of their election by the Divine
will. Those evidences consisted in the graces
of the spirit, chief among which was the grace
of trust. Trust in the infinite mercy of God in
Christ was the main assurance. But as discontent with one's character and distrust of one's
worth are inseparable from the spirit that seriously entertains high ideals, the exercise of confidence in God's mercy became extremely difficult.
And the spiritual distress was aggravated by a
distinction that has long since ceased to exist.
Virtues were divided into natural and spiritual :
the natural were the product of the human will

or constitution, and were in the sight of God worthless; the spiritual were the fruit of the Divine indwelling and were the sole assurance of salvation. It was inevitable that the man who honestly studied himself should be unable to conclude whether what seemed to be grace might not be mere nature. The more conscientious the character the more inclined it would be to interpret itself downward, to look upon its religious interests as but natural selfishness in disguise. This is the vast and terrible shadow that Puritanism cast upon many of the finest spirits of the age. The doubt of the Divine election spread through families and communities. Men had no rights that God was bound to respect; the assertion of God was not of the kind to admit of the moral assertion of the human spirit. The element of gloom in which Puritanism lived cannot be overlooked; the discipline of doubt through which the heroic passed was severe and incessant. It was a common remark that no man should thank God for his existence until he awoke after the sleep of death and found himself in heaven. The judgment of multitudes of the best people was in a pendulum swing between optimism and pessimism as the final word for existence. The uncertainty as to whether God's will was for them or against them was a shadow that was never lifted. This is the tragic element in Puritan biography, the thing that fills it with imagination and that makes characters that otherwise would be commonplace extraordinary and grand. The contest with fate, in these lives, reminds one of a Greek drama ; their sufferings and their horror recall Prometheus and Œdipus. Bunyan's phrase, "the wilderness of this world," was but the echo of universal feeling; and the sad history of his Pilgrim is true to the best life of Puritanism.

The Puritan uncertainty was further complicated by the belief in apostacy. The possibility of apostacy, of breaking away from the Divine election, was stoutly denied ; and the logic was all in favor of the denial. But certain passages of Scripture seemed to make the possibility plain and to warn men against the danger. Apostacy, if it should take place, was final. There was no renewal for those who had put Christ to an open shame by their fall from discipleship. It is this fearful doubt that was working in the mind of Cromwell when he asked his chaplain whether once a Christian meant always a Christian. That he was once a believer he knew, that he had remained a believer throughout his long battle with the world he was not sure ; and he therefore looked to the transcendental link between the Divine will and the human soul for the decisive proof. If the gifts and calling of God are without repentance he was safe ; if apostacy was possible he was uncertain. That life should be invested with moral interests so high and issues so tragically uncertain is profoundly affecting. One must be blind indeed who does not see the moral grandeur of Puritanism, who fails to note its high educational value, and who expects nothing from the races that have passed through this wide and austere discipline. In any just computation of the educational worth of Puritanism large importance must be assigned to the uncertainty with which it charged the human intellect.

The mediæval and patristic doubt, so far as doubt affected the popular Christian mind, was a lower variety of the Puritan uncertainty. Speculative difficulties were of no popular moment until after the Revival of Letters and the Reformation. The belief of the Christian world up to that time was settled by authority. The history of intellectual doubt for this entire period is outside the Christian community. The objects of faith in their essential character were fixed and everlasting; the anxiety that troubled the popular mind was a moral or physical anxiety. The great persistent uncertainty concerned salvation. Salvation meant little more than escape from hell. Through masses of sad superstition and baseness of mind one discerns a salutary suspicion in the custom of postponing until the latest opportunity the rite of baptism. The case of Constantine is typical of a practice that

lasted into the fifth century. The emperor post-
poned baptism until death was near, on the
ground that baptism washed away all iniquities,
and that the sins committed after baptism might
be as few as possible. These sins committed
after baptism were indeed serious. They threw
into grave uncertainty the condition of the sinner after death. And here one gains a glimpse
into the popular mood of those vast periods.
Notwithstanding all the fine ecclesiastical appli-
ances for quieting the conscience, it was felt that
wrongdoing lay heavy upon the soul of the
wrongdoer. It was confessed that unrighteousness did in fact imperil salvation. The operation of a great, crude, moral doubt is discernible.
It was part of the civilizing force of the times.
Without this beneficent criticalness those great
populations would never have emerged into high
social moods. The awful jeopardy in which life
itself was set was an indispensable stimulus to
seriousness. The shadow of hell lay upon Europe for sixteen hundred years; it was the
shadow of an infinite reality, distorted, to be sure,
into caricature. Dante's Inferno lay in the conscience of patristic and mediæval Christendom;
he found it there, and his sole office was to provide for it an adequate symbol. That symbol
remains the monument in literature of the terrible uncertainty under which more than sixteen
centuries of life were passed. The popular

doubt was not of the reality of a heaven for
souls in the eternal world, but about the possibility of reaching it.

That there was profound and anxious questioning in the apostolic age the Epistle to the
Hebrews is the great witness. The Hebrews
who had become Christians had to undergo the
purification, the spiritualization of faith. They
began with the belief in Jesus as the Messiah,
in the expectation of his visible return within
the limits of the first generation of his followers,
in the restoration to Israel of national existence,
in the advent of a new era of power for their
people. They had to flee for their lives from
Palestine, and in the mood of sad surprise they
watched the events that wrought the reversal of
their expectations. They saw the holy city sur-
rounded by Roman legions, the temple in ruins,
their name blotted out from among the nations
of the earth, and still no Messiah appeared on
their behalf. The Old Testament had become
as nothing for this world, and the words and
promises of Jesus had not been kept. It was
into a mood like this that the message of the
great Epistle went. It began with the fundamental truth of a speaking God, it insisted upon
the consummation of the speech of God to men
in the Son ; it went forward upon this basis con-
verting the entire faith and ritual of the Old
Testament into a copy, a shadow, a symbol of

the full Christian truth. Christianity itself became a spiritual faith. The temple of this religion was the unseen, the sacrifice that put away sin was the sacrifice which Jesus accomplished through the Eternal Spirit, the kingdom to be restored was the rule of Divine love in the hearts of men, the city that was now sought was in the heavens. The faith of these Hebrew Christians that it might live had undergone revolution. The temporal elements, the mere accidents of belief, which had at first seemed to be parts of it, had fallen away, and it stood forth an eternal ideal in a transcendent Lord, in whose invisible might the community of believers found an everlasting spring of progress and hope. There has never been a greater revolution in faith since Christianity appeared than that which is both presupposed and recorded in the Epistle to the Hebrews. The attempt there made to estimate in terms of symbolism the value of Hebraism, and in terms of spirit the significance and worth of Christianity, is very great. Events had made the old literal faith untenable ; but the destroyer, time, brought with it an intellect that set the treasure of the Christian heart above time. The worlds of surprise, surrender, and despair that precede this new region of insight, attested truth, repose, and hope, the largest imagination can only imperfectly figure. It is but another proof that the midnight wrestle has always been the heroic introduction to the morning triumph.

For the closest parallel to the doubt of the nineteenth century one must return to the Old Testament. The seventy-third psalm is the type of Hebrew distress over the apparent contradictions in human history of the reality of the moral government of the world. The sufferings of good men and the prosperity and apparent happiness of rascals stirred the Hebrew conscience to its utmost depth. The profundity and the intensity of the doubt that afflicted prophets and psalmists is overlooked because the doubt is never left to stand alone, it is recorded only in connection with the insight or the instinct of trust through which it is dissolved. The fierceness of the battle is forgotten in the greatness of the victory. Still, for the distressed intellect of the nineteenth century dealing with the moral problem of human life there are psalms and passages from the prophets that might stand as its deepest expression. The Book of Job is mentioned by Huxley as the classic of pessimism. On the successive anniversaries of his birth it was the habit of Swift to read the third chapter, which begins with the terrible words: "Let the day perish wherein I was born." It must have been a great comfort to the utter skepticism and profound melancholy of the Dean, who yet had a conventional conscience,

that the Book of Job was in the canon. That
the Bible was adequate even to his moods must
have struck him at times as the irony of revelation. Job was Carlyle's favorite for nobler
reasons. The combination in it of the deepest
piety and the frankest confession of the gravest
questionings respecting the moral order of the
universe, rolled together in the widest sense of
mystery and uttered in the tenderness and majesty of the greatest poetry, made it a kind of
temple for his vexed yet essentially believing
spirit. Few things in any biography are more
touching than those pencilings in Carlyle's journal that picture the old man reading the Book of
Job at midnight when all London was asleep,
pausing for a moment to go to the door and look
out upon the starlit sky, and returning to the
great epic of sorrow, alternating between these
two mysteries, gazing with those unsatisfied and
sad eyes now upon the silent worlds spread before him in the Hebrew poem and again upon
the voiceless brightness and infinitude of space.

The forms of doubt in the nineteenth century
have been mainly scientific, sentimental, and
philosophic. Physical science has seen with
extraordinary clearness the law of struggle in
the life of the cosmos ; it has seen only recently
the law of sacrifice that everywhere precedes and
qualifies it. The cosmos has appeared to modern
science as a universal battlefield ; it has there-

fore been impossible for it to see any moral
character in the Being who gave life to these
fighting legions, and who sustains the conditions
that make the struggle inevitable. Science has
set man and the cosmos at war, as in Huxley's
famous Romanes lecture. Nature's procedure
and human ethics are in eternal hostility. There
is this petty but noble world of human brotherhood inside the vast and unfriendly cosmical
order. Besides, man's higher life is based upon
physical existence, the spiritual part of him is
wholly dependent upon the bodily. That the
cosmos is forever assailing, that it finally under-
mines and overthrows. Indirectly, then, the
deadly enemy of man, the cosmos, accomplishes
the destruction of the individual, and the outlook for the race in the heart of these everlasting
hostilities is gloomy enough. Thus science finds
an unmoral nature, a transitory human being, a
social order matched in unequal conflict with the
universe, and therefore drops at once into the
mood of despair. The facts of existence and
the character of reality will not permit Christian faith. The Christian faith is sublime; it is
the best thing in the world, but it is not true.

The sentimental form of the doubt comes to
its strongest expression in "The City of Dreadful Night." This great poem originates in sympathy with the sufferings of mankind. The fortune of men, the woe which is the common lot,

the darkness and despair which wait upon all
are incompatible with faith in the Christian conception of God. This sentiment has been the
mood of an entire generation of writers. In its
unrelieved pessimism as in the work just named,
in its tempered forms chastened by the strength
and grace of the moral nature as in Arnold, in
its transfigured character as in Tennyson, and
still more in Browning, one must refer to the
literature of Europe as the only adequate illustration of the sentimental doubt of the century.
It has a basis in science, but its origin is human
sympathy.

The philosophic doubt is familiar under the
name of agnosticism. Coming in one stream
from Kant through Hamilton and Mansel and
Spencer, in another from Hume through Mill
and Huxley, strengthened by the thought of
Comte, this movement has a common character. It asserts that all that men can know are
appearances and their ways of behavior, that
ultimate reality in the cases of the world, the
soul, and the Supreme being is simply inacces-
sible to human intelligence. For more than
thirty years this agnostic creed has dominated
vast bodies of thoughtful people. It resolves
itself into the deepest distrust of human reason
in the presence of the ultimate meaning of existence. In Kant, in Hamilton, and in Spencer, it
is a creed elaborately reasoned, and in the pages

of scores of writers of eminence and influence it is sincerely held and earnestly advocated. The agnostic mood is one of the most decided and marked of all the moods within the nineteenth century. As has been said, it seems to mean essentially distrust in the highest in man as the organ of the best in the universe, the fall from the confidence of reason, the loss of faith in the power of thought to read the riddle of existence.

III

Kant's illustration of the relation of the known to the unknown, as an island in the midst of a shoreless sea, is not altogether felicitous. For one thing this island of knowledge is constantly gaining and losing, here science is permanently advanced, there false assumptions are broken up. The territory thus assigned to the human intellect is far from being a definite or even definable bequest. At one point it runs out into new and firm-set continents, and at another it is shown to be not land at all but a mirage. Besides, the ideal of this surprising island will allow of no fixed limitations. It insists that its boundaries shall be pushed forever farther in upon the immeasurable deep. Ideally, the island is the whole, and the prophecy, " there shall be no more sea," must be read as history, " there is no more sea." Knowledge lives and grows because its inspiration is a universe that may be known absolutely.

The actual achievement of the intellect and the possible are ultimately inseparable. Before the reason, as it goes forth on its great quest, horizons recede, limitations are lifted, boundaries are pushed back, the island fills the place of the vanishing sea, the poor actual conquest lives and advances in the strength of the possible absolute conquest. Kant's island is indeed a contradiction to the fact and the law and the ideal of knowledge. The fact is an expanding knowledge, the law is expansion through sustained confidence in the ideal, and the ideal is a universe absolutely intelligible, and for man knowable without assignable limits.

Notwithstanding these obvious infelicities, Kant's comparison is a good introduction to an enumeration of some of the greater sources of doubt. This island of knowledge that rises out of the sea of the unknown rises so slowly, makes its gains at so much cost, holds its ideal of universal emergence against a protest so wide and stormy, that it is not strange that doubt should be one of its inhabitants. The first source of doubt therefore lies in the desperate inequality between the intellectual ideal and the intellectual achievement of mankind. The ideal of the separate sciences is exhaustive knowledge, each of its special subject. Chemistry, physics, astronomy, geology, biology, physiology, psychology, political economy, anthropology may be named as representative. Each of these sciences is but recent in its exact form, each during its brief history has been disturbed by revolutionary ideas, each has had to revise repeatedly its entire achievement upon the arrival of fresh light, each is animated by an ideal that is immeasurably beyond its present attainment. The ideals of science generally are largely unrealized, and no one is wise enough to say when the realizations will approximate the visions. In the sciences there is room for endless dispute, and no one can be quite sure that the discoveries of to-morrow will not overthrow, or generally alter, the conclusions of yesterday. All science is a Columbus voyage from the known to the unknown, and while one may guess and guess with genius, one cannot be sure against what the prow of the ship will eventually bring up.

If this is the case with the separate sciences, with the activity of the intellect when the division of labor has been carried to the greatest extreme, and when the province of investigation has been reduced to the point of correspondence with a single highly specialized faculty, how much more must one insist upon the incommensurateness of philosophy and its ideal. To admit the infinitude of the universe, and to confess the finiteness of human knowledge, would appear like the construction of a syllogism whose conclusion must be the questionableness of any opinion or judgment upon the ultimate character of being. This is the state of the case. Every characterization of the universe is questionable ; not because it may not be true, but because no one knows enough to prove that it is true. In this way one is to account for the atheisms and the theisms, the pantheisms and the materialisms and the nihilisms that like vast armies crowd the field of history. Each is founded upon knowledge, each is too poor in knowledge to support its conclusion by absolute proof. Each claims the liberty of prophesying, of venturing a characterization of the part without a knowledge of the whole, of risking a judgment upon the meaning of the whole from a provisional opinion about the part. Philosophy is not reasoned knowledge, it is reasoned faith. Philosophy is a series of more or less consistent beliefs about reality. Theoretically, atheist, theist, pantheist, materialist, and nihilist are alike in this, that the conclusion of every one of them, as to the ultimate character of the universe, is questionable. One can never be sure that one has before one all possible conclusions, one can never be certain that the disjunctive judgment is complete, that the right guess has not been omitted from the collection of samples. And if all the possibilities were assured, one could not know absolutely which one is the real. The ideal of knowledge is infinite, the object of knowledge is infinite, and so long as the attainment is less than this doubt is possible about the truth of its final characterizations. There is, indeed, no theoretical assurance against doubt this side of omniscience. It is the story of the travelers and the chameleon over again. The first contends that it is blue, the second that it is green, the third that it is black. Debaters and umpire are alike put to confusion by an appeal to the creature itself, when it turns out to be white. Each conclusion was based upon real although insufficient knowledge. The contradictions and mistakes originated in the fact that isolated particulars were turned into general conclusions. Aspects of the animal were converted into wholes, different aspects gave different wholes, and when the appeal was taken to the baffling beast, another aspect, that at once transformed itself into another whole, made confusion worse confounded. Here in parable is the history of philosophies. Aspects of the universe are all that men have. These aspects are indeed constantly expanding, and they are as constantly enriched with fresh varieties. Still, aspects of the Infinite are all that the largest intellect can command; and with different degrees of insight, thoroughness, fidelity, probability, and mastery these aspects of existence are shaped into the whole. Nothing is here hinted against the legitimacy or respectability of this procedure. Indeed, it is asserted that no other is possible. The point is not that the method is unlawful or mean, but that it be clearly understood. Then it will be seen that philosophy is not knowledge but systematized opinion, or as was said a moment since, reasoned faith.

Here, then, is the primary source of speculative doubt. The intellectual ideal is infinite, and this implies that the present knowledge is certainly imperfect and possibly erroneous. Theoretically every man takes his reputation in his hand when he risks a judgment as to the ultimate character of the universe. He may prove to be a wise man, and he may prove to be a fool. The Day of Judgment is the supreme court of appeal. Until the great and terrible Day of the Lord we rest in questionable conclusions. We cannot play the part of the judge; we appear as parties in the eonian trial of truth. Parmenides appears in court claiming that the ultimate thing is Permanence; Heraclitus contends that it is Becoming; Plato and Aristotle come in and depose that it is Mind, while Epicurus and Lucretius witness that it is Matter; Spinoza testifies that it is Substance, and Hume that it is Shadow; Hegel avers that it is Absolute Spirit, and other voices complicate the issue with the characterization that it is the Unconscious. This last contention is so inherently humorous that it nearly upsets the gravity

of the court and all the parties to the suit. To
be dead and alive at one and the same time and
in the same sense, and to have mind and not to
know it, is one of those mirthful incidents that
lighten the hours of the long trial. But it is
no part of the present discussion to expose the
absurdities that may lie in the case of any one
of these militant litigants. They are in court ;
they are arguing their cases ; they are awaiting
judgment. All that it is now in order to say is
that until judgment is given the merits of these
cases are in doubt.

The ethical ideal is another source of doubt.
The world and the ethical ideal do not agree.
What ought to be nowhere is, and this fact gives
rise to the profoundest and most serious questioning. Nature and man are at once friends
and enemies ; but in this connection the friendship easily drops out of sight and the enmity
with astonishing facility occupies the entire field
of vision. Nature does not behave toward man
as man thinks he has a right to expect on the
assumption that it is the order of a Being supremely good and wise and powerful. J. S.
Mill's indictment against nature is the popular
one. "In sober truth, nearly all the things
which men are hanged or imprisoned for doing
to one another are nature's everyday perform-
ances. Nature impales men, breaks them as on
the wheel, casts them to be devoured by wild

beasts, crushes them with stones like the first Christian martyr, starves them with hunger, freezes them with cold, poisons them with the quick or slow venom of her exhalations, and has hundreds of other hideous deaths in reserve, such as the ingenious cruelty of a Nabis or a Domitian never surpassed." [1] Superficial as this is, and onesided to the last degree, [2] it contains an aspect of the truth, and one that appeals strongly to human feeling. The cosmos does not behave toward man as man is bound to behave toward his brother. If one expects from the cosmos the behavior of an ideal man one will be profoundly disappointed. And here the chief difficulty presents itself. When the cosmos is said to be the work of a beneficent Creator it becomes at once the object of an ideal expectation. The doubt that follows upon contradicted hopes is temporarily inevitable. Human life and happiness seem incidental to the purpose of nature, things permissible but unessential. Nature appears in the mood of absolute indifference toward the ends which are of supreme concern to man. Therefore he concludes that it is unmoral and sorrowfully sings : —

> " I find no hint throughout the Universe
> Of good or ill, of blessing or of curse ;
> I find alone Necessity supreme ;
> With infinite mystery, abysmal, dark ;
> Unlighted ever by the faintest spark
> For us the flitting shadow of a dream."

[1] *Essays on Religion*, pp. 28, 29.   [2] See chap. ii.

The want of concert between nature and man is the first source of moral doubt; the inequality between man's ethical outfit and his ideal is the second. The heavenly vision is everywhere accompanied by the surest earthly limitations. The Christian ideal is, " Ye shall be perfect, as your heavenly Father is perfect." [1] Applied to the spirit and achievement of the noblest disciple, this sounds like the irony of the Infinite, as if an infant were commanded to discourse like a Demosthenes. The social ideal is the city of God, and in this light the best city in the world looks like Sodom. The evils of society arise largely from inheritance, general incapacity, and inhumanity. There is a vast mass of evil conditions for which nobody would seem to be personally responsible, as in the cases of inherited physical weakness; there is another and yet vaster mass for which no one would appear to be wholly responsible, as in the remediable social and governmental grievances; there is, besides, the work of man's inhumanity to man within the sphere of clear understanding and unmistakable obligation. The victims of inherited disease, the sufferers from an unjust social order, and those upon whom injuries fall from the working of perverse wills represent the mystery of iniquity born of the solidarity of man and compounded of ignorance and wickedness.

[1] Matt. v. 48.

To these must be added the slow rate of possible improvement. The promised land is almost always sighted a generation before its nearest border can be reached.

Now these things put together, an unmoral cosmos and a humanity unequal to the moral task set before it, seem to argue against the reality of the moral character and purpose of God. These observations upon nature and upon society in the light of the ethical ideal issue, not infrequently, in the last despair. The universe appears to disown and contradict the human conscience, personal and social. All ideal commonwealths are Utopias, all kingdoms of God are but colored and amazing devices of the moral imagination of mankind. Morality is the highest in man, but its cause is hopeless, because the universe is against it. Nothing is more terrible than this fall from faith in the righteousness of the universe. Of all the voices in "The City of Dreadful Night," none are so piercing in their sad significance as these : —

" From prayer and fasting in a lonely cell,
   Which brought an ecstasy ineffable
   Of love and adoration and delight;
   I wake from day dreams to this real night.

" From preaching to an audience fired with faith
   The Lamb who died to save our souls from death,
   Whose blood hath washed our scarlet sins wool-white ;
   I wake from day dreams to this real night.

" From writing a great work with patient plan
To justify the ways of God to man,
And show how ill must fade and perish quite ;
I wake from day dreams to this real night."

There have probably never been so many in any previous century who have fallen from faith in the moral character of the universe ; and the source of this fall is to be found in the stern application so characteristic of the nineteenth century of the Christian ideal to the behavior of the universe toward man. It is suggestive that the person with whom that ideal originated felt no incompatibility between it and the Infinite. It raises the profoundest and most interesting questions as to how much nature was meant to teach of God, and the function of man in this economy of revelation. It intimates that large confusions exist upon the subject, and that there is an imperative call for revised and more adequate thought.

It seems ignoble, but it is nevertheless true, that personal fortune in this world has much to do with the optimistic and pessimistic moods in which men view the universe. One must make room here for a wide and long procession of exceptions. One must not overlook the literal and symbolic truth in the serenity of Epictetus, the slave, and the misery of Nero, the emperor, the chastened but invincible hopelessness of John the Baptist in his prison, and the terrible

forebodings of Herod in his palace, the supreme
trust of Christ upon his cross in the Father of
his spirit, and the fear of Pilate in his high
success. Heroism has the power to transmute
the dross of existence, the injustice and outrage to which it is subjected, into gold; while
meanness of soul reduces the golden triumph
to dust and ashes. There could hardly be a
more fatal mistake than to overlook this double
movement in human history, — the sublima-
tion of sorrow and the debasement of success,
the proclamation of the gospel of love from the
grave of earthly hope, and the utterance of the
evangel of despair from the summit of earthly
achievement. This is indeed the heart of the
most precious tradition of mankind. The men
of whom the world has not been worthy are precisely those who have looked upon good report
and evil as mere incidents in the passionate pursuit of sublime and wholly indispensable ideals.
And upon the negative side the pessimism that
has its origin in egoism is never the most affecting. The despair that issues from altruistic
sources, the negation of faith that has its spring
in pity for mankind, is the really great phenomenon. Rachel in her eternal peace, weeping
for her children, and refusing to be comforted
because they are not, is the type of the despair
that is truly mighty.

Upon the majority of mankind, however, personal fortune does tell. Odysseus's fortune was hard, but upon the whole good. He cannot think ungratefully of the order that gave him Penelope and Telemachus, and that after a career so varied, romantic, and glorious brought him back to the unshaken fidelity and the everlasting affection of his home. With many memories that make him weep Odysseus can hardly look upon the universe with other than friendly eyes. On the other side of the question, if one is supposed to have undergone the horrors to which Œdipus the king was subjected, one would be more than human if the experience left belief in the moral order of the world unaffected. The order that should avenge any conceivable crime by a pre-destination so horrible, that should lead its victim into the snare by the steps taken in all honesty to avoid it, that should make inno-cence the path to parricide and incest, could hardly appear as other than diabolic. It is not implied that this is the whole story, or that there are not larger ethical settings in which the central horror should be viewed. The point made is that one would be more than human if one were able to transcend the personal · abuse experienced at the hands of the universe.

Passing from imagination to fact, it has often been remarked that the healthy optimism of Aris-totle owed something to the rare good fortune of the philosopher. The man who had Plato for his master, Alexander the Great for his patron, one of the happiest of Greek homes, the supreme opportunity of the ancient world for philosophic achievement, and powers to match it unparalleled in their grandeur, could scarcely fail, on these accounts, to think a little better of the world. Few and uncertain as the facts are about the personal fortune of the great Roman thinker and poet, Lucretius, in reading his poem it is nearly impossible to resist the impression that the bitterness of individual sorrow is in it. There is certainly more in it than that. The sympathy that feels the fears with which superstition has afflicted his time, and that would deliver men from their burdens, is the basis of the great poem; but the social purpose is fired by passionate personal grief. The man who wrote that poem had a hard lot in life, and the spectacles through which he looked upon the universe were blurred and darkened by the sad eyes that used them. James Russell Lowell has remarked that the Paradiso was Dante's reward for living. The poet had found the supreme good, and the universe could appear in no other character. Suppose that Dante had stopped with the Purgatorio or with the Inferno. Many men go no farther. An infernal fortune is apt to characterize the universe in its own vocabulary, and according to its own idiom.

All this is unphilosophic in the last degree.

One swallow does not make summer, nor does one flake of snow make winter. Personal fortune, whether happy or unhappy, is an insufficient basis for a general judgment as to the character of the ultimate reality. Nevertheless, as a source of doubt, personal ill-fortune is prolific. The intellectual disinterestedness and the moral heroism that take a man outside of himself, that enable him to regard the universe in the light of pure reason and the glow of a passion for the highest education of man, while they are the double summit from which the only adequate vision is to be had, are altogether too high and steep for the majority of mankind. The personal element in the work of Ecclesiastes and Lucian and Omar Khayyám and Swift and Schopenhauer and James Thomson should not be overlooked. It is the sheer stupidity of a false generosity that cannot hear in the productions of these men the fundamental note of personal failure. The objective truth of their work is secondary, perhaps accidental, and it is certainly severely limited. The primary thing about it is its autobiographic value. The conclusions of Ecclesiastes are inevitable from his premises, and the vital syllogism presented in his pages stands there a painful sign as to where the truth is not to be found. Lucian is a gifted, entertaining writer, and in the great workshop of the world there is something for him to do.

But the man who never takes the world seriously cannot object if it refuses to take him seriously. Omar Khayyám's philosophy would appear to be mightily supported by his practice. Swift, one of the noblest of natures, and one of the greatest of writers, carries up into his work his personal experience in the world. As Christian minister there is no evidence that his eye was single, or that he ever seriously entertained the Christian ideal. The initial horror of Swift's life was that he was in the ministry of self-sacrifice with the purpose of self-assertion. He had neither the comfort of his calling nor the freedom of the man of the world. Disappointed ambition, disgust at the men and the things that united to defeat him, scorn for the weakness and the villainy of the world, magnified by his embittered and passionate imagination, and the saving although savage humor that opened the floodgates for his tormented heart, are the chief sources of Swift's work. One can scarcely resist the conclusion that if he had gone in another direction he would have reached a different goal. Swift is one of the greatest masters of irony, and he felt the irony of the universe when he said of Gulliver's Travels that the book that he had written to vex the world had become the amusement of children. Somehow men are discovered, the sources of their work and the estimate in which it should be held. Schopenhauer is of a more objective character; still, the personal contribution which the pessimist makes to his own creed finds an uncommonly impressive illustration in this writer. The universal value of James Thomson's great poem is evident to every discerning reader. It seems to me the greatest poem of despair in the world; it voices with a terrbile sincerity the hopeless sorrow of mankind. It is the only adequate voice for a large section of the experience of human beings in the nineteenth century. It would be folly to look at it as other than sadly representative; yet one must think that the streets of "The City of Dreadful Night" would not have been so dark had the quantity of Scotch whiskey consumed in them been less. The moral problem of the universe is inseparable from the moral character of the thinker. The pessimism that is in a large measure produced or inspired or colored by the moral failures of the pessimist does not impress the world as scientific. The only really objective and scientifically valid pessimism would be the pessimism of love. Had Jesus Christ in his love for mankind accused the universe of indifference, that accusation would at least be impartial. Had he, in his service of love for men, written a book to show wherein the universe had opposed him or left him unsupported, that book would be the Bible of pessimism. The conditions would be such as to insure, not indeed a necessarily fatal, but the strongest conceivable arraignment of the moral character of the Infinite. Short of this one must have doubts of the doubters and compassionate them.

The terrestrial habit of mind is not without considerable influence in creating a negative mood toward the Infinite. Wordsworth describes it when he writes of the " shades of the prison house " that close about the growing boy, when he accuses earth, " the homely nurse," of doing

> " all she can
> To make her foster-child, her inmate Man,
> Forget the glories he hath known
> And that imperial palace whence he came."

The naturalistic habit of mind represents the working of many tendencies. Agnosticism is partly a result of the desire to reduce the universe within manageable compass. Intellects that love above all things order and completeness, that have a passion for clearness and exactness, that are pained when knowledge is unorganized and fragmentary, are under strong temptations to reduce the object of knowledge. Men like Kant, and Comte, and Hamilton, and Mill, and Spencer are impelled by the whole bent of their minds to make a map of the universe, to divide it into the two continents of the knowable and the unknowable, and then to seek the high excellence for which they are fitted

in the sphere of the finite to which they would
limit the legitimate operations of all human intelligence. The naturalistic habit of mind originates, for the most part, in no agony of baffled
endeavor after the Infinite, but in the desire to
make the universe scientifically manageable. It
is first done for personal convenience; then personal convenience is converted into universal
necessity.

The world is an isolated planet, men are born
and die upon it, the main business of existence
is confessedly with it. The heavens make a
great show and they are not without their uses;
still, both the display and the service are for man
as he lives upon this earth. A terrestrial habit
of thought is instigated by man's visible origin
and end, by the sources and the chief concerns
of his existence, by the order that rounds off his
career with the globe, by the whole appearance
and by much of the substantial interest of his
life. When the lower ends of mere livelihood,
or wealth, or position, or power are the sole pursuit, where thought is never allowed to run out
after ultimate relations and causes, where love
does not enter with its confusing infinitudes,
where ideals for the individual in society and
for society in its bearing toward the universe
make no disturbance, it is not strange that limitation of intelligence and feeling to the earth
should result. When the terrestrial life is taken

as self-sustaining and self-sufficing the reality of
the supersensuous and eternal ceases to be felt.
The bird gets accustomed to its cage; under the
power of habit the world beyond ceases to mean
anything to it. The cage becomes the universe.
To the naturalistic type of mind the sphere of
significance gradually contracts, and the infinite,
as far as it concerns man, is reduced to the
boundaries of the material world. The size of
the universe depends upon the range of human
interests. The withdrawal of interest from any
phase of reality means practically the extinction
of that phase for that person. Dead interests
mean a dead universe. No source of antagonism
to the higher faith of mankind is wider than this
quiet withdrawal of interest from the things of
the living spirit.

Less obvious than any source of doubt yet
mentioned and more fundamental than them all,
I should put the neglect of the negative mood
to look for God through man, and through man
at his best. Cosmical theology has its place;
that place is, however, altogether subordinate
and even insignificant. The way in which it has
been worked has led men to think that when
one looks for God through the material order one
stands on philosophical ground, and when one
appeals to man and his highest spiritual history
one enters the region of faith. Theologians have
taught philosophers to prefer for evidential force

the natural to the spiritual, the outward world
to the human. Theology has suffered for its
lack of humanism, and it has smitten faith with
its own malady. The natural man, the naked
framework of a human being, the person abstracted from his highest life, has been called
into court as a theistic witness. As well call in
the witches that Macbeth found on the heath.
Worse than the injustice thus committed against
mankind has been the consequent failure to
appreciate the meaning of the Incarnation. As
was seen in a former chapter, this failure is by
no means characteristic of the nineteenth century, taking it as a whole. Still, the century is
full of contradictory moods, varying in their
degrees of depth and persistence. And beneath
the negative mood now under consideration, as
its deepest source, there would seem to lie this
neglect to see the significance of man, and of
man at his best as a witness for God.

The life of Jesus Christ is part of human history, it is part of the universe. And if one is
seeking to discover the ultimate character of the
universe, it can be little short of fatal to neglect
its supreme manifestation. The idea of the Incarnation lives in the strength of the axiom of
cause and effect. The cause must equal the product; Jesus Christ is not self-originated. In the
highest metaphysics of theology he is still the begotten of the Father. His advent, his ministry,

his passion, his whole character and career in this world need explanation. The principle of causation cries out for satisfaction here as elsewhere. Christ is a gift, a product, an effect, a manifestation of the universe; and to generalize upon the character of the universe in neglect of this supreme fact is, in the last degree, unphilosophical. In a lower sense this contention holds true of the whole brotherhood of the brave and wise. They could not have been what they were without the endowment, the spirit, the opportunity, and the constant inspiration which they received at the hands of the universe. In the last analysis, therefore, they are witnesses for the universe. The motto written upon the forehead of every wise and just man is in the words: " By the grace of God I am what I am." The case of faith against doubt and denial has too often gone to the jury on the testimony of its least capable witnesses. Worlds that depend upon their association with human thought and feeling for their higher meanings have been called into court as independent and primary; the weaknesses, the crimes, the records of human ignorance and suffering, have been admitted as evidence ; while endowment, opportunity, spirit, genius, heroism, the whole higher outfit and achievement of the race, have been, under the name of revealed religion, ruled out. Man is the real witness for God ; man at his best is the

supreme evidence of the Spirit of God. The
Incarnation is the only adequate and just form
in which to put the case of faith in behalf of the
character of the universe, before the jury of
human intelligence.

IV

To a wise believer doubt must always appear
as a service in the interest of a greater faith.
Progress is achieved through strife; Kant's bird
flies heavenward by impact of its wings against
the resisting air. The victories of truth over
error, of righteousness over iniquity, of society
over anarchy, ultimately viewed, are won by
contributions from all the parties to the conflict.
The law of antagonism and the progressively
victorious effort after reconciliation are the
heart and soul of human life; and it would
appear, in the light of present insight into
man's nature, that should the stimulus of contradiction cease the existence of the race would
be one of stagnation. For the present, at least,
and indeed for a long time to come, the hostile
environment would seem to be absolutely indispensable. Physically, intellectually, ethically,
and spiritually the adversary is essential. This
is the great philosophical truth underlying the
myth of the devil. The universe is both against
man and for him, in the order of nature and in
the human constitution itself; and among the

contributors to the building of the wall that is to surround and shield the city of God there must be reckoned, not only Nehemiah and his brave companions, but also the mocking Sanballat and his stone-throwing and jeering crowd. In the determination of merit there is a distinction to be drawn between these persons wide as the interval between right and wrong; in the estimate of the total force that produced the grand result all must be included, some as divinely ruled, the others as divinely overruled.

This is the principle upon which it is held that great doubters are ultimately great servants of faith. Satan appears among the sons of God, and the first result is that Job is overwhelmed with loss. But this is but the beginning of things. The trial of strength follows between good and evil, between faith and doubt, and the final issue is the vindication of Job. He recovers all that he had lost, and he now holds it in the security of an irreversible victory. For those who believe in the Christian philosophy of history, the drama of redemption is prefigured in the great Hebrew epic. Satan still appears among the sons of God, and here the concern with him is as intellectual accuser. The associations of the name are unpleasant, but one can think charitably of a great function of human thought under the most adverse designation. From the point of view of the believer the purely negative thinker must appear as an adversary. One may think of him as essentially noble, as intrinsically true and tender, but by some calamity compelled to play the part of a Sanballat or an honorable Satan. For it is believed that the restless spirit so designated in the Hebrew poem is absolved by scholarship from all essentially bad qualities. He is the doubter, the inquirer, the spirit that will not believe save upon the application of the severest tests and the last rigors of proof. Upon this basis of respect and antagonism, and not wholly deserted, it is hoped, by the humor that lends sanity to earnestness, this chapter may be fittingly closed with a brief reference to a few of the great doubters and their great services to progress.

The treatment here must be rigidly symbolic, the suggestion of the history and service of doubt through the selection of a few of its more prominent types. And the first observation may well be of the work of the negative intellect in the elimination of superstition. In the death of the follies of Paganism something must be set down to the credit of Lucian. His pages must have provoked laughter in thousands of readers. In the passage of the popular religion of Greece and Rome from the sphere of reality to the region of fable, the great satirist must have wielded an enormous influence. Granted

that superstition is best eliminated by growth
into the truth of which it is the counterfeit,
granted that the affirmative conceptions of Christianity were a surer promise of the early demise
of Paganism than the shafts of the keenest wit, it
still holds that laughter turned against a foolish
creed is one of the strongest weapons. The " Dialogues of the Dead " were intended to do more
than eliminate superstition ; but in removing popular and multitudinous absurdities and horrors
they must have done good service. Popular religious notions had come to cast so dense a
shadow upon human life that Lucretius found
the motive of his poem in the merciful desire
to expose their groundlessness. To the humane
spirit of Lucretius, atheism and a purely terrestrial view of man's existence seemed a sanctuary of peace compared with the horror of the
popular religious notion. Lucretius fought the
superstition that laid the earth in the hopeless
gloom of supernatural terror. His work is great
not only as an expression of the negative mood,
but also as an exposure of intimidating and degrading superstition. Erasmus did much of his
best service in fighting this evil. His " Praise
of Folly " and his " Colloquies " set free the
humor and laughter of the time, and forged
them into weapons for the emancipation of the
spirit from absurd customs and sad superstitions. Voltaire's true place is in this line. In

the progress toward freedom his work cannot be overlooked. He fancied, doubtless, that he had done more than expose enslaving customs, and hence the point of Carlyle's sarcasm: "Old Ludovicus has a story of a clown that killed his ass because it had drunk up the moon, and he thought the world could ill-spare that luminary. So he killed his ass, *ut lunam redderet.* The clown was well-intentioned, but unwise. Let us not imitate him : let us not slay a faithful servant, who has carried us far. He has not drunk the moon, but only the reflection of the moon, in his own poor water-pail, where too, it may be, he was drinking with purposes the most harmless." [1] This sarcasm fits the mood of the Frenchman and his popular critics. To himself and to them he was the destroyer of religion. Here humor and fear run up against the irony of truth; the laugh is on the mocker for his ludicrous mistake, and on the believer for his equally ludicrous ignorance.

But it is essential to distinguish between what men think that they are and what they really are. Because Voltaire was less than he imagined, he may be justly visited with sarcasm, but he cannot fairly be dismissed by it. When the illusion born of vanity has been dissipated, Voltaire's merit is still solid and honorable. The exposure of Antichrist is always a service in the

[1] *Miscellaneous Essays*, vol. i. pp. 460, 461.

interest of truth; the sincere attack upon unworthy forms of the truth is an indispensable
warfare. "De Maistre compares Reason putting
away Revelation to a child who should beat its
nurse. The same figure would serve just as well
to describe the thanklessness of Belief to the
Disbelief which has purged and exalted it."[1]
Much of the religious custom of the age de-
served Voltaire's exposure and mockery. It
was in the interest of a better future than he
himself represented that he spread so widely the
mood of antagonism to ecclesiastical Christianity.
He could not do the highest service, he was unable to discriminate between the counterfeit and
the reality; he was far from being able to dis-
place the floods of error by planting the mountain of the Lord in the midst of them. But
enslaving error, widespread and evil custom
walking under the sanction of ecclesiastical
Christianity, he did smite hip and thigh, and
the wise believer will not fail to remember this
service.

In the nineteenth century, this warfare against
superstition has been carried on by a multitude
of writers through the agency of science. One
vast benefit has certainly accrued to the people
from the silence into which the supernatural has
fallen. During this silence the fear of nature
has been passing away. The cosmos has slowly

[1] John Morley, *Voltaire*, p. 32.

emerged into a trustworthy character. It has been sifting itself into the popular mind as an order, and as an order that stands ready to serve the intelligence that masters it. Witches, ghosts, devils, supernatural horrors no longer people the darkness or lie in wait for lonely wayfarers. There are no traditions in existence to-day like those out of which Burns, at the close of the eighteenth century, constructed "Tam O'Shanter." The serious and terrible traditions of witches and fiends and kindred uncanny presences have become a ludicrous mythology. Common-sense has had a good deal to do with the transformation, but science has been to an incalculable extent its friend and helper. Under the sarcasm of fact, the irony of knowledge, the noble mockery and laughter of truth, whole hosts of imposing superstitions have passed clean out of existence. In cleaning this Augean stable, science has been our Hercules; and one can do no less than commemorate the broom that has swept into tolerable condition such unspeakable spaces.

That ideas should have an opportunity in their best expression to appeal to the human mind is always ultimately a service for truth. The call of truth is for the forcible suppression of no idea. Free speech is the universal and absolute right of ideas ; and it is the privilege that only the true idea can endure. Let an idea

like a man talk, and if it is not true, it will
swiftly give itself away. The seeker for truth
has therefore the deepest interest in the classic
expression of opposing ideas. He wishes to
meet materialism and idealism, atheism and
theism, in their strongest forms. The believer
has the best of reasons for desiring that the
negative moods of the race should attain the
completest expression. The enemy is not overcome until he is crushed in his citadel; a doubt
is not answered until it is met in its highest
form. The answer of Demosthenes is to the
challenge of Æschines, that of Cicero to Catiline,
of Burke to those who skillfully drew " an indictment against a whole people," of Webster to
Calhoun. And along another line the answer of
Plato is to Protagoras, of Kant to Hume, and,
greatest of all, of Christ to Pilate. For pessimism it is believed that the two most powerful
utterances are the literary expression of Swift in
the eighteenth century and the philosophical
expression of Schopenhauer in the nineteenth.
The bitterness of the deepest and sincerest unbelief in man is in every characteristic sentence
that Swift ever wrote. Inside the inclosure of
institutional Christianity, with scrupulous fidelity
to the forms of its service, and with absolute
sphinx-like silence upon the question of its fundamental reality or unreality, and with a personal life wholly free from the stains that so

often pollute his speech, Swift is yet the profoundest, intensest, and completest pessimist in English literature. The vision of the dark side of life is wide and accurate; the expression is deliberate, generally within bounds, and yet deadly in its aim. There is nothing hysterical about Swift's pessimism. Its awful passion is subdued or veiled by the sanest humor. The popular expression of the pessimistic mood could hardly be more powerful, and this of itself is a great service. Here is the mood at its best so far as literary genius is concerned.

It is believed that pessimism has never found a more adequate philosophical expression than in the writings of Schopenhauer. He has discovered the supreme sorrow to be in the will to live. Life is a mistake, its desire to go on is its curse. "That this most perfect manifestation of the will to live, the human organism, with the cunning and complex working of its machinery, must fall to dust and yield up itself and all its strivings to extinction, — this is the naïve way in which nature, who is always so true and sincere in what she says, proclaims the whole struggle of this will barren and unprofitable. Were it of any value in itself, anything unconditioned and absolute, it could not thus end in mere nothing." [1] The nature of will, then, is inherently and endlessly discontent and sorrow. The German

[1] *Studies in Pessimism*, p. 39.

thinker has grounded pessimism in scientific psychology. The depth of the analysis, the finding that accuses the constitution of the will as the fountain of sorrow, the indictment that is so tremendous and that calls in as evidence the fundamental instinct of life, opens the door into an opposite mood. The case does turn upon the nature of the will. In modern thinking there is no testimony stronger than that supplied by the writings of Schopenhauer to the fact that human existence is either evil or good, according as the will is wild or trained in love. The will is the centre either for pessimism or optimism. A wild will generates the data upon which its own hopeless conclusions are founded ; while a will trained in love supplies the new creation upon which the heavenly vision draws for support. But for the powerful and passionate expression of the German pessimist, thinkers would be largely without that consciousness which now obtains of the originative function either for good or ill, for unbelief or faith of the human will. The facts upon which pessimism and optimism build are not ready-made. The same world confronts two persons, and one remarks upon it, " Curse God and die," while the other says, " The Lord gave and the Lord hath taken away; blessed be the name of the Lord." [1] The world may be bent into pessimism or into

[1] Job i. 21.

optimism. It is capable of either conformation, and the character of the thinker exercises a determinative influence. The facts are not furnished by the order of the world independent of personal life. They are supplied by the will renewed in love or left unrenewed and in its unbroken egoistic passion. The kingdom of heaven is within, and the kingdom of hell too.

Naturalism is another great mood. It hardly needs definition. It is the result of the view that regards man as the highest expression of terrestrial or cosmical life and nothing more. It seeks for the origin of man in the life below him and not in any supposed life above him. It makes much of the sensational side of the mind and little of the universal laws of thought. It lays immense emphasis upon outward fact, and notes but lightly the transforming influence of the inward upon the outward. Its passion is for definite and demonstrable views; its spirit is negative toward the spiritual; its tendency is to look upon man's life as nothing more than the climax of the animal life of the world.

This mood has received powerful expression in the writings of J. S. Mill, Huxley, and Comte. It has vanished as philosophy largely because it put itself into forms so strong and full of challenge. This philosophy, whose fountain-head is Hume, has had the merit of embodying one of the sincerest and most influential moods of the

nineteenth century; it has had the further merit
of calling forth an antagonist mightier than itself. Philosophical idealism, in a fair fight with
naturalism, has swept it from the field. To put
an incomplete view of human life, an inverted
and erroneous interpretation of reality in such
form that a final refutation could be given to its
pretentions, is indeed a memorable service. This
was the work of Hume, but the nineteenth century disciples of Hume fixed attention upon their
master. The obsoleteness of Positivism, the dim
distance to which scientific naturalism has already
receded is due, in part, to the challenge which it
issued to thought. That challenge was worthy
of the attention of the strongest. The Philistine
Goliath called out the Hebrew David; the naturalistic warrior discovered for Great Britain
and America the prowess of German idealism.

Christianity, minus the evangelical record,
from the severe naturalism of Strauss to the
historically nude idealism of Thomas Hill Green,
represents still another of the greater moods of
the last generation. With this entire class the
miracle is a myth, the supernatural is either denied or identified with the spiritual, Christian
ethics are cut from their native evangelical
metaphysics and grafted into the Hegelian tree.
The full issues of this mood are not yet in sight.
But it has certainly been arrested in its unhis-
torical treatment of Christianity. And it is

becoming clearer that it is questionable whether theology gains by the indiscriminate translation of its ideas from one philosophy into another. Hegelianism is in every way immeasurably richer and deeper than Calvinism ; and yet theology should live an independent life. It should borrow as much as it may from the " rich banquet of Hegel," and it should do this in the interest of an original construction of its data. Christianity is indeed the wine of existence, but it is open to doubt whether it is improved by being indefinitely poured from philosophic vessel to vessel. The philosophical construction of the universe must have its genesis in Christian interests, its supreme data in Christian experience, before it can be allowed to be identical with Christian theology. Christianity is great enough to grow its own philosophical forms, and while it is essentially the Holy Spirit of inclusiveness, it is equally the Holy Spirit of transcendent insight and worth. It serves man through his numberless moods and their literary expression, yet it should be made subject to no mood lower than itself, and confined to no form other than that which it freely creates from itself. The true theologian of this new time, therefore, is not a mere translator of old thoughts into novel forms, of Calvinism into Hegelianism; he is a man with direct vision into reality, and he seeks for the better intellectual form in the larger

truth.   Constructions that have life in them can
rise only out of original insight working in awe
and joy upon the facts of the Christian consciousness.   Other science than that which accounts
for facts is vain ; other theology than that generated by the best insight working upon the content of the Christian heart is fruitless.   Translation is easy, original interpretation is difficult ;
still nothing less than this new creation can serve
the new time.

The fatal objection to the Hegelian interpretation of Christianity is that it treats the
philosophic system as primary and Christianity
as secondary.   The system is indeed one of the
greatest ; yet it cannot be permitted to weigh in
its own scales the Gospel of Christ.   The mood
which expresses this attempt is full of seriousness
and interest.   It represents at its best so much
truth and so much onesidedness that it is sure to
continue its influence.   And great good must
result from its persistence.   There are fundamental questions to whose solution it should
have much to contribute.   The relations of fact
and law, history and idea, nature and the supernatural, the cosmic and human fields, and the
evangelical truth and grace are sure to come,
under this mood, to profounder and richer expression.

Perhaps the most signal service rendered by
negative thought has been that it has compelled

the reorganization of knowledge, or the discovery of a deeper philosophy upon this subject. Writers like Montaigne, who do not think but feel, who rest in the custom of the senses, whose charm consists in wide and accurate observation of the superficial aspects of life, in picturesqueness and garrulousness, and who whenever they do look at the conclusions of philosophic thought are ready with the question, "What do I know?" are not amenable to argument or insight. For them the better organization of knowledge is a byword and a reproach. The conviction that deeper insight into the structure and process of knowledge may lead to new outlooks upon the universe and to fresh certainties is folly. Writers of the Montaigne type, impossible believers as they are, do nevertheless stimulate the intellectually normal in the desire for truth. But the really great service in this direction comes from men of a far higher order of intellect. David Hume has the distinction of being the greatest negative thinker on record. He took philosophy as he found her; he paid no attention to her achievements in Plato and Aristotle. He found her in her modern form, young, vain, and full of babble upon all high subjects. He did her the unspeakable service of making her, upon her own principles, reason herself into eternal silence. When Hume had done with philosophy she was obliged to find a new set of principles before she

could open her mouth.   Who shall say that this
was not high service.   Who shall say that Hume
did not preach to sensationalism the best sermon
ever delivered to it, and upon the text, "The
mouth of them that speak lies shall be stopped."
Hume is the negative inaugurator of modern
philosophy.   He gave reasoned expression to
Plato's contention that a consistent sensationalism is dumb.[1] But for Hume's destructive criticism the world would have been without Kant's
critical construction, which, as carried upward by
Kant's idealistic successors, has provided for the
total interests of mankind the most adequate
philosophic home that they have ever inhabited.

The doubt that is most characteristic of the
nineteenth century has originated in the quest
for certainty.   The ideal of knowledge has been
high and severe ; followed into the region of the
ultimate meanings of existence, it has become
for many an impossible ideal.   Vast intellectual
desire has met with vast disappointment.   The
suffering has been of two kinds.   It has been
intense but self-contained, full of sadness but at
the same time full of a noble stoicism, as in
Matthew Arnold, who tried so hard to live in

---

[1] *Theatetus*, 205 C. T. H. Green's famous aphorism, that
"a consistent sensationalism must be speechless," is a con-
densed statement of Plato's thought. Of things in absolute
isolation nothing can be said. This is Plato's idea ; and it is
the axiom which Green uses so powerfully in his *Introduction to
Hume*.

the halo of the spirit set in the frame of absolute night. Here the inner sphere of conscience has been kept inviolate, and the shoreless sea of trouble that surrounds it has been sorrowfully acknowledged, and then with calm dignity defied. Moral feeling is supreme for man; the supremacy is attested by experience, and it is supported by the universe; and yet its issue is death. In man's world there is truth, beauty, goodness, peace; still, that world and its high seriousness is but for a day. Hence the joy and the despair. In the author of "The City of Dreadful Night" there is the other type of suffering. It is unmitigated. To this mood there is no place of refuge. The spirit goes mad in the infinite disregard with which it is encompassed. The prophetic note in both representatives is the sincerity of their work. In both truth is still an inner possession, and the spirit keeps covenant with itself. If they have been disappointed in the quest for light they do not pretend otherwise; and they elaborate their moods with complete fearlessness and fidelity as symbols for their brothers in the great communion of contradicted hope.

The wise believer will rejoice in the baffled thought that issues in profounder seriousness and in greater honesty. He knows that without these nothing can be gained in the affairs of the spirit. He will note in the moral strength of

nineteenth century doubt, the preparation for a
new spiritual realism.   Everything must go that
is unreal, in order that everything real may have
due recognition.   Tradition has given a sad significance to the prophet's words about God:
" Thou hast covered thyself with a cloud, that
our prayer should not pass through." [1]   The
concealing cloud, however, is born from below.
It is an exhalation from the ignorance, superstition, insincerity, and perversity of man.   The
cloud of tradition must be blown away, even if
it should seem that in passing faith itself is perishing.   But this is not the case.   Reality cannot be abolished.   And up against the heavens
that doubt has cleared stand the everlasting
realities of human nature.   With the passing of
much that was deemed permanent and priceless,
there have come a new disclosure of the moral
order of the world and a new opportunity for
insight into the moral character of the universe.
The wise believer will find Carlyle and Tennyson better representatives of the spiritual meaning of the nineteenth century than Matthew
Arnold and James Thomson, precisely because
in them the preparation for a new vision of
spiritual reality is larger and more evident.
Carlyle and Tennyson were both great doubters,
but in both the negative movement was emphatically in the interest of discovery.   Arnold sur-

[1] Lamentations iii. 44.

rendered more and more to doubt; while Carlyle and Tennyson, in their unceasing fight against unreality, became witnesses to substantial, benignant, abiding truth. Both have their deepest significance in their discontent with the world's vision of God, and in their strangely contrasted but common call to look again and more piercingly into the heart of things. Tennyson writes: "My chief desire is to have a new vision of God." Carlyle abandons even the most august name, speaks of immensities and eternities, but always that he may gain a deeper and surer insight into the righteous and pitiful heart of the universe. He writes: "The universe is full of love, and also of inexorable sternness and veracity; and it remains forever true that God reigns." The mood of both was a strange compound of sadness and hope, but the motto that was persistently upon the lips of the more melancholy and less believing spirit of the two was "We bid you to hope."

From this high questioning it has resulted that the characteristic intellectual life of our time is pervaded by moral passion. The habit has been generated that regards truth as not for the intellect alone. The insight and candor and patience essential to the vision of reality make the intellect dependent upon the moral will. Truth is the object of no single faculty or fragment of the soul; it is the possession for life. One must

seek truth as Orpheus sought Eurydice; one
must descend into the worlds of darkness, and
with the music of love prevail over fate itself.
Even if the thoughtless glance should rob him
of his beloved, he should not therefore surrender
to despair.   Like the glorious musician he must
die to live; and if truth cannot be brought to the
abodes of man, man should go to the habitations
of truth.   Nothing is impossible to the immortal
lover ; the gates of death cannot shut him out ;
the spirit that asks and receives, that seeks and
finds, that knocks and is met with divine welcome, is his.

A great Christian thinker of the first century,
who was a witness to the deepest revolution in
history, and to the doubt and despair that were
inevitable in the passing away of the old order
and the introduction of the new, provided a philosophy of these crises for all time to come.   He
foresaw the time when the quaking mountain, at
the foot of which Moses and his people trembled,
would be but an insignificant incident in a vaster
crisis, an inadequate symbol of the shaking which
should overtake the whole earth and the whole
heaven, the entire humanity and the entire divinity of human faith.   That tremendous convul-
sion has been going on ever since the prophecy
was uttered, and in the nineteenth century it has
extended to the total spiritual belief of mankind.
Criticism has certainly had free course, whether

it has or has not been glorified. The elemental testing has spared nothing; the century has indeed been a day of judgment upon the worth of the highest possessions of the race. But the purpose of this universal shaking, as indicated by the writer to whom reference has been made, has been the song in the storm. The tumult has gone on, that those things that are not shaken may remain. Underneath the loose rubbish heap of tradition, covered up by accumulations of superstition, false opinion, inadequate notions, superficial, distorted, and incredible interpretations, there is something that cannot be shaken. The doubt of the world, the long and sore agitations of history, the sad intensity of the negative intellect in the nineteenth century is for no other purpose than to free the essential from the unessential, the abiding truth from the beggarly elements, the eternal gospel from the vanishing traditions of men. Slowly through the vast and painful destructive process there is emerging the kingdom that cannot be shaken. The doubt that is instrumental in the discovery of that kingdom is a discipline in the interest of the best achievement and the highest happiness of mankind.

CHAPTER V

THE RETURN OF FAITH

I

To Aristotle's profound remark that man is a social animal, Burke added the penetrating reflection that man is a religious animal. Religious faith in one degree or another, of one sort or another, would seem to be a part of normal humanity. Certain forces in the human soul tend that way with the inevitableness of the tides. Bacon's saying that " slight tastes of philosophy may perchance move one to atheism, but fuller draughts lead back to religion," is indeed true as a general remark upon the discipline of the intellect, but it is far more significant as an interpretation of the discipline of life. Emerson sees nothing more in Montaigne's acceptance of the consolation of the Catholic church in his last hours than the last expression of the skeptic's habitual conformity to custom. There is more in the case than that. Nature defies opinion, she overrides judgment, she takes her own way with the strongest. The home is founded in happy choice, but yet more in unalterable necessity. The social institutions of man are indeed willed into being, but behind the consenting volition there is the irresistibleness of fate. The Greek philosopher's remark touches the social necessities that in one form or another, in noble use or in abuse, always have their way. The wise insight of the British statesman reaches to the spiritual forces in man that whether for good or for evil ultimately assert themselves. Mill's "pale theism" and faint hope in the permanence of the human spirit express the tendency of man's nature, even in the case of the most negative intellect. Something in man moves that way, and even when arrested it seldom desists or dies, but bides its time. George Eliot the thinker is an agnostic, perhaps a materialist, and, for all practical purposes, an atheist; but George Eliot the artist moves in another circle of interests and ideas, and her nature, elsewhere mocked, here finds satisfaction and repose. So great is the witness of the spirit to itself and to its own. Huxley, one of the most interesting of nineteenth century men, and fiercest of all fighters for the agnostic mood, comes at last to listen with patience to the hypothetical plea, "If there be no meeting-place beyond the grave." Below the voice of opinion is the force of nature. And while it is doubtless true that numerous instances could be easily cited in which the discipline of life apparently did nothing to work revolt in the soul against the results of the negative intellect, it would seem to be the case that in persons of candor and complete human endowment, the rule is the other way.

The return of faith comes, then, first of all, with the movement of life itself. Life itself would seem to be in the hand of God. It would seem to be subject to a law and a necessity that lie deeper than the working of the conscious reason. It would appear to represent a reason below reason, a tide of feeling beneath the obvious current, a determination profounder than conscious volition. Impressions are thus made upon the intellect too subtle for analysis, too numerous for tabulation, and which appear only in the modification of former moods. Thus feeling is colored, like the stained window, by an outside influence. Thus a will is formed in the depths, and that puts a new face upon everything. Human life itself acts as if it had independently a thousand eyes. Our civilization is largely but a rude copy of the unconscious soul. By device and effort and correspondence of agency reports of the world's doings are daily poured in upon civilized man. Every home is a nerve-centre whose periphery is the end of the earth. By structure, unconscious operation, and indestructible affinity the secrets of the moral universe are registered in the soul; rational life is in immediate contact with God, and news from the

Infinite is somehow reported. If the communication is frequently indefinable, perhaps indecipherable, it is still strangely influential. It would seem as if the boldest doubt did but describe a circle whose point of departure is faith, and whose final resting-place is faith.

In the return of faith which would seem to mark the last twenty years, there must be noted the power of reaction. Under this law, no mood appears final; by it, ideas of superior worth cannot be read out of one tendency as opposed to another. In itself, the law stands for nothing other or higher than alternation. One mood temporarily exhausts itself and another contrasted mood succeeds. Now it is theism, and again it is atheism; yesterday it was optimism and to-day it is pessimism. The interests of the race are apt to become one-sided and exclusive; the various dynasties revenge themselves upon one another, and thus by turns they come to power. The inveterate drunkard illustrates the law upon the lowest plain. He turns from his cups in temporary disgust. He betakes himself at times to the cultivation of abstinence with the zeal of an ascetic. Between the moods of drunkenness and soberness his life alternates. When the power of one mood is, for the time being, spent, he betakes himself to its opposite. This rhythm, founded as it is upon the appetitive nature, repeats itself over the entire circle of vice.   The accomplished sensualist alternates between the parlor, where he appears as a charming gentleman, and the den of infamy, where he is a lineal descendant of Judas Iscariot. Where there is no character, where will interposes no check, where impulse has free course, one spent condition is succeeded by its opposite.

This law of action and reaction is obvious in its influence upon the higher levels of human life.   From 1859, when Darwin published his "Origin of Species," until about 1874, when Green published his edition of Hume, the popular mood at the universities, and, indeed, in all the centres of intellectual life, was the evolutionary mood.   For about twenty years, evolution was the romance of the intellectual world.   The world was drunk with it, the season of inebriety was long, and the condition unusually heavy. Darwin, Wallace, Spencer, Lewes, Haeckel, Huxley, Tyndale, Fiske, and scores of others were the names that monopolized attention. Evolution as an intellectual interest was universal and sovereign, and mainly, although not exclusively, in its materialistic form.   Evolution was the fad of the intellectual world, and that means that it must surely pass.   The mental organism of mankind could not endure this spell forever. The mood was too intense and one-sided to last. It spent its force twenty years ago ; it no longer lives except in a transformed existence, and as a minister to interests mightier than itself. It has given place to the science that has at least the will to believe, and especially, in Great Britain and America, to the idealistic movement in philosophy. A generation ago the majority, perhaps, of those of the medical profession who had obtained a European education were agnostic; the exact opposite of this may be said to be the case to-day. Materialistic science thirty years ago controlled the larger body of its students; to-day science is delightfully surprised by the fact of religion. In the succession of the moods of materialism and of idealism there is of course much more to be noted than mere alternation. But the primary element, nevertheless, is in the tendency of moods temporarily to exhaust themselves.

No better representative of this rhythm between contrasted moods could perhaps be named than Amiel. His profoundly interesting journal has its chief value as a singularly faithful account of a series of opposite moods. Belief in him exhausts itself, then is the opportunity of unbelief. The will in the man seems to be wanting. Thoughts stay with him only so long as they can maintain the mind's interest in them. What one would describe as the influence of character upon the hospitality of the intellect is nearly absent in Amiel. He is by turns idealist and materialist, optimist and pessimist, high be-

liever and utter doubter. He is a mirror in
which the mind of every man, and especially
the mind of the nineteenth century, is seen as it
is affected by the simple law of action and reaction. Discount will, — and will must be discounted in a sense for very many, since it is a
late development in all, particularly in those
addicted to reflection, — discount will, and one
may be sure that if the world is unbelieving in
one generation it will be believing in another,
if it is pessimistic to-day, it will be optimistic
to-morrow. This rhythm between opposites, between the drunk condition of the intellect and
the sober, is a law of the human mind.

On the higher levels, and where obvious abuses
are excluded, it should not be difficult for the
wise thinker to see the temporary necessity of
this alternation. The swing of the pendulum
seems meaningless enough, but it marks the
progress of the day ; and successive and apparently endless alternations of belief and unbelief,
naturalism and supernaturalism, hope and despair, really register the advance of the divine
education of man. One mood, however high, is
insufficient for human development. The universe is one, and therefore it must have one ultimate interest, one final character ; but the mind
of man moves toward this last aspect of things,
as the plant goes on its single path, through a
vast variety of moods. The living earth needs

all her contrasted seasons, all her variety of
weather; for humor and pathos, for wit and
irony, for critical depth and creative force, for
seriousness and prevailing strength the human
mind requires the discipline of many moods.
The greatness of Shakespere is both the condition and result of his many-sidedness. Nor must
it be overlooked that the same atheisms and theisms, optimisms and pessimisms, naturalisms and
supernaturalisms, do not return. They return in
new, and in their typical instances, in deeper
forms. Under this law of action and reaction
doubt and faith are profounder to-day than they
have ever been. The play of the negative and
positive intellect is like the play in the St. Go-
thard tunnel. It is in and out of the same mountain, it is light and darkness in apparently unmeaning succession; but the alternation is always
upon higher levels, and the play ends upon the
summit with its supreme outlook. This would
appear to be the teleology in the endless alternation of these great contrasted moods of our humanity. Certain birds, like the pheasant, mount
as they fight. The spirit of man rises through
conflict. The atheism and the theism in him
and in his kind must have it out; the battle is
upon successively higher levels, and while the war
seems interminable, man finds himself in more
and more commanding heights. The summit
is yet afar off; but it is the ideal to be realized

by the discipline of doubt and the assertion of faith.

In the return of faith that characterizes the last decades of the nineteenth century one must note the resurgence of the religious need. Monasticism was upon the whole an outrage upon the social nature of man; and it may be said that whatever is in its deepest character an outrage upon humanity cannot last. At least the period of submission will inevitably give way to that of protest. Here is the fatal defect in the positivism, the agnosticism, the naturalism that has been one of the great moods of the century. It is an outrage upon the religious nature, and therefore cannot stand. The scientist is first of all a man. His humanity is the aboriginal and permanent force in aim; and the science or the art or the philosophy that goes against any great and abiding interest of mankind cannot last. The criticism to which they will be subjected, however objective and calmly impartial it may be, will be instigated and necessitated by the rights of human life itself. Normal man must worship. J. S. Mill, whose career is instructive at so many points, is in evidence here. He was brought up without a religion, he confesses that he did not feel the need of a religion, and yet his " pale posthumous theism " and many pages of his autobiography remain to attest not only his need but also his endeavor to gain a

religion. The worship of humanity which positivism inaugurated, and that strongly appealed
to Mill and others, was a concession to the im-
perialism of the heart. Carlyle's hero-worship
is another concession of the same character. In
the foundering of faith, men betook themselves
to all sorts of spiritual life-preservers. In the
sad periods in which the old dies before the
new is born, these Platonic rafts deserve deep
respect.

It must be added that concession to the religious need means ultimate surrender. If some
sort of religion is allowed as a necessity, it follows, as matter of course, that the best religion
will be felt to be the supreme necessity. The
highest ideals of mankind, the noblest conceptions of man, and of man's universe, that the race
has reached, cannot long remain matters of indifference to the individual, even if he should
continue unconvinced of their objective validity.
They are even to him more than the mere subjective glory and dream of the race ; they are
the supreme paths along which the desire of all
nations is realized — reconciliation with the universe. The rebel mood toward the Infinite is
destructive of the best humanity ; the mood of
indifference by a less violent process comes to
the same thing. *Sursum corda*, lift up your
heart, is the language of human nature struggling to retain or to recover its integrity. The

everlasting reality, the essential humanity of the
religious need, is given in the Hebrew psalm:
"My soul thirsteth for God, for the living
God." [1]   Schleiermacher's genius is at its best in
his plea for religion as an interest essential to
man.   There is in man " an immediate relation
to the Highest ; " the sense of that relation is
the beginning of religion.   The relation persists
in spite of all theoretic slights and outrages ;
and in the starved heart of a generation it nour-
ishes its great avenger.

In the return of faith to which attention is
now directed the sense of the preciousness of life
has played a part.   Mill's theory that life is for
knowledge is reversed by Mr. Spencer.   Knowledge is for life.   The issue between these two
thinkers is fundamental ; it is a sort of parting
of the ways toward negation and faith, a watershed where one opinion inclines surely toward
the extinction of personal religion and where the
other makes it certain that the current of existence must seek a religious goal.   Where knowledge is the ideal, other interests appear upon the
whole as incidental ; where life in largest amount
and in highest quality is the chief end, a new
standard of truth is introduced.   Life is allowed
to discover and determine reality ; the function
of the intellect is that of the interpreter.   Life
with its thousand needs pursuing their appropri-

[1] Ps. xlii. 2.

ate satisfactions, growing into something more and better in this process of victorious pursuit, is in a way discovering and indicating the truth of its objects. The growing man, the greatening soul, is the primary attestation of the reality to which its growth and greatness are due. In the paralysis that has fallen upon the intellect this has been the saving strength. The puzzled and negative intelligence has consented, under pressure, to allow the heart, the human life, to have its own way. The fundamental axiom has been that what supports life must be true.

Life is instinctively rational, and under the force of its higher needs it goes, not infrequently, in its instinctive rationality with elemental strength. No weapon formed against it by the negative intellect can prosper. The Arminian and Wesleyan protests against Calvinism are primarily protests of life, and as such they prevail. In Browning, who lived through the scientific mood of the century, and who is the witness of a profoundly religious philosophy, the plea that life makes for itself has large utterance. In Stevenson there is this character. His religion is tradition, purified by life and attested by life. The sense of the supremacy of life in the home, in the fellowships of trade, and art, and learning, in the relations and interests of the citizen and the man, has never before, perhaps, attained to equal volume and force. In the last quarter of the nineteenth century it has simply demanded, in innumerable instances, the right of way. The passion of life disregards obstructing philosophies as serenely as the passion of love in a Hartmann laughs at pessimism. Of all illogical creatures, the pessimist who marries and becomes the father of children is the supreme instance. The rational strength of life, the optimism of love, is too much for the false logic of the pessimist. It must be the richness of his humor or the appalling lack of it, which led Hartmann to think of marriage and population as the method of the unconscious for passing into consciousness with the view of finally reaching the heaven of universal and absolute suicide. This theoretic justification of marriage on the part of the pessimist is immensely interesting. It is meant, possibly, to complete a system and to justify action under that system. It is the humorous monument of the weakness of a false philosophy in the presence of the fullness and power of life. As is the witness of marriage among the pessimists, so is the significance of religious feeling and religious action and life among the agnostics. The ripple upon the surface of the sea in response to the wind off shore may hide, but it cannot arrest the power of the incoming tide. To the final decades of the nineteenth century knowledge stands to life as the superficial to the profound, one is inclined to say, as the finite to the infinite. Pessimism saved by marriage, and agnosticism preserved by religion, remind one of Lot's wife. She was turned into a pillar of salt because there was no other way of keeping her pure. Take the happy humanity out of German pessimism and the noble piety out of English agnosticism and they would revert to Sodom.

In this great return of faith, for Great Britain and America, the new interest of the universities in idealism has had large influence. There is in the educated world to-day a new science, new in the attitude of feeling and mind toward the great fact of religion. There has been at work for twenty-five years in the English-speaking world a new philosophy, new in the sense of a more widely understood and influential movement of thought. German idealism reconstructed by British and American thinkers is fundamentally friendly to the highest interests of the human spirit. Whatever its limitations may be, and its errors, this movement of thought has put a new mood into a multitude of leading minds. The totality of man's life is receiving at its hands a treatment profounder, nobler, more vitally practical than it has hitherto received from writers in the English tongue. This great wave of thought has passed over the English-speaking races, and wherever it has gone, it has profoundly affected man's attitude toward the things of the

spirit. And of all names connected with this interpretation of human problems, that of Thomas
Hill Green must rank first. Hardest of writers,
he is yet the most thorough and commanding.
It would seem as if among British thinkers of
the last thirty years he at least had done something that would not have to be done again.

Of all these forces that have been making for
a return of faith Romanes is perhaps a representative example. In 1878 he published " A
Candid Examination of Theism." This book
expressed the mood of atheism to which his scientific studies had led him. It is a book of intellectual vigor and great moral intensity. Its
value for this discussion is its human value. It
embodies the conviction and the passion of the
negative mood. But by the simple law of alternation, by virtue of the rhythm in man's nature,
it might have been anticipated that this mood
could not last. It had spent itself in expression.
Slowly the opposite mood replaced it. Atheistic
fatigue yielded to the returning freshness of the
theistic mood. The law of action and reaction
had another brilliant illustration in Romanes.
At length there appeared the resurgence of the
religious need. The mind in its uncertainty did
not oppose the heart in its strong claims. Human life itself began to plead with great power
in favor of its high distinction, and Christianity
as the vindicator of human life became a new

object of interest. Finally there is evidence that a new way of thinking was gaining upon Romanes, and the hope is not without grounds that if he had lived a few years longer his deepening religious experience would have found support in a profounder interpretation of the universe.

II

The faith to which there is a return involves, as all faith must, a theological construction of Christianity. The basis is the same, the gospel remains essentially unchanged, but the theological construction is new. There can be no return to the old theology unless faith be defined, in the terms of an Oxford undergraduate, as the "faculty by which we are enabled to believe that which we know is not true." There is still extant a good deal of this sort of faith; but those who have broken away from it are not likely to return to it or to do anything to incite a return in others. While doubt has gone as deep as the fundamental positions of the gospel itself, while the whole case of atheism against the noblest theism has in the nineteenth century stated itself with unwonted sincerity and strength, and this because of the pure passion for truth, it is yet true that Calvinism has had much to do with the production of unbelief. For the race as a whole, and for the thinker who judges schemes of thought from their bearing

upon the interests of mankind, there is indeed
little to choose between Calvinism and atheism.
The soul of man has had a sad time under all
forms of that nightmare.   As long as it seemed
to be the truth men had to endure it; now that
it has become incredible either as an interpretation of the gospel or as an exposition of theism,
something other and better must be found.   To
Melanchthon, Calvinism appeared as a revival of
stoicism.   With this penetrating insight before
them, the praises that learned historians have
bestowed upon Calvinism are inexplicable.   Calvinism has done some good; it has asserted the
priority of God, but the kind of priority asserted
and the incompetence of man to pass judgment
upon it have been an incalculable damage to the
conscience of Christendom.   More than anything
else the traditional theology has discredited itself
by its scorn for the critical conscience.   Against
the protest of the moral reason it has elaborated
systems of opinion, trusting for victory over its
invincible enemy to bad exegesis of Scripture,
poor views of history, and to the inequalities of
human life on earth.   That there are in these
systems great and permanent truths is freely
admitted; that they truly represent either moral
theism or Christianity is emphatically denied.
They are interesting as a Kenilworth is interesting, for their large plans, their massive masonry,
their commanding situations, their magnificent

and tragic associations. They are objects of pious pilgrimage and a world of sad thoughts; but they are no longer habitable, they are ruins. Faith may visit them, muse over them, profit by them, but if it is to live its home must be elsewhere, and of another style of architecture.

A generation ago signs were occasionally seen in England with pictures of the Four Alls. The picture of the king had under it the motto, "I rule all," that of the bishop, "I pray for all," that of the soldier, "I fight for all," and that of John Bull, the farmer, "I pay for all." In other centuries John Bull the farmer was placed last because he was held to be of least account. There has been in the nineteenth century a reversal of judgment upon this point. The king and the bishop and the soldier have been made amenable to the person who pays for all, the ruling and priestly and militant functions of human life have been subordinated to the best interests of the life that supports them. The supremacy of John Bull the farmer, who pays for all, has issued in a new government, a new church, and a new army. Politics, ecclesiasticism, militarism, have a relation to the people profoundly new, and what has been accomplished in these spheres of interest must be repeated in the sphere of faith and theological belief. It is the race that ultimately pays for all; humanity really carries the purse for all offices and occu-

pations; John Bull the farmer is supreme over
king and bishop and soldier. No scheme that
ignores his rights can last. No theology that
discounts his existence can now intimidate him
into paying for it.

It is John Bull the farmer who has inaugurated the movement of moral reason in theology,
under what may be called the logic of alternatives. John Bull and his constituents are ready
to support a theology, but it must be a theology
worth supporting. All theories of the universe
are on probation; none of them is demonstrably
true. This is the situation that gives faith its
opportunity. Ultimate beliefs appeal for supporters by the evidence in favor of them, by
their inherent reasonableness, and in one case
by the additional claim of absolute nobility.
Christian theism blends in its appeal these three
voices. It is able to produce evidences of its
truth that rise to high probability; it may confidently assert the inherent reasonableness of its
interpretation of the universe; and in its highest
form it adds the further attraction of utter nobility. The union of these three claims — evidence, reasonableness, worthiness — constitutes
the unique power of Christian theism over the
mind of civilized man. The third element, in
the absence of perfect knowledge, is of supreme
importance. After it has been granted that
there is evidence of the Divine existence, and

when it has been admitted that the conception
of the Supreme being is a reasonable conception,
it remains to ascertain the character of the fact,
the significance of the idea. The fact of existence merges in reasonableness, and the idea of
reasonableness issues in the assumption of goodness. Deny the absolute goodness of God, and
for man he ceases to be God. The life of belief
in the Deity is bound up with confidence in his
infallible righteousness. Nothing but the wor-
thiest can fulfill the office of the Highest.

It may be said here that men create God and
then fall in love with him. That has often been
said, and in one sense it is true. It is true in
the sense that the moral ideal of the supreme
man is the supreme witness for the character of
God. The true believer cannot allow that God
is less worthy than the best human thought of
him. Christian theism contends for the infinite
transcendence of the Divine reality over the best
human image of it. It still repeats the noble
confession of one of the greatest of its forerunners : "For my thoughts are not your thoughts,
neither are your ways my ways, saith the Lord.
For as the heavens are higher than the earth, so
are my ways higher than your ways, and my
thoughts than your thoughts." [1] It forever
seeks to know the love of Christ that passeth
knowledge. By the very terms of the final dis-

[1] Isaiah lv. 8, 9.

covery of God in the highest moral conceptions of the race, nothing can be admitted as true of God which contradicts the Christian conscience. We do not go to God to have our best ideas set at naught. He is not given in the facts of the cosmos and in the course of history and in the Old and New Testaments as something independent of the highest human expectations, and the noblest standards of worth. He is recognizable in those only in so far as he is discovered in these. When, therefore, it is said that notions, however humane and exalted they may be, count for nothing against the facts, the obvious reply is that in ascertaining the ultimate character of the Creator the highest notions are the highest facts. The heavenly body is greater than the greatest image of it in the earth, and God the Creator is at least equal to the best thought of himself that he has breathed into the human reason.

The Christian idea of God is of a being whose moral perfection is absolute. For theology this idea is fundamental and finally determinative of the whole. And the return of faith is a return to the Christian conception of God. The traditional theology is tried by its own ultimate assumption and is found wanting. The Christian conception of God has in no striking instance found logical expression in modern orthodoxy. That orthodoxy is therefore dead at the root, and the truth that it contains needs to be grafted into a new principle before the decay reaches higher. This may be said to be the fundamental issue in theology to-day. There is the traditional conception of God's relation to mankind, and there is the Christian conception as justified in the Incarnation: "For God so loved the world that he gave his only begotten Son, that whosoever believeth on him should not perish, but have eternal life." [1] Here the purpose of God in the advent of Jesus Christ is the salvation of the world. The effectualness of the purpose is indeed conditioned upon belief, but upon its own side the Divine intention is absolutely unlimited. Other texts there are which look toward restriction; whether they actually involve the limitation of God's moral interest or not is for scientific exegesis to say. But the Christian thinker is independent of these witnesses. He assumes the reality of the Incarnation; he takes that event at its word when it asserts that the Divine purpose in Christ is inclusive of mankind. If there are texts against this truth so much the worse for the texts. The believer in the universality of God's love in the advent of Jesus will allow nothing that contradicts that assumption to be a genuine part of the gospel of the Incarnation. Is Christ divided? The question leads back to another more fundamental yet, is God divided?

[1] John iii. 16.

While nothing but respect is here felt for the great representatives of New England theology, it is only common honesty to say that in their conception, God is at cross-purposes with himself. The great founder of American theology writes : " Thus it is necessary that God's awful majesty, his authority, and dreadful greatness, justice, and holiness should be manifested. But this could not be, unless sin and punishment had been decreed." In the same connection this profound but bewildered thinker asks whether it is not proper to say " that God would have it be, that Judas should be unfaithful to his Lord." And he argues that since the sin of crucifying Christ was foreordained of God, and since that is the head and representative sin of the world, it follows " that all sins of men are foreordained and ordered by a wise providence." [1] From first to last there is no essential disagreement among New England theologians upon the question of the relation of God to mankind. Hopkins and Emmons, Dwight and Taylor, Henry B. Smith and Edwards A. Park all built upon one foundation. That foundation is courageously indicated by Dr. N. W. Taylor as follows : " That God has eternally purposed to renew, and sanctify, and save a part only of mankind." [2] And upon no other basis has traditional theology rested since the days of Augustine.

---

[1] *Edwards' Works*, vol. ii. pp. 516–517.
[2] *Revealed Theology*, p. 374.

The imperative demand to-day in the theologian is for the courage of his convictions. The Christian community still waits for a declaration of principles from the professional theologians of the country upon this supreme issue. Is the practical life of the church to go on upon the assumption that the Divine purpose is inclusive of mankind while its intellectual life is based upon a restricted grace? How long is this seesaw to continue? Whom shall plain men trust, the gospel that reveals God as on the side of mankind, or the theologians who limit the saving intention of God to a part of the race? The business of Christian living waits for a theoretic basis adequate to its need. The call is for a theology that shall embody the Christian idea of God as given in the Incarnation. Why should it be considered an indication of a sound mind to give allegiance to a theology that has no longer any relation to the moral ideal of a good man and a living church? The radicalism for which the best people are longing is that which will make it clear as sunlight that the orthodoxy of to-day holds God in his eternal intention and everlasting endeavor, free from all logical evasion and hide-and-seek methods of explicit and hidden decree, and in absolute honesty, for humanity. The seminary that shall take that position may receive persecution, but it will command the men who command the future. The frank avowal of the inclusive purpose of God as the basis of Christian theology to-day, in contradistinction to the restricted Divine intention which has served as the immemorial foundation of the traditional theology, it is believed, would create a national interest in the theme, and inspire a national movement in religious life. Ideas are the ultimate forces of the world, and Christian sentiment is ineffectual without the tidal pull of the Christian conception of a God forever on the side of mankind.[1]

The faith, therefore, to which it is believed that there is a return, is the faith in the God and Father of Christ. The truth of that sublime conception cannot be demonstrated; but it is as likely to prove true, to say the least, as any alternative that can be named. Besides, it is worth while to contend for such a faith. Granted that the truth may prove to be that physical force is the ultimate thing in the universe, or un-moral intelligence, or a being to whom man's existence is only incidental, or a God with a limited regard for the human race, or a God of absolute love. These are the conceivable forms of the truth. These and others like them are the possibilities of the case. The disjunctive judgment is applied to them by faith. Granted again that philosophy is unable abso-

[1] For a fuller discussion of the subject, see *The Christ of To-day*, pp. 166–206.

lutely to decide as to which among them is the valid idea. Philosophy has her choice, and she is able to say much for her favorite, whichever that may be, and much against her non-elect. But when she is sane she does not pretend to settle beyond all peradventure the nature of the ultimate reality. Plato and Aristotle say that it is mind, and they say more for their contention than Democritus and Lucretius are able to say for their opposite conclusion. Berkeley and Hegel find in spirit the key to the final character of the universe; but they are met by Hume and Spencer, who ignore the spiritual view. One may be quite willing to confess that idealism is deeper far, and better reasoned than material-ism, that theism can say immeasurably more for itself than atheism; and yet be obliged to con-tend that the best and most widely attested thought of the universe falls indefinitely short of a demonstration of its truth.

Here comes in the option of faith, particularly the faith that would seem to have command of the future. It selects from the possibilities of the case the idea that is the highest, that has the most and the best to say for itself, and that is wor-thiest of support during the hours of darkness. Faith is essentially choice, at least it involves this function. It is a selection from among competing notions of the one that is the likeliest to be true, and which, in the absence of complete proof, is best deserving of human devotion. And upon this ground there cannot be a moment's doubt as to the choice which an unfettered faith will make. The process of elimination begins; possible truth after possible truth is ruled out until the last and best is reached. The basis of the universe is either non-mental or mental, atheistic or theistic. These are the ultimate possibilities of the case. The non-mental or atheistic view is allowed to speak for itself. It represents a mood through which many serious minds have gone in these days, and few who deserve the name of thinkers find themselves unable to enter into it with sympathetic comprehension. The human life, that began in the ante-natal sleep, seems to end in the sleep of death. The organism is the main thing; consciousness is incidental. Mind is an inexplicable concomitant, a beautiful or absurd excess upon organic processes. Neither at the first nor at the last is thought essential to the human organism. Mind, therefore, is an incident in the history of the body in its passage from birth to death. What is true of the body may be true of the universe; the mind in it may be incidental and temporary; the basal and enduring fact may be blind force. Thus a materialistic psychology becomes the basis for a materialistic ontology.

Faith rejects this mood upon several explicit grounds. The rejected mood assumes that appearance is reality. The organism seems to begin and end in thoughtlessness; it seems to be independent of mind in its main functions; therefore human life is in its ground non-mental. One on an island who should see sunrise and sunset but once would be under the power of a parallel experience. The sun comes up out of the sea, and it is day; the sun goes down into the sea, and it is night. Darkness preceded and followed the intermediate phenomenon of light; therefore the world is based upon darkness. The sun was seen to rise but once, it was seen to set without return, therefore when it sank in the sea it was quenched. Such is the appearance to one observation; but it is false. It may be that the appearance of the incidentalness of mind to a temporary organism is likewise false. Materialism is grounded upon an assumption that what appears to be really is.

The rejected view inverts the order of reason; it makes the lowest chief, it makes the highest of least account. When physiology is primary and psychology is subordinate and incidental, all rational notions of value are upset. The inversion is expressed in the maxim, " live to eat;" which is an admirable summary of physiological ethics. The contrasted maxim, " eat to live," implies an order where the organism is subordinate, and where the rational character which it supports is supreme. Materialism is the degra-

dation of mind and the consecration of mud. It
puts the government of the universe upon what
is lowest and of least account. It subverts all
man's ideas of order, worth, and reasonableness.
That the seed of the woman should bruise the
serpent's head is the expectation of reason; that
the cunning physical force should overwhelm
the moral puts thought in hopeless confusion.
This monstrous inversion of values, this unac-
countable placing of the last first and the first
last, this ghastly ὕστερον πρότερον is absolutely
fatal to materialism.

The rejected view is in antagonism to the
higher interests of human life. If it were demonstrably true, one would be obliged to accept
it notwithstanding this enmity. But inasmuch
as the best that it can say for itself is that
it is possibly true, the fact that it is inimical to
the whole high distinction of man is an argument against it, which, for human beings living
in the strength of their humanity, must be final.
That cannot be true which if heeded would
make impossible the noblest tradition of mankind. That cannot be true which if acknowledged would reduce to an idle dream the best
in the thought and in the character of the race.
If the competition is between two possible delu-
sions, let the moral will defend itself, and brand
the materialism that would reduce it to folly as
the superlative impostor. When one reflects

that the absolute primacy of the organism implies the mere incidence of the thought of Plato and Aristotle, the works of Homer, Dante, and Shakespere, the intelligence represented in the universe as understood by science, the genius that speaks in the high art of the race, the constructive reason that appears in language, in social institutions, and in the organized life of mankind, the moralism and theism of the Hebrew prophets, the mind of Christ and his character, the position becomes incredible. Between a universe grounded in mud and a universe based upon mind the choice and devotion of faith go to the latter. Thus faith makes its first disjunctive judgment. It is either atheism or theism; it is not atheism, it is theism.

But theism divides into alternatives. The ground is debated by Calvinistic theism and Christian theism. Calvinistic theism is the general name for all forms which involve restriction upon the Divine interest in man. The traditional form is familiar enough. It asserts or implies or harbors or refuses to expel a limited elective purpose on the part of God. It looks upon man as depraved, that is foreign, until regeneration intervenes, to the Divine nature. It provides both a limited sphere — this world — and a limited time — the earthly life — for the redemptive purpose of God. It grounds salvation upon a grace that is severely narrow; it

involves the perdition of the overwhelming majority of mankind. It presents a spectacle of
ruin and calamity so vast and hideous, and, according to its scheme of Divine sovereignty, so
needless and pitiless, that the recoil from it to
atheism is like going from infinite horror to infinite peace. Granted that the scientific doctrine
of the survival of the fittest is but the shadow
of Calvinism in nature, or its counterpart rather,
since shadows can never be so loaded with darkness; granted that much in the history of men
and nations goes to show that the weak are
driven to the wall by the strong; granted that
much in the Old Testament and here and there
isolated texts in the New Testament assert or
imply that the saving grace of the Eternal is
restricted, — that does not prove that the doctrine is true. The believer in God's love for the
whole world in Jesus Christ simply calls in
question the competency of the witnesses. He
refuses to find the final expression of God's
relation to the race anywhere save in the highest. Christ is God's witness that God is for
the race. All other testimony, whether scientific, historical, or Biblical, where it conflicts
with the witness of the Incarnation, is invalid.
And if it should be shown by pure exegesis that
in the teachings of Jesus there are expressions
that imply a restriction upon the grace of God,
the consistent believers in the Incarnation will

not allow that these expressions are adequate reports of the sayings of the Lord. The fundamental position is that Christ must not be set at variance with himself; the universality of God's love in the Incarnation must not be affirmed and denied in the same breath. Thus, after all that it can say for itself from Scripture, history, the present condition of human society, and the scientific view of the struggle for existence, Calvinistic theism is rejected. It is not demonstrated; and it is not worthy of the risk of faith and high devotion.

It remains to adopt the sublime alternative of a God absolutely on the side of mankind. It is not contended that this position is proved, or that it is at present susceptible of complete proof. But it is the gospel of God according to the Incarnation. It is the position for which Christ is the supreme witness. It is the contention to which goes, upon the whole, the support of the New Testament. It is seconded by the moral reason of mankind. All that is best in human thought, and character, and history sanctions the belief that God is not a partial Father, that in divers times and by different methods he has an equal and endless interest in every soul that he has made; that restricted election as a finality is a contradiction of his being; that the limitation of his redemptive endeavor to this earthly life is incredible; that annihilation of

the morally unfit at death is an impossible confession of Divine weakness, a fragment from a
system of opinion that divides God and humanity by an impossible gulf, that has floated into a
strange place, a veritable Satan among the sons
of God; that the movement of the whole moral
power of the universe is toward a racial redemption, and that whether he shall succeed or fail
God would have all men to be saved. But is
this not universalism? No. Universalism is
bold to forecast an issue, to determine a result,
to assert a fact; the position here maintained is
that God's love and endeavor are for all his
children, and for them all forever. If this is
universalism, so be it. What is the alternative?
That God's love and endeavor are not for all his
children, and that his gracious regard for mankind is limited to the uncertain period of human
life upon the earth. That is the open door to
atheism. One is pained to hear of a gospel for
mankind unsupported by the Divine purpose for
mankind, a religion for the race resting upon
limited election, good news for humanity backed
by the logic of atheism.

Faith is ultimately the choice among alternatives. It is the selection for human devotion of
the view that is intrinsically the noblest, that
has the most and the best to say for itself. To
the candid mind the Christian conception of God
appeals in this way. It has the supreme witness

of Christ in its favor; it has the witness of all
that is best in human history; but it is not
proved. It is something offered to faith, that is
to choice, to devotion, to experience, to the heroism of insight and trust. Other competing views
from the lowest extreme of atheism to the ideas
of the traditional theology are rejected, either
because they are worthless or because they are
of inferior worth to that which is chosen. This
procedure of faith among these numerous competitors finds a striking illustration in the selection of David from among his brethren for king
of Israel. Jesse called his sons and made them
pass before the prophet. There was the hand-
some and commanding Eliab, and, as he passed,
the confident father says, "Surely the Lord's
anointed is before him." But the Lord thought
otherwise, and speaking by his prophet replied,
" I have rejected him." Then Jesse called •
Abinadab, and made him pass before Samuel.
And he said, "Neither hath the Lord chosen
this." Seven sons in succession were made to
pass before Samuel, and the answer was, "The
Lord hath not chosen these." The youngest of
all, the shepherd lad with the ruddy and beautiful countenance, was sent for, and the Divine
intimation to the prophet was, "Arise, anoint
him: for this is he." He was the best available
candidate for the throne, and while he was far
enough from being an ideal choice, the rejected

competitors fell indefinitely short of his fitness.
Among theories of the universe there is a similar
contention. They pass in review commended
and applauded by their various sponsors. One
by one they are rejected, the candidates for devotion reduce themselves to the supreme instance.
The conception of God embodied in the Lord's
prayer, the God and Father of Christ, appears
to the mind in search of a governing idea, in-
comparably the best. It is in itself of ideal
perfection, it is full of the richest promise for
the individual and the society that stand in surrender to it; and while the future is uncertain,
and the last nature of the universe still remains
to be attested, yet Christ's thought has the most
and the best to say for itself, and it gives the
strongest pledges of its likelihood to prove the
complete and everlasting truth.

III

The return of faith is but the return of humanity to itself. The nineteenth century has
been great as a century of scientific discovery.
Alfred Russel Wallace, himself one of the foremost of scientific discoverers and writers, credits
the nineteenth century with about double the
number of great discoveries, to those contributed
by all other centuries together.[1] The benefit to
society resulting from these scientific triumphs

[1] *The Wonderful Century*, p. 150.

may well be admitted to be beyond estimate.
Still, the same authority frames against the century a tremendous indictment, chiefly for its
inhumanity. Mr. Wallace does not see any relation between the century's success in science and
its failure in humanity. Failure in humanity
relative to previous centuries he would not admit; the failure which he notes is the failure
implied in the abuse of the greatest privileges
ever granted to any century. This is doubtless
true. Yet it means more than it seems to mean.
It implies that the race has been carried away
from itself by its scientific interest, that its humanity has been for the time being overmastered
by its physical discoveries, that it has not been
able to assimilate the vast and sudden additions
to its knowledge, that it has been living in two
unreconciled spheres — the world of outward investigation and the world of the humanities.
The radical reason for the century's doubt lies
here. Scientific interests, methods, researches,
discoveries, and utilitarian results captivated the
leading intellects during the middle third of
the century. The immense gain implied in
this involved at the same time a corresponding
loss. The loss was the inevitable consequence
of this wholesale interest in a subject relatively
foreign to the humanities proper. As was shown
in the first chapter of this book, the loss was but
temporary. The question was whether science

should master man or man science. Science did for some time master man; the return of faith is but the shifting of victory from man's subject to man himself. So far as his published views intimate, it would seem that Mr. Wallace himself has passed through no such period. But Darwin is a conspicuous example of the success of the scientist and the failure of the man. The loss of his passion for poetry, the fading out of his interest in music and pictures, the intimation that he gives that his chief æsthetic pleasure, the beautiful in nature, was on the wane, the gradual extinction of religious feeling, coupled with a helpless intellectual swing between atheism and theism, show the captivity of the man to his subject. Darwin is the type of the century's success and failure for the period to which he belongs. The world beyond man laid its spell upon the period; human things came to cosmic laws and natural history for judgment; human values were not to be determined by human standards; the spiritual possessions of the race, which are in the best sense human possessions, lost command of the esteem and allegiance of scientific authorities. For about thirty years the outward man was renewed day by day while the inward man was left to perish.

But the century that had Hegel and Coleridge in the first third of it, Carlyle and Maurice in the second, and Tennyson and Browning well into the last, could not but set up a reaction in favor of man and his human possessions. Philosophy returned upon victorious science and took her captive. She is now a peaceful servant, a mighty helper in an idealistic view of the world. She is all that she ever really was ; she has been made subject to man instead of supreme over him. And the idealistic philosophy has been caught and converted into a servant of religion. Thus has man asserted the sovereignty of what is highest in the soul over all forms of intellectual activity and achievement. It has proved that in exploring the stellar universe, in discovering the laws of the cosmos, in investigating the history of the earth, and in speculating upon the genesis and development of life, science has been but finding and clearing new continents for religious faith. Since the amazing achievements of science have been made, the universe has acquired an immeasurably increased value for the intellect; that is a step toward theism. The result of these scientific discoveries upon the self-consciousness of man has begun to tell. The discovering intellect and the discoverable universe have emerged at the close of the century with greatly increased significance for thought. The human intellect has proclaimed its uniqueness in the fields of being over which it has gone ; and the universe that has shown itself amenable to the forms of thought, that has proved itself

intelligible, has thereby declared that it is the
expression of living intelligence. Through the
achievements of science, nature and spirit understand each other as never before ; man calls with
new confidence and the cosmos answers with
new depth of meaning. In the large answer-
ableness of man and nature each to the other,
in the intelligence of the one and the intelli-
gibleness of the other a deeper basis is laid for
the theistic significance of the universe ; and in
preparing for this result science has done immense indirect service. She has been like a
star intent upon nothing else than burning ; and
yet the fulfillment of this office has brought with
it guidance for the wayfarer and a new vision
of the infinite.

A vast section of the century's best thought
cannot be expressed as a return to faith simply
because there has been no departure from faith.
This is true of many of the ablest representatives of the higher criticism of the Bible. Men
like Ewald and W. Robertson Smith were conscious of no break with the faith which they inherited. In their hands it became something
larger and deeper, but this was accomplished
through progress. Perhaps the chief meaning of
Dean Stanley is here ; he is a type of the continuous and peaceful development of faith inside
the church, the happy union of the critical and
the believing spirit. For the vast majority of

the Biblical scholars, at least in Great Britain and America, this tradition of faith and criticism has descended. Perhaps this has been too much the case. The critical habit has been, perhaps, too much spent upon documents and too little upon dogmas. The fact of wide and thorough criticism of the Bible is found not infrequently in conjunction with little or no insight into the spiritual process that is the everlasting basis of revelation, with little or no appreciation of the revolution in theology demanded by fidelity to the consciousness that is under the sovereignty of God in Christ, and that would be true to its Lord. Biblical scholarship has been leading the way to a new interpretation of the Christian religion, and in this way must count as a force in the making of the new faith to which there would seem to be in progress a return. The school of theology that dates from Schleiermacher and Ritschl is a type of opinion profoundly influenced by philosophy, and yet, at the same time, sure of its faith. The progress in that movement, both of criticism and of religious life, has been equal ; and while the earlier faith and the later are widely unlike in their forms, still there has been no lapse, only continuous and free development. It may be said of many of the highest servants of faith in the nineteenth century that they went without catastrophe from the less to the greater, from the traditions of men to the Word of God. Maurice in England and Bushnell in America grew into the greatness of their faith; they were makers of that better thing to which thousands but loosely connected with organized Christianity, and wholly cut off from traditional orthodoxy, are in return. In less profound and massive forms, but with a wider sweep of influence, Henry Ward Beecher and Phillips Brooks did a similar service. Channing's name must be added; for in the whole century nothing is more important than his witness for the divinity of man. Meagre in its conception of God, poor in its Christology, the strength of the Unitarian tradition has been its assertion of the divine worth of human nature. It has seen from the beginning human nature as free, inspirable, and necessarily operating in some measure of self-sacrifice. It is bound to receive wider and more grateful recognition for this magnificent service. In its conception of man as naturally in league with God, and the organ of God because he is the son of God, New England Unitarianism has recovered one of the great traditions of the Christian faith; and within the larger and deeper theology in which it would seem to be the destiny of Unitarianism to be absorbed, there should be an everlasting remembrance of its singular and happy merit. The " I am a worm and no man " philosophy might have effaced the consciousness of the Incarnation, and emptied of all its meaning the phrase " there was a man sent from God whose name was John," had it not been for the clearness and persistence, the rational and spiritual strength of the Unitarian counter-assertion.

For the greater part, theology in the middle of the century, and later, like the Spanish fleet in the late war, was of little or no use when the trial came. Julius Müller was a profound and powerful thinker ; but his work was simply un-available in the crisis. The historical work of Dorner was of a high order, yet here again it must be said that for the new need his theology seemed to be ineffectual. Generations of preach-ers were trained by these thinkers, as by their parallels in this country like H. B. Smith, Shedd, and the Hodges, and this was a great service. These thinkers were masters in the church, and the living interests of the church flourished under them. But when it came to dealing with the fundamental schism of the century, the rent between theism and atheism, it was philosophy and not theology that was the champion of faith. Dogmatic theology was old and spent when the great crisis came ; and to the might of reason in another field the church is indebted for the greatest service in the interest of faith.

It was said at the close of the second chapter of this discussion that the century had been enacting the Parable of the Prodigal Son. That would seem to be the widest and deepest account of its departure from itself and its return. The method of the return, from the point of view now reached, appears to call for another symbol. Perhaps the century is a kind of Odysseus, abandoning its humanities, forsaking its Ithaca, its Penelope and Telemachus for Troy and the adventure and glory of conquest. It has, like the Greek hero, enacted an immense romance and achieved unexpected renown. Like the Greek hero, too, it has felt that somehow the worth of this new achievement depended upon that which had been left behind. And now the point of the parallel becomes embarrassingly obvious. The return of the Greek adventurer was an epic of ludicrous situations, hairbreadth escapes, sweeping sorrows, and deferred hopes. The return of the nineteenth century to faith has been with similar embarrassment. It has frequently seemed to be a struggle against preternatural forces. Occasionally it has been through experiences humorous and pathetic, and even tragic. The progress has been slow, and yet amid long delays and many temptations, and confronted by seeming impossibilities, the holy dream has been cherished. Calypso has pleaded in vain, Circe's wand has been powerless over the master spirit of the time, Siren songs have been discounted in advance, Cyclopean brutality has been vanquished by an invincible humanity, and the enmity of earth and sea and air has been overcome. And this inevitable return has set the old possessions in the freshness of its own romance. It has made it clear that the new renown is for the sake of the everlasting humanities, that Troy is for Penelope and Telemachus and not they for Troy, that science and art and philosophy are for human life, and that Christianity as the supreme consecration of life is sovereign over all.

There are, doubtless, aspects of this return less happy than the foregoing remarks would seem to imply. For very many of the finest spirits the dogmatic form of faith has had the fate of the apostolic ship. It has run aground where two seas meet, — the demands of science and the needs of the heart. The generation represented by the Newmans, Carlyle and Emerson, Sterling and Clough, Martineau and other high names found itself obliged to abandon the ship at sea. Those who were self-sustaining, good swimmers like Carlyle and Emerson and Martineau had but an exhilarating contest before they reached the shore. Others had a harder time. John Henry Newman went shoreward upon the plank of authority; Keble and Pusey upon another plank, high Anglicanism; Sterling and Clough and Arnold got through the waves on other things from the ship. And so it came to pass that a multitude of fine spirits who underwent shipwreck of faith escaped safe to land. The land was hospitable, but still barbarian. It was indispensable and yet it was but a temporary abode. It was an island on which to linger until another and stancher ship should arrive to carry its passengers, British and American, and the vaster multitude who in this epitome of the spiritual history of a generation are only silently represented by them, on a happier voyage to their common destination.

CHAPTER VI

NEW HELP FROM HISTORY

I

THERE are two widely contrasted moods in which the study of reality may be pursued. One is the purely individualistic mood. The student regards himself as face to face with truth, and his mind he assumes to be representative of the mind of man. Thus out of the individual vision of truth he proceeds to deliver oracles for mankind. And it must be confessed that when this daring individualism is represented by a Rousseau, and still better by an Emerson, something may be said for it. It is then a revolt against mere tradition and the worthless heaps of opinion that stand between men and the truth. Rousseau's appeal to nature, and Emerson's plea for a first hand relation to reality, as a revolt from a dead past to a living present, are essential to progress. Still, the availing protest is in danger of becoming obsolete through its provincialness. The single vision unextended and uncorrected by the universal human vision is not an unsetting star, but a rush-

light whose service is brief. Emerson would
have done better for his insight if he had been
more "retrospective." It would have added to
his joy in "an original relation to the universe"
if he had occasionally built "the sepulchres of
the fathers." In raising a war-cry between "the
poetry and philosophy of insight" and that of
tradition, he was not improving the prospects
of his faith; in setting "religion by revelation
to us" against the history of revelation, he was
inflicting damage upon his own high cause.[1] This
individualistic mood dominated the eighteenth
century. Hume indeed sums up the meaning of
English philosophy; but of the reality of things
outside of England and imitative France he
knew nothing. How the universe appeared to
Greek thought Hume had neither impression nor
idea. Leibnitz is under the same condemnation.
His optimism is founded upon *a priori* reason-
ing, and takes no notice of fact. Theology is
equally provincial. It is Calvinistic or Arminian, and therefore is ignorant of what in the
consciousness of the church is opposed to itself
or indifferent to it. With all our just pride in
Edwards, it is evident that he reasons too much
and inquires too little. Owing to the narrowness of outlook upon the field of human life,
reality often fares hard at the hands of Edwards's successors. To gain the widest insight

[1] *Nature*, p. 10.

into reality, one "must study in more than one school."

There is, however, another mood in which to approach the study of truth. It is the historic and philosophic mood. The history supplies the fact; the philosophy tries to ascertain the value of the fact. The two greatest representatives of this mood are Aristotle and Hegel. Aristotle's uniform method is the combination of the historic and the philosophic. He looks at reality through the thought of other men. His predecessors are his teachers; the experience of the average man is important; the maxims and proverbs that coin the common-sense of mankind are always considered. His first aim is the search for reality in and through his own thought and the thought of the world; his second aim is the proper valuation of what has been found. Thus it is that Aristotle sums up all ancient knowledge and carries all ancient insight to its full maturity. He makes the reality tell through the compass and validity of the thought which he shapes for it out of the more elementary and fragmentary thoughts of other thinkers. Hegel sustains a somewhat similar relation to the modern world. He understood the history of philosophy as no one has ever done; and he found its meaning for the modern world in a way hitherto unequaled. He is in the first third of the nineteenth century the

fountain of historic impulse, as Darwin is in the
last half. The impulse is not pure in either
case, but it is far purer in the Hegelian Baur
than it is in the Darwinian Spencer. Whatever
may be said of Hegelianism as a system, it is
clear that Hegel has had no equal in modern
times in associating reality with human thought,
and in appreciation for reality of the whole historic toil of man's intelligence.

II

In the modern meaning of it what is history?
It is the study of reality through the process of
its development. He knows the river best who
has gone with it from its source to the sea. He
knows best any given piece of reality who has
traced it from its earliest beginnings to its full
maturity. He knows the mountain best who has
studied it upon all sides, and in all lights, and
from near and far. He knows the total reality
best who has looked upon it through the widest
association of human thought and feeling, who
has seen its image in the largest expanse of
man's life, and who as thus discovered has tried
with high judgment to appraise its worth.

That history is essential to the full ascertain-
ment of truth is the universal assumption of the
time. Here both faith and skepticism appeal to
the same fundamental maxim. History is essential to the demonstration that there is no ascer-

tainable reality. The universe is a chameleon. If that is the conclusion of negative thought, it can be justified only by history. The chameleon universe, to recall a former illustration, must be seen to take its character from the mind upon which it fastens. It is blue to one, green to another, black to a third; and when the three observers are together and all in a new mood it is white. But the investigation cannot pause at this point. It must run through all the colors, finding the universe each by turns, before its utter subjectivity and illusoriness can be made out. The world is truth and righteousness. That is the affirmation of faith, and again it can be made good only by an appeal to history. One man, one generation, one century is insufficient evidence. Ages, historic time, must be called into account.

This is to-day the method of intellectual life. It moves through an increasing range of history upon its new conclusion. Astronomy is more than the study of present magnitudes, numbers, and relations among the heavenly bodies; it is, in addition, an attempt, in the interest of science, at a history of the stellar universe. Geology is plainly the history of the formation of the earth. Biology is the history of the behavior of life in its earliest forms and among all living things. Physiology is the history of nervous systems and the relation thereto of intelligence.

Psychology is the study of mind in the light of its history, individual and racial. The ethical constitution of man is best seen through the record of its development, the moral endowment through the historic expression. The greater ethical insight is won through the wider and more intelligent study of ethical fact and theory with which the past is crowded. Political and social science can understand its own ideals, shape them into governing influences, and keep them from revolutionary and destructive effect only by the knowledge of human nature and the sober wisdom that come from history. Philosophy can hope to become a new and greater insight in no other way than through the discipline of the history of philosophy. The new philosopher must see the successive achievements of philosophy before he can intelligently set himself to remove defects. What has been done must be seen and appreciated before one can wisely plan new conquests. The philosopher who should take to his task without knowing where philosophy was left by Berkeley and Hume, Kant and Hegel, would surely make himself ridiculous. So essential is it that the new thinker should understand the old, if thought is not to sink into a confusion of tongues. And it will be found that we have here the sign of the pivotal thinker in all departments of speculative concern. The world is

full of the babble of blind learning and wild individualism representing nothing but their own
immaturity and vanity. In the midst of this
unmeaning activity the real thinker now and
then puts in an appearance. He understands
the past along his own special line; he sees
what others have done to further his interest,
and what they have failed to do. In reverence
for what has been done, in the clear sense of
some part of that which remains to be done, he
girds himself for his high enterprise. Thus
Plato succeeds Socrates, and Aristotle Plato;
thus Origen follows Clement, and Athanasius
Origen; thus even Calvin takes up the work of
Augustine, and Edwards that of Calvin. And
underneath all is the Eternal spirit that makes
all honest thinkers, and especially all men of
genius, destroy and build better than they know.

This at once suggests the new help that faith
is beginning to receive from history. The help
lies in the new conception of history. It is the
record, not of mere opinion or feeling or fortune,
but of the process whereby truth develops its
full character. In 1564, on the banks of the
Avon two children were born. Each looked,
let us say, as promising as the other. One
became Shakespere because he was Shakespere; the other became little or nothing because he was little or nothing. The world is a
a reality whose character makes itself known

through human thought. Human thought is its
organ, and in that organ there is an infancy;
there is, besides, a process whose goal is maturity.
The infant organ, that seems to do nothing but
sleep in the presence of the world, becomes with
the process of the suns the world-seer, the world-
interpreter. Thought with its insight and its
art promises to master the world. The world is
real, and in the apprehension of its reality there
is an apostolical succession which means progress. The science, art, philosophy, and religion of the world are an evolution in response
to the power of reality over man; over his sense
of fact, beauty, truth, and goodness. The task
of science, art, philosophy, and religion belongs
to the race. The revelation of reality is in progress, and it will be complete for man when
human history is complete. Faith thus becomes
the attitude of the individual mind toward this
historic process, this racial enterprise and hope.
It is of the nature of insight, prophecy, and
adventure; it sees, it anticipates, it is ready to
take risks. And the help which comes to faith
is through the new conception of history as the
form that reality has taken; it comes in the old
ways of sentiment, humor, ethical wisdom, and
religious insight. In history one sees, as nowhere
else, reality in feeling; one sees it in the perspective and incongruity and irony that appeal to
humor; in the fruitful labor of the intellect

working upon the sense of the moral order, and in the consciousness of the Infinite love. Faith comes to mean sympathy with the race at its best; and the polemic of faith is then but the struggle of the individual to keep the race true to its highest insight and its grand, historic vocation.

III

At first sight sentiment seems to be a foreign accretion upon reality, and not an essential aspect of it. It is the mist from the earth that rolls upward, that gathers into clouds which block the sun's path, which obscure or color its face, but which are no part of the sun. Sentiment thus appears to be a human exhalation, through which reality is forced to blaze its way; it has much to teach one about man; it has nothing to say about the truth of things.

That this is a superficial view soon becomes evident. Feeling gets at the heart of truth in its own way. It is the basis of the achievement of the intellect along all lines. For men of genius it is the sure prophecy of the approaching poem, symphony, discovery, and the deeper solution of old problems. These interests are the out-posts of the intellect. They discover the enemy, and their shots bring on the great engagement. The difference between Philistine service and genuine intellectual achievement is here appar-

ent. The Philistine covers the subject, but he
has no instinct for any part of it; while the true
workman is led by feeling and his work is based
in it. For the average person feeling does the
work of thought; and if the two are to be sepa-
rated, if thought and feeling are to be divorced,
feeling is infinitely to be preferred. It is to be
preferred because it always implies some sort of
a relation to reality. And here one comes upon
the soul of feeling. It is receptivity. Individual feeling is capable of extension through
imagination into a kind of racial feeling. The
sense of the humanity embedded in the world
or cosmos is but individual feeling or receptivity,
extended by imagination, into racial feeling or
receptivity. Man and the cosmos play into each
other, and the first form of the play is feeling.
When the individual looks at outward or inward
reality, not only through his own association
with it, but also through the association of the
race, there is true gain. The figure that seemed
to prove the subjectivity of feeling does in fact
attest its objectivity. The mist that becomes
cloud, that gathers into the gates of morning
and evening, serves as prism for the advancing
or retreating day. It is the condition of a genuine disclosure of the nature of light. And
in the same way the feeling of the individual
in the presence of reality, broadened through
imagination into the feeling of the race, is not

only atmosphere for the transcendent truth, it is also a condition through which is revealed the character of the truth. The value of the truth for one man is increased by the sense of its value for all men; and these values of the ultimate character of the universe are owing both to the character of the universe and the nature of human feeling. Nowhere does the apocalypse of reality complete itself in feeling; there are other media of revelation. Intellect and will, always present in human feeling, rise from the position of servants to that of masters. Then new insights and assurances are gained. But the first and widest appeal of the universe is to feeling; in that deep well the image of its face is earliest cast and seen.

Can it be maintained that the external world gains anything from or becomes anything for feeling? Let it be understood that feeling is instinctive intellect and there can be no great risk taken in an affirmative answer to this question. Let it be conceded that nature as force and order and law, as a system of differentiated objects, is the work, not of feeling, but of reason. The whole mind must come to the world before the world can reveal its truth and order. And yet even here feeling is by no means unimportant: feeling for nature, and feeling for nature through the feelings of other students. The insights of Newton and Darwin began in feel-

ing; and this feeling owed an immense debt to
the feeling of predecessors. A true psychology
of scientific genius would show it, in the first
instance, clinging with an inexplicable tenacity
to nature, attached to it by unquenchable interests, and, at the same time, bound still closer to
the great object of affection by the history of
scientific enthusiasm. The feeling of the math-
ematician, from Archimedes to Benjamin Peirce,
has been strengthened by the succession; and
each, as he has become great, has felt for his task
by the power of all. The same is true of chem-
ist, physicist, biologist. The passion for the
scientific object is the promise of discovery; the
increase of this passion through sympathy with
predecessors means an increase of promise. The
scientific conception of nature is thus evolved,
through feeling for nature immediate and sympathetic.

But the scientific aspect of nature is by no
means the whole of nature. There is the human
value of nature, the part that it has played in
the education of man. The physical life has
been developed through its sympathies and hostilities. The tissues of the body are stored with
mute memories of summer's heat and winter's
cold. Exhilaration of animal existence carries
in it a tacit reference to nature, and sickness
has a pathetic association with it. The strong
world that keeps one well, and the fierce world

that will not allow one to get well, alike tell upon feeling. Birth, home, early association, love and grief, all the great experiences of life, taking place as they do under the silent witness of nature, bring out of it a new meaning. The education of the poet and artist is typical. Colors, harmonies, wide fields and sweeping streams, woods and hills, seas and stars, are more to them than they are to other men. Still there is in every one, in some degree of strength, both poet and artist; and the influence of nature in awakening intelligence is large and constant. If it is true that nature owes much to man, it is equally true that man owes much to nature. If nature must wait for human eyes and ears, for man's feeling heart and seeing spirit, the first awakener of the soul outside the family circle is nature. Nature in literature, in painting, and in music, is but the enlarged and transfigured image of nature in ordinary human feeling. This way that the race feels about nature is a revelation of the character of nature. That character is at once friendly and unfriendly toward man; and the bearer of it is implicated in the whole gain and loss of human existence. Nature wears both an immemorial smile and frown; she is brightened with the joy and covered with the sorrow of the race.

The humanity embedded in the cosmos is thus discovered through sentiment. The feeling soul in the feeling of the whole race sees in the cosmos a new character. The value of the earth for physics is one thing; its human value is another. The first value it owes to itself in connection with human thought; the second value it owes to itself in connection with human feeling. The estimate to be put upon it, owing to the composition of its rocks, its soil, its seas, and in virtue of its intrinsic character, may or may not rank it high among the countless worlds of space. But there can be no doubt of the supremacy to be given it, at least from man's point of view, because of the human history with which it has so long been identified. Should it become a dead planet, it would still be the ruined temple of humanity, more precious in death than the multitudes of the living that blaze around it. Its significance for feeling, for rational life, would still remain incomparable. And even should it be dissolved into atoms, and dispersed like flying dust, among the original forces of the universe, still each whirling particle, each lonely bit of the poor dead earth, would bear with it forever the shadow of a great history, the mark of an imperishable association, the touch of a sublime sanctity, and would stand, even in its infinitesimal form, more august and beautiful to imagination than suns and constellations. To this extent has the race and the globe run the one into the other. The earth is

forever saturated with humanity, and its high
distinction, living or dead, intact or dissolved,
must be that it abides the symbol of the career
and conquest, the sorrow and hope of mankind.
And it is through sentiment that this great
aspect of the earth, and indeed the cosmos, is
discovered. The cosmos becomes something new
through the history of human feeling. It was
fitted to touch the race in this way, and through
this vast medium the individual man looks into
the face of nature to find there a higher meaning.

Humanity, the human race as constituting one
kind, as forming, in spite of endless diversities,
one family, is for this generation an objective
truth. It has come to appear as part of the
nature of things, an ultimate premise of sound
social philosophy. And it is at first difficult to
see how feeling for the way in which man has
felt toward himself can add to the range or cer-
titude of this conception. It is obvious that for
the practical force of the idea sentiment is supremely important; but that feeling can shed
any light upon it or make it more authentic,
seems to be claiming too much.

This is, however, the very point to be made.
And the fundamental position from which to
present the contention is that reality is best
known through its history. The ideas of philosophy, because of the abstract form in which

they necessarily live, often come to appear as
the idealism of arbitrary minds, as the inventions
of noble but lawless genius. These ideas are
indeed the product of the historic process; but
they have forgotten their parentage. In the interest of their validity, it becomes essential to
look at them in the light of their origin and development. And a new certificate of truth can
be given them, when they are seen to emerge,
gradually and inevitably, from the human mind
in its long, sore, and yet grand wrestle with the
reality of things. This induction of truth is
always an induction from feeling. While the
result is something different from feeling, the
process by which the world of outward reality
and the world of inward reality is built begins
in that mystic phase of mental life. The particular truth of the unity of mankind began its
evolution in feeling; and to survey the truth in
connection with human feeling does indeed im-
part to it a profounder reality and a clearer
inevitableness. The immanence of the plan of
the stellar order of to-day in the primitive fire
mist, if made good, cannot but implicate that
order with the heart of cosmic reality; and the
presence in human feeling of the unity of man,
even if it must be allowed that this feeling
is crude, would seem to imply that this idea is
forced upon man by his own nature, that it is
indeed in the constitution of the human world.

The influence of heredity and environment is first of all an influence upon feeling. The power of ancestry, of home, of the social group, of the business guild, of the patriotic appeal, is primarily power upon sentiment. In this human order the fountains of emotion are first opened. We do not go to history to find our hearts; we go there to have them enlarged. Because of the immediate and ineffable humanities into which men are born, and in which they come to the sense of love and sympathy, they wish to extend, or rather they are unconsciously impelled to extend, their relations with their kind. They have felt, in the quiet harbor of home, and friendship, and social union, the softer ripples of the tides of humanity, and they are now driven by instinct to the exposed shores and the far extending promontories that the mightiest surges may break over them.

A piece of pottery dug from the ruins of ancient Rome has a value quite independent of its beauty or utility. It is a symbol that makes possible a vivid appreciation of the way that man has felt about his life. It may be a household utensil, striking neither for its æsthetic features nor its convenience; and yet because it had a place in the homes of millions of mankind, served the uses of their table, was among the gifts at weddings, and handled and admired by friends, identified with the history of the children, and passed on from generation to generation, covered with an increasing cloud of rich and transfigured memories, it cannot but possess for the beholder an immense human value. A tablet impressed with Assyrian characters, preserving on its surface the correspondence of kings who lived more than forty generations ago, or revealing the business methods of times and peoples of remote antiquity, or allowing the scholar to look in upon the domestic life and to note the bright hopes set in the black framework of despair, or voicing the penitence and aspiration of religious faith and taking one into the sanctuary of races and civilizations that have utterly perished, must serve as an affecting symbol of the way in which man has thought about his own existence. Art, in all its forms, has perhaps its chief interest here. It is an authentic interpretation of the ways in which human beings have felt about life. The Odyssey is greatest as a witness to ancient feeling, the Divine Comedy as a voice for ten silent centuries. Art is an original and an authentic interpretation of man's heart. And the feeling for art, on the part of men at large, becomes part of the power of art itself. The Sistine Madonna is great in itself, and it is great through the appreciation and confession of its greatness by so many generations of students. The Republic of Plato is something more than one of the masterpieces of phi-

losophy. It is, besides, an old book, and the
reader who holds it in his hands to-day is looking upon the page upon which a multitude, that
no man can number, of the wisest in all these
generations have looked. He is following the
course of thought that such imperial minds as
Berkeley, Butler, and Bacon; Kant, Leibnitz, and
Descartes; More, Erasmus, and Luther; Augustine, Origen, and Clement; Tacitus, Virgil, and
Cicero; Plutarch, Alexander, and Aristotle followed. The book has become a symbol of the
way in which men have felt about life and the
universe. That this is true of the Bible in a
far higher sense will be noticed presently. At
this point it only remains to be repeated that the
successively loftier ways in which men have come
to feel about themselves are an important part
of history. In one aspect history is sentiment;
and through this evolving sentiment the idea is
seen emerging of the unity of mankind. It is
the sense of brotherhood in solution in the feeling of the race that has controlled the moral
plagues that otherwise would have blotted man
out of being, as it is the salt in the tidal movement of the sea that enables it to sweep the cities
of their sewage and to remain sound. The history of the ways in which the race has felt toward
itself shows many sad things; but it presents
above all a vast testimony to the idea of the
unity of man as an authentic part of the order
of things.

There is the same relation of sentiment to
God. The sense that men have felt after him
if haply they might find him relates the race to
the highest reality by the elemental force of instinct. The successively higher ways in which
the race has come to feel toward the Infinite is
of large importance for faith. The final emergence of the idea of God has been out of a world
of feeling. It has been like a polar sunrise.
There have been alternate advances and retreats,
yet the advances have been more than the retreats could cover. The luminous promise has
waxed and waned only to wax still more and
wane less. At length the red dawn has come,
and out of this transfigured passion of the human heart the notion of God has risen. To con-
nect the ideal possession with the long prophetic
passion through which it was won is to secure
its validity.

It is natural at this point to mistake an association of a great idea with human life for the
witness of human life to the truth of the idea.
When the Hebrew, recently returned from captivity, broke into the hymn, "Blessed be the
Lord, the God of our fathers," [1] two thoughts
were doubtless in his mind. There was the
sacredness that the conception of God had acquired through long and tender association with
his ancestors ; and, for the power of the concep-

[1] Ezra vii. 27.

tion, this high association is of the utmost importance. This supreme idea is never a bare insight of the individual mind. That experience is now impossible; it is nearly inconceivable. The thought of God is dyed in the rich and tender humanities of the ages. It is impossible to get at it as it shines beyond the atmosphere of human association. The love, the truth, the longest reach of memory, the deepest and tenderest feelings of generations, have gathered round the sublime conception, and it enters the mind of the individual believer with this human power. Veneration for man attaches itself at once to man's highest thought when the thought is believed to be true. When the apostle speaks of the God of his fathers, and the God and Father of Jesus Christ, one intention certainly is to mark the gathering and consummated sanctity which the truth receives from association with heroic men, from the ineffable association with the Divine man. The believer is indeed beside himself who does not open his spirit to this appeal. Emerson sings of the "accent of the Holy Ghost" which he thinks the "heedless world has never lost." His fine insight may be deepened to the heart of things and carried to their utmost bounds, and still be essentially true. What is now claimed is the human accent that the Holy Ghost has never lost; the human accent that has become more and more unmistakable and precious as the ages have come and gone. The Lord's Day, Baptism, the Lord's Supper, the great hymns of the church, the gospel and epistle, the Hebrew psalms, the real Bible within the Bible, Christ himself, and the God and Father of Christ come upon the sympathetic, imaginative believer and worshiper of to-day in the sacred strength of a human association that no mind can measure. If it is true that the light of the Divine ideal is everywhere upon human life, it is equally true that the pathos of humanity is everywhere upon the Divine ideal. And this general statement has its greatest force in reference to the highest things. If " a day in thy courts is better than a thousand," it is owing to the immemorial association of God's house and human need and triumph. If the conception of God is the mightiest of all thoughts, it must not be forgotten that the thought is the best tradition of humanity, and that it comes in the power of the highest humanity.

This observation has been made, however, that it may not be confounded with another now to be made. Human feeling as an association with the idea of God is one thing ; human feeling as a witness to the truth of the idea is another. It is with human life as a witness to the reality of God that we are here properly concerned. And this is the second thought that

the Hebrew must have had when he shouted,
" Blessed be the Lord, the God of our fathers."
Ancestry was a lengthening witness for the
truth of contemporary faith ; the vista into the
history of his race was a new assurance of God.

Feeling toward the Infinite has assumed many
forms. Strange and tragic and hideous they have
often been ; sane and wholly serviceable to life
they have become only within the last few thousand years, and that only in the best specimens
of the race. And yet the feeling for the Infinite
has been universal and ineradicable. It has been
inevitable, and as such it is the witness, not only
to the constitution of man, but also to the constitution of the universe. It has been inevitable
and it has risen into successively higher forms.
It has become finally the feeling of Jesus toward
the Infinite, and Jesus in his feeling for the Infinite has become the type of the race. The Divine
reality is embedded in the passion of Christ. He
grows up into these ways of regarding God even
before the full advent of his gospel, we may well
believe. Being such as he was, the universe
affected him in this way. And it may be that
the feeling of man for the Infinite finds its full
interpretation in the feeling of Christ.

Sentiment is not new, but history as the sense
of the evolution of reality through human feeling
has new help for faith. The primary attach-
ments of man to reality are feelings. Nature,

human nature, and the Divine nature are in aboriginal contact with sentiency. In the world, and in the soul, and in God, the reality is wound round by the instincts of man. Back to this primary source it is essential to carry the elaborated ideas of science, anthropology, and theology. They become, in a sense, independent of feeling; their ultimate judge is their author, reason. Still, when they are overtaken by skepticism, as they often are, and when they become mere notions, idealisms in the air, "cloud-capped towers" with no base in reality, it is necessary to return to the emotive, instinctive sources of knowledge. The first association of reality is there; it is an association, constant, universal, indestructible. The history of this association between human passion and the Divine aspect of reality gives to faith, in its essential spirit and content, the sanction of the constitution of man and the constitution of the universe. Man has felt this way because in this way he has been affected by the truth of things. "Your feeling is piety in so far as it is the result of the operation of God in you by means of the operation of the world upon you." [1] Schleiermacher plead for feeling as the sphere of religion; his plea is true, although it is not the whole truth. And when to feeling is added the history of feeling, the immediate contact of

[1] Schleiermacher, *Speeches*, p. 45.

the soul with the Divine reality, for which
Schleiermacher contended, becomes an ampler
and more significant experience.

IV

Humor is no new thing. If it were new, it
could not be of any possible use in this discussion. It is fortunately as old as man. From
the beginning it has entered into human life
as a great educational force. It has been an
immeasurable security against the possibility of
universal and permanent madness. The growth
of humor may well be regarded with religious
interest; for it is a happy sign of increasing
mental health and reasonableness. Humor is in
fact an essentially logical exercise. More perhaps than anything else, it is the varied play of
the laws of logic upon the self-conscious spirit,
amid the bewilderments of this world. Its precious emotional accompaniment is apt to conceal
its essential and piercing intellectuality. It is
of the essence and finest life of reason. And on
this ground it is of high importance for faith.
History as humor means here the humor that
works through the annals of the race, in favor
of possessions that are precious to the race.
Besides other high services that do not now concern us, humor is a force for truth and beauty
and goodness. Religion and art and character
of the highest order are inconceivable without

humor. It is the unerring discoverer of false magnitudes, the revealer of bad perspective; further, it is the sense of incongruity; finally, it is irony, or the seeming assent to ideas, customs, and institutions, which really means the steadfast purpose to overthrow them. Conceit, for example, personal, domestic, and national, appeals to the element in humor first mentioned. It is a case of bad perspective. Cases of incongruity are seen in the matter of names, — the colored brethren who are known as George Washington this or Abraham Lincoln that. The New England fashion of giving Biblical names to the children is another witness to the fact that among the many high possessions of the Puritan the sense of humor is not to be counted. The conjunction of Jeremiah and gay youth, of Jerusha or Jemima and a fine fascinating face, do not seem to be particularly congruous. A good example of irony would be a letter of thanks from Washington, and in his polite and serious vein, to Benedict Arnold, after his treachery, upon his unbounded loyalty to the American cause. With this intimation of the three aspects of humor that concern the present discussion, it is next in order to ascertain their bearing upon it.

History is seen as humor through the revelation of false magnitudes. All conceited persons are not cured by the discipline of experience any

more than all who engage in battle are at any
one time killed. The fool makes his escape even
more miraculously than the soldier. Still, human
beings do pass through an extraordinary transformation of opinion concerning their own magnitude in the course of a lifetime. Those who
founded the " Edinburgh Review " took for their
motto the words, " The judge is condemned
when the guilty man is absolved or escapes
condemnation." " It is said, that of the persons who felt themselves called to this office,
and who formed this determination, scarcely one
had passed his twenty-first birthday. That may
appear an early time for men to take their seats
upon the bench; yet many of us can recollect
that at that age, though we might have few or
none of the gifts which these Edinburgh Re-
viewers gave ample evidence that they possessed, we thought ourselves perfectly competent
to assume the same position and to pass sentence
upon the universe. If we did not think so then,
we probably should never have arrived at the
belief afterwards; for as we grow older painful
doubts of our infallibility spring up within ourselves, and they are encouraged by the persons
with whom we converse." [1] There comes a time,
as Young says, when a man suspects himself
a fool; and this is followed by another, when,
again according to Young, he knows it. The

[1] *Friendship of Books*, F. D. Maurice, pp. 354-355.

geocentric mood is the primary mood of the natural man. The centre of the circle formed by the horizon is the spot whereon he stands, and the zenith of the sky is directly over his head. Thus illusion becomes reality, and every man seems to himself to be at the heart of things. Thus egoism finds its symbol and its apparent justification. To undo this habit, to reveal the ludicrous perspective involved in this notion, and to destroy the false magnitudes which it sets up, is one great office of humor. Probably no wise man has ever been able to estimate his debt to humor; and it is more than probable that no man ever became wise without the aid of the world's humor. The education which children get from children at this point, and youth from youth, and men of the world from men of the world, is beyond valuation. The conceit and snobbery and nonsense are in this way taken out of the mass of mankind. And even those who are uncured know the times and the seasons for the restitution of the ludicrous perspective. Such men, be they farmers or merchants, doctors or lawyers, ministers or politicians, know enough not to brag or put on airs among their peers. They select their victims with the greatest care, and always from the ignorant and credulous class. And until they feel themselves secure they proceed with infinite caution, making for themselves apologies at every forward step, as if they were intrenching against the keen and merciless humor of the world. Very few indeed are the shameless egoists. The world has so far prevailed over conceit that even when it is not cured it knows how foolish it is and how heartily it deserves the world's laughter. For whatever adjustment of personal merit to personal merit, of family pride to family pride, of national egoism to national egoism, has been achieved, the obligation to humor is great.

The great joke of history is ignorance pretending to be knowledge, falsehood assuming that it is the truth. The relations of Charles I. and Oliver Cromwell furnish a typical example. For two centuries and a half English historians persisted in asserting the reality of King Charles's magnitudes. He was as great and essential as he thought that he was. His cause, his opinions, his methods, his views of England were genuine perspective. Things in their essential character were as he saw them. On the other hand, Cromwell was false and wrong beyond description. His magnitudes and relations were a lie. His cause, ideas, spirit, religion, and general view of the nation were a vile and calamitous want of perspective, enough to make angels weep because it was so tragic ; enough to make devils laugh because it was so comic. This is one of the standing jokes of modern history.

For two hundred and fifty years ignorance is allowed to have her way and to exhaust her power in making herself ridiculous. When she has thus prepared herself to be the butt of the world, knowledge comes in as an aid in the appreciation of the figure. Within the last fifty years the verdict upon Charles I. and Oliver Cromwell has been reversed. History has overthrown the false magnitude and wiped out the bad perspective.

To multitudes of his contemporaries the claims of Jesus seemed to be absurdly false; to an equal number the opinions of the chief priests and Pharisees about Jesus, and about life and the universe, appeared to be profoundly and permanently true. He went to his cross as the assertor of false magnitudes, as the author of an impossible perspective. In the mockery of the soldiers, "Hail, King of the Jews," and in the jeers of the crowd that stood under his cross, there is reflected the common opinion concerning his preposterous pretensions. The work of ignorance is here so supremely tragic that one cannot speak of it in other than the most serious manner. Yet it is plain, in the light of history, that the magnitudes and relations of Jesus are real, that in his perspective lies the truth about himself, human life, and the universe. History has turned the mockeries of the soldiers and of the mad crowd upon those who for the moment triumphed over Jesus. Slowly their self-consciousness has been shown to be self-conceit, their teachings to be caricatures of reality, and their conduct the wildest distortion of humanity. For their magnitudes and perspective they have become the sport of mankind. They are the saddest, and at the same time the most instructive, instance on record of the humor of history. The Hebrew psalmist has anticipated the mood into which mankind has been brought upon this supreme subject, · by the humor of the centuries : —

> " When the Lord turned again the captivity of Zion,
> We were like unto them that dream.
> Then was our mouth filled with laughter,
> And our tongue with singing." [1]

The revolution wrought by time, through the increase of knowledge, upon the false estimates of man, is an epical showing of the service of humor in behalf of truth.

History determines size and relation. It discovers its real heroes and expels from the temple of fame those who have no place there, or lowers the rank of those who have been too swiftly promoted. To his age Voltaire seemed to be the greatest man that the world had ever seen. The sense of humor working through time has long ago reduced his dimensions. Goethe, on the other hand, was surpassed in repute during his

[1] Psalm cxxvi. 1, 2.

lifetime by a score of writers. In the generation following his death there were few who
would have put him unconditionally above
Schiller. But perspective improves with the
lapse of time, and the preëminence of Goethe as
a man of genius over all his German rivals has
won nearly universal consent. To half his nation, if not to more than half, Sir Walter Scott
appeared to be a greater nature than Robert
Burns. Such a judgment is nearly impossible
to-day, for an intelligent person. When Plato
died Aristotle was not chosen to succeed him;
another man whom time has proved to be a
popular nobody received that honor. Yet in
utter disregard of the votes of the Academy history has constituted Aristotle the sole successor
of his master. Shakespere had to wait until
the world's humor discovered his real magnitude. Fluctuations of taste apart, and the literary insanities that occasionally afflict men discounted, time discloses a procession of thinkers,
poets, artists, rulers, and makers of the world
up toward the zenith, where they remain forever;
and another procession of intellectual usurpers
and poor inflationists of many kinds down from
the heights to which they have been undeservedly
raised, into the rest of oblivion. Nothing better illustrates the sense of humor in man than
this achievement of a juster perspective with
the lapse of time, and the discrimination, on a

broader scale, of true magnitude from false.
One feels perfectly secure about the position of
the Bible. Time has wrought great havoc with
man's theories about this great literature; but
concerning the literature itself, so long as the
sense of humor remains in man, to say nothing
about the sense of religion, the ages as they run
can only discover its immeasurable superiority
to every other literature in the world. And
with still more confidence this may be said about
Jesus Christ. Humor is not the author of
Christologies, although it may prove a powerful
weapon against false doctrine here as elsewhere.
But humor is the instinct for truth. The supremacy of Christ is his own achievement through
the appeal that he makes to this instinct. Not
until all sane judgment about the magnitudes of
men and their work is gone, not until all just
perspective is lost, will Jesus Christ pass away
from the sovereignty that he has won.

It is owing, in some degree at least, to the
sense of humor that certain ideas about the universe fail of general assent. Atheism is an impossible doctrine for one with any measure of
sanity in the perspective of things. French vanity is responsible for the famous reply of Laplace
to Napoleon's question about God : "Sire, I had
no need of any such hypothesis." To assume
that the universal order can come from original
universal confusion, or that an intelligible world

has risen from a non-mental source, is the superlative speculative joke. Atheism is with Cicero, and with every other person gifted with the sense of humor, as credible as would be the supposition that nothing more is needed for the production of the Iliad and the Odyssey than to keep tossing the Greek alphabet into the air. Such miracles do not occur. For this reason, Hume who is the strongest reasoner against theism, is no atheist. His moral sense offered, perhaps, little embarrassment to the scheme, but his humor made it incredible. And if the mind of man could be fully sounded, it would be discovered that atheism is rejected, in part at least, because it is ridiculous. It is one of those inversions that imply, in their performance, immense mental agility, but that always impress the sane beholder as supremely funny. The amount of knowledge necessary to establish the universal negative, there is no God, would equal omniscience; so that the successful demonstrator of atheism would be himself the Deity. And again the scheme is transfixed by a shaft of humor. It is, perhaps, not too much to say that in the general abandonment of speculative or scientific atheism the sense of impossible perspective has played an important part.

Pantheism is a system that witnesses to the profoundest truth. Its great merit lies in the emphasis it puts upon the identity that pervades the universe, and without which there could be no universe; its fatal defect is in its denial of substantial reality to the difference, the variety in the world. It offends the philosophic sense by the reduction of all reality to a bare universal; it violates the moral sense by its consecration of all that is as inevitable and inevitably right; it runs against the sense of humor by its false magnitudes and ridiculous perspective. When one hears of a divine man and a divine oyster, one is likely to answer with honest laughter. The failure to perceive that what makes man divine is not that he shares in the one life of the universe, but that he shares, as the lower creatures do not, in the moral reason which is the essence of the Deity, is a blunder that may well appeal to mirth. What is needed to kill abominable idolatries and to cleanse the Augæan stables of Hindu temples, which are the foul and prolific issue of the pantheism that regards all life as equally of the essence of God, is not so much a true philosophy or a genuine religion as the wide cultivation of the sense of humor. Were this sane instinct educated, as it easily might be, the lapse of a generation would see the end of these hideous distortions. There is a Lucian somewhere in every man, and a Christian Lucian present in the mind of every foreign missionary should be a necessary qualification for appointment to that service.

Theism lives and prevails because of its inherent sanity. The best theistic argument is that which seeks to unfold this fundamental consistency. That order should come from an ordainer of it; that law should imply an originating and a supporting will; that humanity should be regarded as having its source in an Eternal humanity; that human history should be believed to be part of the Divine plan in cosmic development, having a character, function, and worth of its own; that moral reason should seem to be the best description of the ultimate reality, and righteousness with an endless opportunity the essential vocation and highest hope of man, is only what one might expect. The scheme is in fundamental accord with the permanent instincts of the soul. It could be shown to be the best philosophy; that it is the highest wisdom would seem to be implied in all the greater and more thoroughly reasoned systems that the world has seen. That it wins to its support the sense of humor is obvious. Its magnitudes and relations are reasonable; its perspective is permanently sound.

The second element in humor, incongruity, is separable from the first only for purposes of exposition. In all the instances given of false magnitudes and bad perspective, the incongruous has been present. The word is but the name for a new aspect of a mental power that is one spirit in many forms. The sense of false magnitudes exhibits humor as the servant of truth; the sense of incongruities shows it as the servant of beauty. It is the incongruity in things more perhaps than any other perception that excites mirth. In an interesting essay upon "The Physiology of Laughter," Mr. Spencer asks: "Why do we smile when a child puts on a man's hat? or what induces us to laugh on reading that the corpulent Gibbon was unable to rise from his knees after making a tender declaration?" The physiological answer is left for Mr. Spencer to furnish; the psychological answer is plain. The sense of incongruity is the source of the amusement. The amusement would be equally great if the man should appear in the child's hat; or if the fair one to whom Gibbon made his knightly vows should have been altogether such as he, and, on joining him in his humble posture, should have been equally unable to rise. It is this element of incongruity which affects one on reading the reproachful cry of the poor woman who had treated D'Alembert as a son: "You will never be anything better than a philosopher, and what is that? 'T is a madman who torments himself all his life, that people may talk about him when he is dead!"[1] The same thing convulses one on imagining Falstaff hidden in the basket of dirty clothes, carried down to the river and emptied into it.

[1] *Diderot*, vol. i. p. 126. John Morley.

Turned upon higher subjects, this aspect of humor appears as the sense of moral incongruity. And only stupid custom prevents one from seeing how great has been the influence of this gift in exalting the supreme art, the art of righteous living. The terrible humor of Burns in "Holy Willie's Prayer" is the best sermon ever preached against hypocrisy. The merciless exhibition of the incongruity between the elder's profession and his practice has stung a whole church into higher ethical feeling. The companion piece upon "The Holy Fair," which exposes the fearful abuses that attended the celebration of the Lord's Supper in Scotland in the eighteenth century, has been equally effective. The laughter and mockery of a nation, inspired by a noble humorist, have had an immense moral influence. Humor has had much to do with the purification of political life. When the community sees a judge sending a man to jail for a breach of the peace who is himself living in violation of the laws of purity, the incongruity appears monstrous. Pilates as rulers and Felixes as judges have sorely tried the patience of mankind. At length, however, there has come the exposure of the villainous incompatibility, and the mockery of the world has told upon the cowardly governor and the corrupt judge. It was the national sense of heinous incongruity between political leadership struggling for the betterment of a race and the life of an adulterer that drove Charles Stuart Parnell to the wall. And the political history of the world, especially of the last two centuries, is a continuous testimony to the growing power of this saving grace.

In all departments of life the same fact is seen. Social customs and industrial methods are subject to humor, because they are held up in the light of the brotherhood of man. That idea is essential to the modern world, and it has become the mighty vantage ground of the high humorist. It is impossible for society to continue unmodified in its heartlessness in the presence of this divine mocker, or for industry to remain unimproved under the merciless jeers of Christian humor. This work of grace extends to all who claim a place among the serious servants of man. The teacher of an idea must be a worthy representative of his idea; otherwise the world will laugh him down. The moral incongruity presented in the lives of the leading French thinkers of the eighteenth century, for example, has contributed not a little to the oblivion that has overtaken them. Rousseau represented something worth while, but unless society can make a better use of his wisdom than Rousseau himself made, his teaching is vain. Between the gospel of human perfectibility as preached by the Encyclopædists, and the brutal impurity of their lives, there is a ghastly incompatability. Society is willing to pardon weakness and to condone unintentional folly, even in its accepted spiritual teachers; but since the verification of spiritual truth is ever through life, the shameless will must always be a fatal embarrassment to the brilliant intellect. The dictum that the validity of the sacrament does not depend upon the character of the priest is doubtless sound; yet the sacraments will swiftly become obsolete if men do not insist upon clean hands and a pure heart in those who administer them. Immoral genius is unequal to the task of adequately interpreting human life; and the truth upon which it is able to lay hold is likely, in course of time, to find a worthier representative. For this reason Goethe suffers. He is not good enough to see the highest meaning of human passion. He is not what he might have been. Between his life and his gospel of culture there is a grave incongruity. Imagination is the servant of life, and not the substitute for its ethical strenuousness. The sense of humor demands that the epic poem shall come out of the epic character. Between the teacher and his ideas there must be a profound reconciliation; otherwise the mockery of the world will reprobate him, and another will take his bishopric as a worthier representative of the kingdom of truth.

Hebrew humor is applied, for the most part, to the moral aspect of life. It is this fact that has led Carlyle and others to the monstrous conclusion that humor is foreign to Hebrew genius. In the stories of David and Goliath, and in the Samson legends, there is humor upon the ordinary level, and by no means of the fastidious sort. The Jonah parable is full of humor; and from nearly every book in the Old Testament instances of humor, in the common acceptation of the term, might be gathered. Still, Hebrew humor finds its object, as far as the second element in it is concerned, in moral incongruity. The humor and pathos of the opening words of Isaiah's prophecies can be missed only by the mere nominalist: "Hear, O heavens, and give ear, O earth, for the Lord hath spoken: I have nourished and brought up children, and they have rebelled against me. The ox knoweth his owner, and the ass his master's crib: but Israel doth not know, my people doth not consider." [1] The incongruity is incredible, pathetic, ridiculous. Duller than an ox, inferior to an ass is the atheistic man or nation. Surely there is matter here both for tears and laughter. In an admirable essay Dr. A. P. Peabody has called attention to the humor shown by the man who was born blind, as recorded in the Gospel of John.[2]

[1] Isaiah i. 2, 3.

[2] *Internal Evidence for the Johannine Authorship of the Fourth Gospel.*

"Why, herein is the marvel, that ye know not whence he is, and yet he opened mine eyes."[1] The incongruity of the situation, to this humorist, lies in the fact that the Pharisees are unable to see that the beneficent act of Jesus issues from a divine source. The perplexity of the Pharisees is plainly seen to be pure hypocrisy, and this humorist's exposure of it is merciless and amusing. That Jesus saw the moral incongruities of his time is manifest nearly upon every page of his teachings. "But whereunto shall I liken this generation? It is like unto children sitting in the market-places, which call unto their fellows and say, We piped unto you, and ye did not dance; we wailed, and ye did not mourn. For John came neither eating nor drinking, and they say, He hath a devil. The Son of man came eating and drinking, and they say, Behold, a gluttonous man, and a wine-bibber, a friend of publicans and sinners! And wisdom is justified by her works."[2] Here again the perception opens the fountains both of laughter and tears. The twenty-third chapter of Matthew is a terrible instance of Christian humor, dealing with monstrous moral incongruity. The passion of the divine speaker is too high for laughter; but the merciless exposure of tyrannous hypocrisy must have moved to convulsive laughter the poor and oppressed persons who lis-

[1] John ix. 30.   [2] Matt. xi. 16–19.

tened to his address. "Ye blind guides, which
strain out the gnat, and swallow the camel."
"Ye cleanse the outside of the cup and platter,
but within they are full of extortion and excess."
"Ye are like unto whited sepulchres, which outwardly appear beautiful, but inwardly are full
of dead men's bones, and of all uncleanness."
"Ye build the sepulchres of the prophets, and
garnish the tombs of the righteous, and say, If
we had been in the days of our fathers, we should
not have been partakers with them in the blood
of the prophets."[1] This exposure of the whole
hypocrisy of an age is unequaled for completeness and power, and the effect of it upon the
sincere mind of the world is the highest kind of
happiness.

Christian humor is thus a mighty weapon
against pretense. Moral incongruity lies indeed
in the attitude of man toward the ideal. No
one can take as his ideal Christ's words, "Ye
therefore shall be perfect, as your heavenly Father is perfect,"[2] without perceiving an irremediable grotesqueness in his assumption. But the
incongruity that is inseparable from finiteness,
and that which is deliberately brought into existence, and fostered by an evil will, are to be
sharply distinguished the one from the other.
In any case, man measuring himself against the
Infinite is a ludicrous spectacle. Where the in-

[1] Matt. xxiii. 24, 25, 27, 29, 30.   [2] Matt. v. 48.

commensurateness is part of his being the ludicrousness is inevitable, and the amusement to which it gives rise should enrich the universe. But the ugliness of human history lies largely in man's pretense. Hypocrisy is an eonian disgrace. And for the last two thousand years it has met a force in Christian humor that has pressed it hard. Erasmus, and Luther, and Knox were humorists, and in a way they are typical of the reforming instinct in man. In its warfare against moral ugliness it has come to depend much upon the mockeries that are developed through the sense of incongruity.

The third aspect of humor to which attention is here called is that known as irony. Irony is the serious form of humor. It is humor conscious of its own purpose, and while it always adopts a manner calculated to disguise its end, it pursues that end with steady, subdued, and imperious passion. It is a sort of logical strategy; it has its origin in the duel between reality and illusion, and in the circumstances that complicate this fight, and that make it, in the last degree, serious and difficult. Under utter inward revolt, it is the urbanest assent to dogmatic and otherwise incurable folly, in order that through the large opportunity thus given to it, folly may effect its own complete exposure. In argument it is often the last resort. It is frequently the only effective way of dealing with pretentious and aggressive ignorance. By the politest manner toward this strange union of intellectual incapacity and conceit, it is in a way put off its guard; it is beguiled into the didactic mood, made to advance its notions, evolve its own absurdities; and when this process has gone far enough irony simply confronts the pretender with the ludicrous impossibilities to which he has given utterance. Irony in argument thus means that one man is led by the seemingly perfect assent of another to his definitions, and by the apparently innocent questions of this second person from absurdity to absurdity, until in his utter bewilderment he becomes aware of his own pretentious and ridiculous folly. This is the famous Socratic irony, the method by which declamatory nonsense is exposed, the process which begins by accepting the premise of the fool, and which ends in the amazing achievement, the demonstration to the fool that he is a fool. Of this achievement the Platonic Dialogues are the classic example. The method by which Plato's master convinced the conceited persons who came to him, thinking that they knew all about temperance, friendship, courage, justice, knowledge, and being, that they knew nothing about them, shines in these dialogues with a bright and an everlasting light. To the irony of argument that appears in these compositions there is no parallel in the literature of the world. The

Socratic irony is merciless, and at the same time it is genial; it is in dead earnest in the pursuit of its end, and yet it is always ready to pause to make room for an interlude or episode; it is severely intellectual, and still it is abundant in mirth-provoking power. The Socratic irony is an illustration of the remark made above that humor is essentially a logical exercise upon the absurdities of thought and things.

Swift is perhaps the greatest master of irony in the English language. The first and second parts of Gulliver are consummate specimens of irony. The story of the Lilliputians and that of the Brobdingnagians read like genuine history marvelously well written. These two voyages form perhaps the best book for intelligent children that was ever made. And this is the very highest tribute that could be paid to the author's ironical purpose. It is the perfection of art to conceal art. Only the mature reader sees the insignificance into which Englishmen and Frenchmen, who were then in dispute for the leadership of the world, are thrown, first by the terribly serious suggestion that they are as Lilliputians to Gulliver, and second by the equally irresistible hint that they are as Gulliver to Brobdingnagians. The irony is in the whole plan and execution of these parts of the work down to the minutest detail; yet it is detected only by the strange impression upon the adult reader of an ulterior purpose. The reader has been listening to a pleasant story which suddenly develops into the song of a siren. He is charmed by a narration which becomes, as by the stroke of magic, the bitterest indictment of mankind. It is not necessary to agree with Swift in order to admire the skill and power with which he pursues his deadly aim. A specimen of Swift's irony, as admirable as it is consummate, is found in his "Modest Proposal" for the relief of the distresses from which the Irish people were suffering, and the sight of which went like a knife to Swift's heart. In the calmest economic manner he proposes that babies be fattened for the market and turned into a luxury for the tables of the rich. The irony lies in the piercing suggestion that this would be in accord with the economic treatment to which Ireland has been subjected, that it would be in full harmony with the spirit and methods of the English landlords, and that the cruelty and horror of the proposal would be immeasurably less than the inhumanity of the present order. Through the loathsomeness of the proposal the yet profounder loathsomeness of English neglect of Irish sufferings is made terribly plain; and thus what compassion could not do irony has achieved.

Illustrative instances of irony in speech will readily occur to one. Macaulay remarks that "a drayman in a passion calls out, 'You are a pretty fellow,' without suspecting that he is uttering irony." This has its match in the form which passionate indignation against a blunderer takes among our own people: "You are smart?" Carlyle says that his father's speech was full of metaphor, although he could not have told what a metaphor was. The same is true of irony. It is the path for the lightning in the speech of the world. A fine example of irony is Lord Sherbrooke's reply to the modernist, who said to him, "I have the greatest contempt for Aristotle," "but not that contempt which familiarity breeds, I should imagine." The former master of Trinity College, Cambridge — Dr. Thompson — has left several famous specimens, one of which must be quoted. Preaching in Trinity Chapel on the Parable of the Talents, to an audience that considers itself the most highly endowed in the world, the master began his sermon thus: "It would be obviously superfluous in a congregation such as that which I now address to expatiate on the responsibilities of those who have five or even two talents. I shall therefore confine my observations to the more ordinary case of those of us who have one talent." [1]   At the time when Mr. Ingersoll was noisiest in his talk about the mistakes of Moses, a bullet from a careless hand went through the window of the study of a

[1] *Collections and Recollections*, p. 174.

professor of divinity in Yale University, grazed his head, and lodged in a Hebrew Bible; whereupon Professor George P. Fisher remarked: "Another instance of the popular attack upon the Bible." Professor Edwards A. Park of Andover was a master of this gift. His sermon is still remembered by the older men in which, after giving a detailed and painstaking description of a kind of ecclesiastic particularly odious to the preacher, he gravely remarked, "If the clerical estate of man is his best estate, then truly every man at his best estate is altogether vanity." Professor H. B. Smith, who was his fellow-traveler in Europe, used to tell how Professor Park overwhelmed with mock politeness and assumed ignorance a ridiculously egotistic servant of the Bishop of Gloucester, to whom he had a letter of introduction. He crept up into the presence of this person strutting in his imposing livery, and with an air of supreme concern and deference inquired, "My lord, are you the Bishop of Gloucester?" The instantaneous collapse of the poor man is an admirable illustration of the effectiveness of irony upon windy characters. It may now be assumed that the nature of "verbal irony," as Bishop Thirlwall calls it, has been made sufficiently plain.

This primary form of irony has been dwelt upon at some length for the purpose of distinguishing it from that which is about to be named, and which is of chief importance here, the irony of life. This kind of irony represents in the vital process what is otherwise found in argument or in the forms of speech. It implies two persons; one who constructs the order and who foresees the inevitable issue of every violation of that order, and another who in the abuse of his freedom assails it, dreams of success in his assault, for a while even seems to be infinitely secure in his success, but who is being led steadily onward to the demonstration of his folly. The irony of life is divine or diabolic according to the view taken of the character of these two persons. If the ordainer of the vital irony is blind fate, and if the subject of it is caught by it through unavoidable ignorance, the process in its origin, operation, and issues is simply diabolic. Scorn and horror are the only proper human feelings in the presence of such a universe. If, however, the predestinator of this process is Infinite love, working for the evolution of manhood from brutehood; and if the subject of it is led into it as much by perversity as by ignorance, then it becomes a method of education for which one can have the deepest respect. Whether, then, under the irony of existence, one is bound upon a wheel of fire or is a spirit on the way to bliss depends upon the previous question, What is the character of the Author of this irony?

Sophocles is the great classic example of this sort of irony.[1] This poet's most impressive specimen is given in "Œdipus the King." Sophocles exhibits the irony of existence in the case of this man, to whom a revelation comes from Apollo that he would kill his father and marry his mother, flying from his home in Corinth that he may escape these woes, arriving at Thebes, where he weds the queen, is blest with children, attains great renown, and finally, awaking to the awful fact that his glory has been his shame, that in his flight from these foretold horrors he has but taken the steps leading to his own doom. If this is a plot of the gods against a wholly just or an unavoidably ignorant man, then the gods are execrable, and their victim is the object of the deepest and purest pity. But, as Thirlwall contends, the poet's conception of the author of this terrible irony is of inscrutable and yet unerring justice, and his idea of Œdipus is of " a headstrong, impetuous character " whose "blindness, both the inward and the outward," is after all " self-inflicted."

Other instances of the irony of existence in forms that no longer commend themselves to the moral sense of mankind, and that nevertheless possess permanent illustrative worth, are the stories of Sisyphus and Tantalus. The irony consists in the hope which fills the hearts of

[1] See Thirlwall's essay, *Essays and Reviews.*

these tormented ones of attaining the unattainable. They strive as if they were sure that the struggle would sometime prove availing; when to the ordainer of the struggle it is foreknown to be forever in vain. Homer's description is really of a law whose origin and character and application were beyond his insight. None the less striking, however, is his exhibition of the irony of existence. " Tantalus, too, I saw in grievous torment, standing in a pool. It touched his chin. He strained for thirst, but could not take and drink ; for as the old man bent, eager to drink, the water always was absorbed and disappeared, and at his feet the dark earth showed. God made it dry. Then leafy-crested trees drooped down their fruit — pears, pomegranates, apples with shining fruit, sweet figs, and thrifty olives. But when the old man stretched his hand to take, a breeze would toss them toward the dusky clouds." "And Sisyphus I saw in bitter pains, forcing a monstrous stone along with both his hands. Tugging with hand and foot he pushed the stone upward along a hill. But when he thought to heave it on clean to the summit, a mighty power would turn it back ; and so once more down to the ground the wicked stone would tumble." [1] A far happier instance of Homeric irony is found in the

[1] *The Odyssey*, bk. **xi.** 583–600. Professor Geo. H. Palmer's translation.

fortunes of Odysseus. He seems to be over-matched by the forces that oppose his return. The sea and its ruler, Poseidon, Circe, Calypso, and Polyphemus and a hundred other hostile powers would seem to be completely sure of overwhelming the adventurer. But, unknown to them, the secret of the universe is with him, and he is at length restored in spite of all, and by the aid of all, to Ithaca, Telemachus, and Penelope. The fate of the suitors and of all the persons and forces that combined against his life and honor is the obverse of this same irony.

In the Old Testament this serious humor plays a large part. The historical epic of the exodus is a striking instance of irony. The course of events through which the oppressed gain their freedom seems to culminate in each instance, as in the successive plagues, in a still more hopeless impossibility, until, with the Red Sea in front, the mountains to right and left, and the pursuing Egyptians in the rear, their doom appears to be sealed. The irony lies in the deliverance of the hopeless sufferers, and in the destruction of the confident oppressors. Still grander is the irony in the epic of Job. The confident Satan, the dogmatically certain friends, are driven into shame and confusion of face, and the pure sufferer, who meanwhile has lost everything but the sense of truth and his trust in righteousness, receives an unexpected and a joyous vindication. The trial is permitted by the Lord, who knows the integrity of his servant Job, and who foresees that the whole course of his losses and sufferings will but contribute to the final overwhelming demonstration of the lofty disinterestedness of his soul. In the Joseph story there is hidden a philosophy of the Hebrew nation. The victim of jealousy and cruelty, the slave of the Midianites, the servant of Potiphar, who again suffers ignominiously, the prisoner who becomes the interpreter of the king's dream, the wise statesman in anticipation of famine, and ultimately the veritable ruler of Egypt, is an instance of Hebrew faith in the moral government of the world, which reduces to nothingness the guilty in their triumph, and lifts the righteous out of the dust and sets him upon a throne. Here the irony is in working out through the designs and infamous doings of iniquity its final overthrow, and in advancing through each new step into suffering the righteous man on toward his unexpected but divinely foreseen triumph. In line with these illustrations of Hebrew irony is the idea of redemption that is attached to the story of the fall. The defeat of man is really the path to a mightier victory, and the mockery that overtakes the serpent is that in bringing disaster upon man it has been contributing to his greater life and destiny.

The irony of Christ is the consummation of the classic and Hebrew forms of it. In the study of the irony of Christ two things are essential. The fact must be made clear, and the point from which this fact may be consistently interpreted must be reached. To establish the fact it is only necessary to name certain of his teachings. The wise and foolish builders furnish one illustration. Both build, both build in hope, both live in what they have built with equal security. But the searching universe through its rains and winds and floods ridicules and destroys the false hope; and it justifies honest confidence. In the story of the rich man and Lazarus there is another instance. The righteous beggar, full of sores, laid at the rich man's gate with apparently only dogs to comfort him, is shown to be in a process that carries him into eternal peace; while the man who fared sumptuously every day is seen under the awful reverse of torment which is the issue of his real character, for a while hidden but now revealed. When Jesus said of Jairus's daughter, " She is not dead but sleepeth," they laughed him to scorn. The child regained her consciousness under his power, and the laughter and scorn were then seen to belong on the other side of the controversy. For the establishment of the fact that Jesus used irony one more illustration must suffice. There is the parable of the man who had not where to bestow his goods. We are made to see this person, in his supreme joy, meditating how he shall find room for his increased wealth, concluding to pull down his barns and to build bigger, gathering in imagination into these new accommodations his affluence, and ending with the glorious self-congratulation, " Soul, thou hast much goods laid up for many years ; take thine ease, eat, drink, and be merry." The irony here is indicated by the words, " Thou foolish one, this night is thy soul required of thee ; and the things which thou hast prepared, whose shall they be ? "

The point from which to interpret the irony of life as it lies in the teaching of Jesus is supremely important. The determining principle must be the consciousness of his mission to man as his deliverer. In his own thought Jesus was the spiritual redeemer of men. He could not, therefore, have construed the irony of life in a way to contradict that central thought. It is reasonable, then, to seek for the mind of Jesus upon this subject in the parable of the lost son. Instead of the fate of the Homeric representations, and the inhuman justice of the Sophoclean drama, and the restricted sympathy of the Hebrew Deity, we have the Father. He ordains the order of life, he overlooks it. In calm sorrow he sees the willfulness of his son. Nothing can be done but to allow him to have his own way. That way the Father knows is one of sin and suffering and shame. But he also knows that the successive disappointments of it, ever deeper and more bitter, can have only one effect. They will bring the son to himself; the way into the far country will curve into the way home; and before the circle is covered the will-fulness and the vanity will have passed out of the afflicted life; and the Father who surrendered in sorrow will receive in joy. This is the irony of existence lifted into accord with the supreme conception of God. The origin of the difficulty is in the ignorant and perverse will. The way to reclaim an evil will is through the discipline of woe which it makes for itself. The high and tender composure of the Reclaimer is that he knows man, and that he sees that the steps that take him away from God are but the accumulating compulsions that assure his return.

Instances of the irony of life are too numerous and striking to have passed unnoticed. But they have stood out in their isolation from the general movement of history, and they have been regarded as hardly more than suggestive of irony. The fall of Napoleon at the height of his power and through the ambition that had led him to power, the advance of Charles I. to his death through the tricks and the mendacity by which he felt sure that he would recover his throne, have impressed certain persons as exam-

ples of the irony of life. It is not difficult to
see the irony in the debaucheries of Louis the
Beloved, and of others like him, chosen for the
sake of pleasure and issuing in unspeakable disease and death. But this does not carry one
very far. The question is whether there is evidence in history as a whole of the working of
moral irony. The affirmative answer to this
question is, of course, beset with difficulties;
and yet it would seem to be the proper answer.
The Hamans of history are not always hanged
on the gallows which they have caused to be
erected for the execution of good men. The
Nebuchadnezzars are not always humbled in the
enormity of their pride, and driven in the moment
of their supposed supremacy and security to live
with the beasts of the field. When attention is
confined to particular cases, as many instances
can be cited against the existence of moral irony
in life as can be placed to its credit. A better
statement would perhaps be, that in most cases
it is difficult or impossible, for lack of knowledge, to apply the idea. As in the Sophoclean
drama, in certain plays the ironical purpose is
indisputable, while in others it is difficult to be
sure that it is present at all; so in life judged
in individual cases and over a narrow margin
of time. But when history as a whole is taken
into account, and the evolutionary perspective
of man's life upon the earth is adopted, it is

hardly possible to miss the presence and agency of a terrible moral irony. The brutal civilizations or kingdoms of the East, confident in the saving efficacy of brute power, came to their doom one by one, by the spirit and methods which they had chosen as their security. In this way, Greece fell, Rome fell. Modern nations, like Spain, have risen into power, and passed, in consequence of the means chosen to perpetuate that power, to utter ruin, or to the rear of the march of civilization. Over the vast field of history it is possible to see the working of an irony which means the *reductio ad absurdum* of evil. Sensuousness is shown to be ridiculous. Brutality is discovered to be suicidal. Selfishness is revealed as an impossible basis for human society. Profligacy, chosen on account of pleasure, turns out to be an engine for the production of pain. Unmoral power becomes a device for its own overthrow. An ironical Presence permits the willful choice, allows the cruel career, lays no restraint upon the brutal power, refuses to arrest the inhuman civilization ; but time passes, life comes to its climax, historical movements reach their crisis, and then that same ironical Presence confronts the individual or social or national folly with the mocking demonstration of its fatuity.

The Greek sense of this inevitable Nemesis has been rendered by Longfellow : —

"Though the mills of God grind slowly, yet they grind ex-
ceeding small,
Though with patience He stands waiting, with exactness
grinds He all."

This is the irony of history. It receives its
typical expression in the fate of Jesus and his
enemies. Apparently he was defeated; seemingly they triumphed. But his personal defeat
was the path to historical triumph; their immediate success was the assurance of the permanent overthrow of their cause. As history has
dealt with Christ and his cause, broadly considered, it has dealt with all just men and their
causes. The great judgment parable of Christ,
whatever else it may be, is the interpretation of
the course of the world. The infinite surprise
of defeat awaits successful inhumanity; the
infinite surprise of success awaits defeated humanity. The omission of the note of essential
kindness is fatal to the selfish conqueror, the
presence of this note in the oppressed servants
of righteousness is the power of an absolute
reversal. The irony of the judgment parable is
to be interpreted through the conception given
of the supreme ironical Person in the parable
of the lost son; still, it is an irony whose comfort lies in its absoluteness.

V

In addition to the witness in history of sentiment and humor to the moral order of the world, there is the testimony of conscience. In history the heart speaks, humor breaks in upon the silence with her playful and yet profoundly serious words, and conscience utters her great message. Indeed, sentiment and humor are but the right and left wings of the grand army of faith, of which conscience is the centre. Without the purpose and support which this centre gives to them, the wings would be useless and unmeaning. Sentiment is not self-explaining; humor is rooted in something deeper than itself. Underneath both is the human nature which is through and through ethical. The verdict of conscience, therefore, upon the character of the order in which men live is of supreme moment. If any vindication of the ways of God to men is possible, if the construction of a theodicy is in any measure within human power, it is because of the human conscience. The moral reason of man is the organ through which is discovered and declared the reality of the moral order of the world.

The most amazing of all facts is the fact of the human conscience. Here is a moral idealist in man, a moral judge, a penal power in the interest of moral ends. The conception of what

human life ought to be, the honest discrimination between the ideal conception and the actual
behavior, and the power by which shame and
remorse, repentance and hope, are used for moral
improvement, reside in the conscience. The full
exposition of the conscience would carry one
amazing distances. Here it is simply noted that
this spiritual presence in the natural world is an
astounding thing. And if conscience is an evolution, the fact is, if possible, still more significant. If man is a product of the cosmos, if all
that is in him came to him from without, if he is
only the conscious image, the living picture of
the laws and forces of his environment, his conscience must mean not less but more. For the
cosmos cannot put into its product what it does
not itself contain. To give a conscience implies
the prior possession of the gift. If the sense of
a moral order has been slowly developed in man
out of purely animal instincts, it can only have
been a development in response to the reality of
moral order. The genesis of the conscience is a
profound subject; but this much about it would
seem to be clear, that the origin and evolution
of it are an indubitable witness to the reality of
the moral order of man's world.

Theodicies are of four kinds. There is the
personal theodicy, the social, the historic, the
metaphysical. One can think of a career like
that of Joseph or Daniel in Hebrew history, or

like that of Alfred the Great in England, or of
Washington in America, as in a way self-sufficing. For that life the ways of God with it are
justified out of life. Rarely fortunate lives for
themselves possess this value. The Christian
idea would seem to be that this supreme good
fortune, under some of its aspects, is the possibility of every man. Maurice, Bushnell, Stanley, and doubtless a host of others, repeated with
their last breath the apostolic benediction. Life
came to this sense of its meaning and issues, and
the invocation of the peace of God that passeth
all understanding upon the receding world of love
and beauty is itself a personal theodicy. Paul's
words: "I am already being offered, and the
time of my departure is come. I have fought
the good fight, I have finished the course, I have
kept the faith: henceforth there is laid up for
me the crown of righteousness, which the Lord,
the righteous judge, shall give to me at that
day," [1] constitute his theodicy. The world is
alive with these confessions of the saints. The
Stephens that entreat God for those who are ston-
ing them, the Jobs that find within them a reason
for trust in the Eternal that death cannot touch,
form, at least, a sublime tradition. And there
can be little doubt that the way into a true
philosophy of history is through the sense of an
adequate meaning found in personal life. A

[1] 2 Tim. iv. 6–8.

theodicy of a broader character is hopeless without the vision of this personal achievement as a universal possibility.

The best form of social theodicy known to the writer is to be found in Plato's "Republic." There justice or righteousness is defined, first, as the harmony of the soul with itself, and, second, as the harmony of the state, or society, with itself. The question is raised whether, were it not for the penalties involved, all men would not prefer injustice to justice as being pleasanter, as bringing in more satisfaction. To expose the baselessness of this position the criminal is imagined to possess immunity from outward detection. He is presented with the ring of Gyges which makes the wearer invisible; and as an impalpable wizard he is allowed to go his iniquitous way. He robs temples, desecrates homes, and commits wholesale outrage upon life, yet he is all the while outwardly unanswerable for his infamy. And this is not his entire immunity. He is further supposed to be supremely skillful in his wickedness; "for it is the perfection of injustice to seem just without really being so." This adept in villainy is able to acquire the reputation for the highest justice, and all the emoluments of that character are his without any of its disabilities. It is still further supposed that the just man shall seem to be unjust, and that while the highest servant of the state, he shall, like Socrates, be put to death as a criminal. Justice is stripped of its good name and its high honors, it is reduced to its essential self, and then it is loaded with the infamy that comes from the misunderstandings of men, and put to death as an enemy of society. Injustice is cleared of its bad repute, made incognizable, lifted to that perfection of art whereby while supremely wicked it seems to be supremely good, and in this character secures all the good fortune that usually goes with justice. Thus stated, the case goes up for judgment. And even upon this statement of it, the case of a bad man is pronounced to be undesirable. In his own nature a sacred order exists. Reason was made to rule the whole man; spirit was created to fight the battles of the reason, and not to breed insurrection by its vehemence; appetite was born to serve. The bad man in violating this order, in overthrowing this constitution, fills his own soul with hideous anarchy. This pitiless anarchy and its issues of woe protest against the choice of injustice over justice, and demonstrate that injustice with the universe as reward is still the supreme horror, and that justice with nowhere to lay its head, and even upon the cross of agony and shame, is still the superlative joy.

This is the personal aspect of a theodicy which Plato makes for his own time. The social implication of this theodicy is what mainly concerns us here. There is a social order which human volition did not make, and which it cannot unmake. Reason as wisdom, as social good, is represented, in Plato's "Commonwealth," by the governing class; enthusiasm, courage, temperance, and power are represented by the soldier class; industry is embodied in the third class. The way is open for the dunce to descend from the highest class to the lowest, and for the man of genius to rise from the lowest to the highest. This is the serious and yet humorous way in which Plato sets forth his sense of the social justice, without which society cannot exist. There is a place for everything in social man, and when everything is where it should be social justice is the result. In the nature of men there exists the necessity for moral harmony, and this inward necessity is enforced by an outward necessity. According to Plato, the rise and growth, the maturity and permanence of human societies are thus dependent upon social devotion to the moral order within, and upon regard for the infinite surrounding cosmos that supports this august order. For the magnificence and high passion with which Plato elaborates his profound insight, the reader must go to his work.[1] Here the ethical idealism found in the nature of social man is outlined as being one of the earliest, and, on the whole, the best expression of the moral

[1] *Republic.* Books ii., iv., and x. in particular.

consciousness essential to social existence, under the sanction of the world-environment. It is the ideal of the social theodicy, or that view of the moral consciousness of man which is limited to contemporary life.

An historical theodicy may fairly be said to be among the new things under the sun. It has risen out of the immeasurable vista into the past opened by the scientific conception of the origin and development of life. Evolution has resulted in putting an immense emphasis upon the doctrine of ends or final causes. The aspiration of life from the beginning has been shown to be toward humanity. The unceasing struggle of life has resulted in an astonishing ascent. From the forms of life that were practically chained to one spot there have come the swift-footed animal, the free swimmers, and the flying fowl. Finally the ascent has come to moral self-consciousness in man. A great end has here been attained, and a new epoch has been begun.

The supremely important thing, however, has now to be stated. It is the actual improvement which evolution finds has taken place in human history. The depths that have been left behind and the heights that have been gained fill the mind with amazement. This truth is indeed stranger than fiction. There is among the fairy tales of the world no romance that can begin to equal the romance of human existence according to the scientific conception of it. Before the currency of the modern idea of development, and the enormous expansion of history implied in it, the battle between optimism and pessimism was fought chiefly on philosophical grounds. History was the last field to which men would have ventured to appeal in support of the moral order of the world. The predominant mood upon the relation of history to optimism, no farther away than the eighteenth century, is shown in three characteristic books, Voltaire's " Candide," Johnson's " Rasselas," and Goldsmith's " Vicar of Wakefield." The optimistic mood was to the brilliant Frenchman, with his wide knowledge of the worst side of the world, the supreme farce. The butt of Voltaire's scathing sarcasm is the optimism of Leibnitz and his great principle of the sufficient Reason. It is impossible to do other than admire the acuteness and dexterity of the ugly little Frenchman as he presents the veritable Satan of history among the sons of God of the great German's optimistic abstractions. The blockheadism, the barbarity, the vice, the ingratitude and loathsome deceit of the race are marshaled with inimitable skill and scorn in proof of the proposition that this is the best of all possible worlds. Voltaire has made his optimist the silliest of fools ; and the mockery with which he treats his own hero is fundamental. It reflects the author's

view of human history. The debate is carried
out of the region of philosophy; the appeal is
made to the actual condition of mankind, and it
is there that the gospel of hope receives its
death-blow. In " Rasselas " Johnson does not
mock; he treats human aspirations with a sad
reverence. At the same time, he fulfills to the
letter the prophecy of despair with which his
famous opening sentence is charged: " Ye who
listen with credulity to the whispers of fancy,
and pursue with eagerness the phantoms of
hope; who expect that age will perform the
promises of youth, and that the deficiencies of
the present day will be supplied by the morrow,
attend to the history of Rasselas, Prince of
Abyssinia." The argument from history, drawn
out with much wisdom, free play of imagination,
and frequent bursts of boisterous humor, is supposed to be conclusive against hope. And in a
way equally impressive, although far more genial,
Goldsmith has depicted the same mood in his
" Vicar of Wakefield." The good vicar is the
victim of the world, and his life, so full of
worthy belief and noble hope, is driven at last
under a succession of ever fiercer storms into
utter wreck. Nor is it to the point to say that
with Johnson and Goldsmith a distinction was
made between earthly and unearthly hopes. The
vision is fixed upon history, and history is recited
as the record of man's defeat. We may mock

at it with Voltaire, sigh over it with Johnson, or laugh and weep over it with Goldsmith, but the fact, as they understand it, remains unalterable.

It is almost incredible that within a century that which was assumed to be conclusive against optimism is to-day regarded as the strongest argument for it. Mankind began in the depth of animalism. It began with a psychic change that told to the eye of the Infinite, but hardly to any other, that a new race had appeared, that the last and greatest epoch in the life on this planet had arrived. It began with nothing but possibilities. From that remote and almost unimaginable position the race has come to its present attainment. Between the worst man and the best, the loftiest saint and the lowest sinner, the mind of the man of genius and the intellect of the savage, the distance, enormous as it is, is as nothing when put beside the interval that separates mankind to-day from mankind at its origin. So far the race has come in intelligence, morality, and power, in the fruits of a complex and marvelous civilization. It started with nothing but needs and powers, and in an unsubdued environment; to-day it moves in an order of achievement that is simply inconceivably rich. The improvement, to every one who will take the trouble to represent it in thought, is a supreme wonder. The migrations with which the Hebrew race and Puritan America began justly impress the imagination, but they are insignificant compared with the migration accomplished in humanity, from the mood and condition of the brute to the spirit and life of the modern world. The great feats of individuals, like the first voyage of Columbus, or the circumnavigation of the globe by Magellan, are but trifles measured against the feat achieved in the historic career of mankind. The race is the incomparable hero. Its literatures, arts, governments, religions are the monuments of an attainment beside which all others are contemptible.

The question is inevitable, If the race has come so far, why should it not go on? If it has established such a record of progress, why should the progress not continue? Are we not justified in doubling the life of the race on into the future, and in trying to conceive what mankind shall be when it has added to its age another equal length of time? It is indeed true that an unpicturable mass of selfishness and suffering has attended the course of human life, that the condition of man to-day is still a sad sight. But the point established by history is the progressive elimination of moral evil and suffering from human society. Thus much the new vista of history seems to make good, that injustice and inhumanity are not here to stay. The moral evil of society is among things temporal. It is a stream whose fountain-head and tributaries are becoming less and less. Again and again brutal ideas have risen into power and uttered their scorn against the moral idea of society only to be eventually hurled from their eminence into the dust. In 1855, David Christy published his book, "Cotton is King." It was the inhuman answer of the Southern slaveholder to the Northern abolitionist. It is a good symbol for the claim of the brutal idea of human life to sovereignty. When this claim was made they were few who would have ventured to predict that within ten years the sovereignty of the cotton interest would be surrendered to the sovereignty of the national conscience. Such is the fact. The American civil war was fought to determine whether cotton or conscience is king, and the principle and issue of that war yield the true philosophy of history. The growth of the moral idea of society has been painfully slow but irresistibly steady. No weapon formed against it has finally prospered. The movement of the moral idea is ever in upon new territories of human interest, and in greater strength over the old. Inhuman purpose is compelled to play the part of the hypocrite. More and more the voice of history is that "the earth is the Lord's and the fullness thereof;"[1] and the Lord is not cotton but conscience.

[1] Ps. xxiv. 1.

The cheering note in the historic evolution of man is the note of improvement. For the race as a whole this note has scarcely been heard until within the last hundred years. The fact of improvement was denied; and a philosophy of history based upon the continuous moral progress of mankind would have impressed thinking people as in the highest degree ironical. And at this point scientific theory has done an immeasurable service to faith. It has discovered the fact of improvement upon a scale unimaginably great, and from this it has elaborated its optimistic philosophy of human history. Upon a subject of the deepest moment a revolution has thus been wrought in man's view of his race. Mankind has left behind countless evils; that is fact. No evil need last forever; that is inference. And the inference has taken possession of the leading minds in all parts of the world with a depth and force that would seem to insure great issues.

So long as disease was believed to be inevitable and incurable, organized and effective human effort against it was impossible. The educated mind is now possessed by a new idea. It is now seen that within certain limits nature works for health, and that the encouragement of disease is the issue of ignorance and vice. The limits within which disease may be confined, in the estimation of the educated mind, and in the

judgment of the prophets of the great profession
of medicine, are indefinitely narrow. That is, no
one will venture to say that pain is an element in
experience that cannot be reduced almost to the
vanishing point. Even for contemporary man
the horror of physical suffering is subject to
great mitigation; and for the coming man that
mitigation may be carried very far indeed. Relief began to come the moment that it was discovered that physical suffering is neither inevitable nor permanent. The hope of the medical
profession is a scientific hope, and the higher
character that this profession is acquiring is
coming out of the successful struggle to which
its scientific hope is devoting it.

The same line of remark is true of education.
Until recent times popular enlightenment was
believed to be a hopeless impossibility. The
general incapacity of men was regarded as a
fatal barrier. The want of leisure was felt to
be another obstacle. Interest in the subject was
further deadened by the feeling that enlightenment would make the masses of mankind less useful and more ungovernable. Revolution would
follow in the path of knowledge, and anarchy,
and a social conflagration in which all the high
values of civilization would perish. These are a
few of the opinions and sentiments which led the
ruling classes to regard, for thousands of years,
the idea of the general education of the people

as among the wildest absurdities. And even in
the most enlightened nations, until the middle
of the nineteenth century, illiteracy was widespread. The only education obtained by the
masses of men, until recent times, was obtained
largely through physical labor, chiefly through
its problems and incentives, and by means of
human association in this service. It followed
that from any share in the best intellectual and
spiritual life of the race the overwhelming majority were excluded. The Bible in the speech
of the people is a fact of very recent date. The
modern classic writers had to make the tongue
in which they wrote. Down to the sixteenth
century the entire spiritual treasure of the race
was locked up in two or three dead languages,
accessible only to the privileged few, who were
seldom disturbed by the sense of social obligation. A single phrase from early and fervent
Puritan prayers, which may still be heard in the
meeting-houses of New England, is an impressive
reminder of the recentness of privileges that are
now common. Men may still be heard thanking
God that they "live in a land of gospel privileges," that they have "the Bible in their own
tongue." The restriction upon popular religion
was the last consecration of the prohibition
served upon popular enlightenment.

This order of thought, once as apparently fixed
as the nature of things, has gone. The force

that began its disintegration was set free when
it was seen that ignorance is not necessarily permanent, and that its abolition is for the interest
of society.   From that day to this the campaign
of popular enlightenment has gone steadily forward.   The movement for universal education
is supported by the conviction that ignorance is
not an immutable fact, and by the further assurance that marked social progress is impossible
without widespread and reliable knowledge.   In
this enterprise the general capacity for knowledge has been a surprise; the elastic nature of
time, which has enabled workingmen to rise to
high levels of intelligence, has been another surprise; while the public utility of this popular
increase in intellect and in information has been
the crowning surprise.   There is no reason why
a new world of intelligence and the values of
intelligence should not eventually emerge from
these and similar discoveries.   If righteousness
is the reasonable life for human beings, there is
the best of all grounds for hope that with the
new development in rational power there will
come a new passion for righteousness.

At the present time society is distracted over
a yet profounder problem.   Is the present organization of society, coming as it does out of unequal ability and of free opportunity, the best
that man can achieve?   Are the enormous evils
that accompany the working of this order inevi-

table? Should ethics have a profounder influence upon economics? Is it possible for man's humanity to exercise controlling power over man's animal interests? Must the food-problem always stand off by itself, subject only to the law expressed in the brute struggle for existence? Is the organized selfishness of the economic order a measure of safety against the enormous unorganized selfishness of mankind? And does society in its inhumanity rest upon the inhumanity of man, grounded upon the inhumanity of the universe? Such are some of the questions that are agitating the economic world to-day. They are immensely significant. They indicate a new sense of the economic situation, a new consciousness of the economic affliction. They show a growing appreciation of the magnitude and complexity of the problem. Social forms are expressions of social man; and those who are out are not any juster or nobler than those who are in. Society in consenting to be reformed has to take measures against being abolished; in admitting the redress of wrong, it has to guard against the introduction of other and greater wrongs. The depth and intricacy of the problem started by Socialism has yet to be comprehended. Social philosophers do not yet know enough, nor are they wise and powerful enough for the high enterprise proposed. But the general belief that the present order of society is not the final order is wholesome and prophetic. The conviction that no enemy of human welfare is necessarily abiding is inexpressibly precious. The assurance that the injustice of the present industrial order is doomed will yet generate the wisdom and the power necessary to secure its overthrow.

The times in which we live are marked by an immensely influential and spreading belief in man's power to improve his condition. Man has found that what he was made to do for himself God will not do for him. Trust in God is ceasing to be a substitute for human exertion; it is becoming the sublimest form of self-reliance. What man is able to do for himself is the supreme witness of God's kindness to him, and the trust which he is coming to put in his own powers naturally flows out into deepest trust in God. Whether it flows out to its final end or not, man's confidence in his power over his lot is on the increase. He has found in science the Promethean fire. The advance in science is one great feature of recent history, and the advance in the application of science to the purposes of human life is another. From this process, still in its morning hours, two results are already clear. One is an immense vitalization of scientific pursuits; the other is the consciousness that scientific discoveries are availing only for the sincere; that is, for men and women thor-

oughly in earnest and of distinct moral purpose.
It is generally apparent that the business of
reducing the evils from which men suffer is dependent upon knowledge and character. And
the woe of existence when wasted, and the joy
of it when inspired with high hope, are the
twofold aspect of the fundamental motive upon
which reformers are coming to rely. Life itself,
under the discipline of the universe, generates
the impulse that makes for sincerity, and that
enables society to profit by the ministry of science. The instinct for essential good is in the
human soul; experience operates in favor of the
growth and strength of this instinct; and all
exact knowledge thus becomes more and more
availing.

The chief issue of this serious application of
knowledge to human life is the conviction that
the moral improvement of man may be immensely accelerated. Not only is moral evil im-
permanent, but its life may be indefinitely short-
ened. Hitherto progress has resulted largely
through the operation of environment upon instinct. On a wide scale there has been little
serious effort at the elevation of human character. The moral elevation of man has never been
the vocation of the many. This greatest of all
tasks has never yet been seriously confronted
by society. This neglect of the supreme social
interest cannot last. It is for man's interest to

cease being a mere animal, and to rise to full
manhood. And the knowledge that has transformed production and exchange, that has revo-
lutionized government and social distinctions,
that in biology, and in all related sciences, is
working with such grave intensity for the limitation of disease and the full normal health of
the body, that is seriously and incessantly questioning the legitimacy of the reigning industrial
order, that insists upon the universal application of instructed intelligence to the business
of living, cannot be forever cowed by the moral
problem. What has wrought so mightily elsewhere should have an adequate trial here. For
religious teachers, salvation for the few has
always been an accepted possibility; salvation
for man, redemption to the righteous and joyous
uses of life for all men, is bound to become the
accepted and inspiring possibility. The new
faith is founded upon the new assurance that
moral evil is not necessarily a permanent element in human existence, that the number of its
days is not infinite, and that this number may
be indefinitely cut down.

The final battle of man will be with his inhumanity. Progress upon the lower levels of existence will compel him to feel more keenly the
calamity that overspreads the highest level. Victory against other enemies will stimulate him to
undertake the greatest of all campaigns, that

against the reign of the brute in human society.
The believer in man must think of the consciousness, into which the makers of society are
yet to come, of the fact that moral evil is neither
inevitable nor everlasting, and of the further fact
that, under such an attack as may be made upon
it, its life may be made astonishingly brief.
After the gestation of centuries nations are born
in a day. After millennial preparations there
will come forth the great conscious struggle of
man with his inhumanity. And as part of the
historic theodicy there must be recorded this
final battle the character gathered for it from
the world-environment, the prevailing spirit in
the last and deadliest encounter with the brute,
and the militant moral equipment developed
through the struggle. It may prove to be the
fact that the conscious overthrow of the historic
Satan has been the final stage in the evolution
of the historic paradise. If the devil can be
turned to a good use, it should be put to the
credit, not of the devil, but of the world-environment in which men live. At this point possibilities amount to indications of superhuman
sympathies, and the struggle for righteousness
that is an increasing success may well seem to
say that the stars in their courses are fighting
against unrighteousness.

The witness here to the moral order of the
world may not be all that one could wish, still it

is of great weight. It does not explain the historic mystery of iniquity, but it does show that mystery passing away; and no evil that is temporal should permanently baffle faith. Under the august pressure of the universe inhumanity is dying; the campaign of the Infinite in history is slow, but it is finally fatal to lies, lust, and all brutality. Thus far the world-environment is revealed in the annals of the race. Its ultimate demand is the dethronement of the brute and the kinghood of the man. Its ultimate character is seen to be an eternal power not ourselves that makes for righteousness. Thus out of human history emerges a conception of God that transfigures Goethe's song of the Earth Spirit in " Faust : " —

> " In the currents of life, in the tempests of motion,
>   In the fervor of act, in the fire, in the storm,
>   Hither and thither,
>   Over and under,
>   Wend I and wander,
>   Birth and the grave,
>   Limitless ocean,
>   Where the restless wave
>   Undulates ever
>   Under and over
>   Their seething strife,
>   Heaving and weaving
>   The changes of life ;
>   At the whirring loom of time unawed,
>   I work the living mantle of God."

The historical theodicy prepares the way for the metaphysical, which, however, does not concern us here. It is certain that the metaphysical theodicy will not make moral evil a necessary part of the universe. The Leibnitzian theodicy was constructed when there was no vision of the self-destructive nature of iniquity, under the operation of the world-environment. It was thought out in the atmosphere of the Augustinian theology, as revived by the Protestant reformers. That theology made sin an immeasurable and abiding fact in the earthly career of man, and an eternal fact in the world beyond death. History as thus read could say nothing of the passing away of this awful mystery, nor could it mitigate the deep shadow which it cast upon the face of the Infinite. The new metaphysical theodicy will do well to be modest in its propositions. If it can show where the insoluble difficulty lies it will do some service ; and if it is sane enough to refuse to identify sin with the will that is working through history for the extermination of it, it will cancel the contradiction that theology has for many centuries planted in the heart of God. Working both by the sense of what cannot be ascribed to the Supreme will, and by the vision of the historic victory of good over evil, the metaphysical theodicy may accomplish much for the relief and the illumination of faith in the moral order of the world and the moral character of God.

VI

Religion is no longer regarded by any school of reputable thinkers as an invention. History has shown that it is part of normal humanity. It belongs in the same rank as the sense of humor, beauty, obligation, and love; as the appreciation of cause and effect, purpose and result in life; as the perceptions of time and space. The normal mind sees things in succession or in coexistence. Infinite room, both temporal and spatial, is an indispensable requisite for making a beginning in understanding the world. Even if time and space are simply the colored spectacles through which the world is seen, since every man wears them, they are valid for man and universal. Whatever outward reality there may be stands under the colors of these spectacles, and can appear for human beings only in this way. There may be no humor, beauty, righteousness, love in the universe; still, man is not man without some share in these perceptions, and the greater his share in them, the richer is his humanity. Cause and effect, purpose and result, may be real only for the human mind; yet, as they are real for all human minds, they cannot be ignored. Religion is real for man; the sense of the Infinite is practically universal, and in one form or another, the feeling of dependence, and the sense of obligation in the presence of the Infinite. Religion can be treated as an illusion or as a disease only by those who reduce to the same level the whole law and content of the human intellect. The utter subjectivity of religion involves the absolute subjectivity of all knowledge. If there is nothing in religious feeling but feeling, there is nothing in any other feeling but feeling. If the skeptical Samson insists upon pulling down the temple of piety, he must overthrow along with it the entire edifice of knowledge. Either universal experience is a revelation, and an attestation of reality, or it is not. If it is not, the negation must be an impartial negation. It must hold over the whole field of experience. If the negation is changed into an affirmation, and it is granted that universal experience does involve reality, again, the affirmation must be an inclusive one, and the faith that brings back knowledge must reëstablish religion.

The concession may be assumed as made that universal experience involves reality. That space and time, cause and effect, purpose and goal, humor, beauty, moral order, and love, denote something real other than themselves, may be taken for granted. What the nature of this reality is does not concern us here. It is sufficient to point out that it is assumed. Science investigates and discovers in a real world; in that world there is some basis for the sense of

humor and the play of other universal instincts.
The serious work of the world goes on upon the
basis of reality.   And, in the same way, religion lives on the basis of reality, and that reality
is involved in the life of religion. Under all the
sciences is knowledge and its real world ; under
all religions is religion and its real world.

> " As the hart panteth after the water brooks,
>   So panteth my soul after thee, O God." [1]

The reality of the water brooks is given in the
universal desire and satisfaction of the animal.
The distress and the relief of the animal are a
transaction in fact. The reality of God is given
in the thirst and the refreshment of the soul.
The pain and the comfort are again a transaction in truth.   If there were in the case of
the animal never anything but panting, and
in the case of the soul never anything but thirst,
the mere subjectivity of the experience would
be clear.   If in the case of the animal the passion and its object exist, and if in the soul there
were only the burning need, the inference to
God would be from the general meeting of desire and satisfaction.   The eye and the light
match each other, the fin and the water, the
wing and the sky, the need of food and the fact
of food ; and, therefore, analogically, the thirst
for God and the reality of God.   That there is
some force in this analogy, when carefully stated,

[1] Psalm xlii. 1.

is not to be denied ; but that force is never more than probability, is never anything other than prophecy. It is not the certainty of the religious soul. There the hunger for God and the bread of heaven are included in the one experience, the distress and its relief, the agony and the consolation. Religion is not only a hunger and a thirst after the living God, it is also the consciousness of being filled with his presence. And, therefore, in the universality of religion as in the universality of science, the reality of the object is given.

History has established the practical universality of religion. It has shown that religion has played, for weal or woe, the supreme part in the life of mankind. To endeavor to explain the family life of the world, or the art or politics or social customs of man, apart from religion is in the last degree unscientific. And this means that religion has stood, for the implication of human life, in one form or another, with the unseen and Infinite. The concern of the religious spirit is with that which is above man. In the baser religions, even, there is hardly ever wanting some hint of this. In the nobler religions the central fact is the consciousness of the Infinite, and the sense of dependence and obligation growing out of that consciousness. Thus far, then, history declares the object of religion to be real, and the reality to be the Infinite.

History implies that the progressive rise in the character of religious conceptions is the result of the pressure of the Infinite upon the spiritual nature of man. Deliverance comes in this way from the suspicion that the supreme religious conception is an invention, a beautiful but wholly arbitrary imagination. That the Infinite is simply baptized into the name of the highest man often torments the modern thinker, as very possibly the truth. If we were without historical perspective, if the highest religion were without any prior historical development, it might be difficult to expose this fallacy. But the growth of religion, like the growth of science, implies the profounder appreciation of the character of the reality with which it deals. The best in the religions of Egypt, Persia, Greece, India, Arabia, the best in the religion of the Hebrew people, implies a prior discipline which means the ever higher pressure of the Infinite upon the conscience of man. Religion, in the light of history, is a growth; and the growth is not alone the work of man; it is the ever higher result of man's response to the appeal of the Infinite. And here is another great declaration of history. Religion is the revelation of the character of God; the continuous ethical rise of religion is the more and more adequate revelation of that character. The material world gives up its secret to the scientific genius; the supreme vision of God is imparted to the religious genius. Neither makes the character of his object; each beholds and declares it. Behind inadequate science is the patient cosmos; behind imperfect religion is the long-suffering God.

History has another declaration to make. Since Christianity is the highest religion, it is therefore the highest revelation of God. Christianity is not the dream or the invention or the teaching and ideal of Jesus; it is the revelation of God to him and through him. The weakness of our generation lies here. We discuss the conception of things, the conception of God, of the moral order, of immortality; and we refuse to commit ourselves to the further position that these conceptions are real. We discuss the ideas of Jesus in this way; we exhibit their depth, comprehensiveness, self-consistency; we admit that they lift religion to its highest conceivable form. Here men pause. They are slow to identify the teaching of Jesus with the ultimate truth. Christianity is haunted with this terrible suspicion of subjectivity; it is always tending to become for men of our time the highest tradition of humanity and nothing more. A fatal dualism between the highest thought of the world and its true character infests our age, a skepticism about the validity of the best conception as a witness for reality, a strange incapacity for getting, in the great ideas, close to the heart of things. This is the act of faith for which multitudes are apparently unfit.

The answer to this mood is threefold. Instinct is insistent that beneath the universal interest there always is the real world. Analogy presses the same contention. The world of science, of political economy, of every-day life, is assumed upon the strength of instinct to be real; and the general trustworthiness of the human intellect is another fundamental assumption. In like manner, we take for granted that under the universal religious interest there is a world that answers to it, and that answers to its highest form. History is, however, the great deliverer from subjectivity. In the light of the historical development of religion, Christianity is seen to be the result of the pressure of the Infinite upon the soul of Jesus. Nothing is his but his sublime soul, his transcendent receptivity. This he presents to the universe, and the issue is his gospel. The prism is at last found that reveals the heart of the Eternal light; the soul finally arrives whose divinity receives and declares the inmost nature of God. The universe that made Jesus, made his mind, and put within it its sublime conception of God. Jesus is not the author of reality; he is the highest product of reality, and therefore the supreme revelation of its character. The consciousness

of Jesus Christ is not the self-creation of one
in utter isolation from the order of the world,
inspired by goodness and glorified by devout
imagination ; in the light of history it appears
as the inevitable issue in the soul of the Master
as he stands in full communion with fact.   Emerson's beautiful lines upon the Æolian harp
have a transcendent application to the teachings
of Christ : —

> " Speaks not of self that mystic tone,
> But of the over-soul alone ;
> It listens to the cosmic breath
> And as it heareth so it saith."

History has become a new authentication of the
claim of Jesus, made in the final days of his
life, and in a manner of the highest seriousness :
" The words that I say unto you I speak not from
myself : but the Father abiding in me doeth his
works." [1]

[1] John xiv. 10.

CHAPTER VII

THINGS EXPECTED

A NEW beatitude has been coined by an American humorist of the last generation: "Blessed are they that expect nothing, for they shall not be disappointed." There is wisdom no less than humor and pathos in the remark. Concerning every judgment about the future disappointment is always a possibility. Absolute certainty covers only what has been and what is. And in the widespread contradiction which meets human hopes, it would be strange if in many instances expectation were not greatly moderated or even altogether abandoned. There is naturally in man a Prometheus, a divine foresight that steals fire from heaven for the sake of human progress, and that usually comes to grief in the furtherance of its high schemes. The reason is that rashness enters into the undertaking. Audacity and ignorance bring the suffering that occasions the delay, and the prophetic mood chained to the rock gives way to despair. Disappointment is so large an element in life that hope is often enough sorely beset: —

" The best-laid schemes o' mice an' men
Gang aft agley,
An' lea'e us nought but grief an' pain,
For promis'd joy."

In the face of this experience many settle into the conviction that prevision is an impossibility, and that definite expectations are entertained at too great a risk.

In the discipline of the nineteenth century, what has occurred, however, is not the expulsion but the sobering, the purification of expectation. Kant's mood at the beginning of the century reappears as the inevitable human mood at its end: "What do I know? What ought I to do? What may I expect?" Knowledge and duty issue in expectation. The past and the present have their full meaning in the future, and while no mortal can comprehend that meaning, to be sure that there is meaning and to reach the least insight into its nature are no ordinary gains. And it is remarkable that prevision is part of human life. It is based upon experience; it is qualified in assurance according as experience is uncontradicted or otherwise in an increasing measure. We expect that day and night will continue to succeed each other, that the seasons will observe their immemorial order, that seedtime and harvest will not fail, that the heavens above and the earth beneath will keep their ancient covenant with man. We expect this with perfect assurance, because the expectation is grounded upon an uncontradicted experience. Science is an attempt to conquer new fields of uncontradicted experience. The experiments in chemistry and physics, the conditions being the same, give uniformly the same results; in biology and physiology, allowing for the nature of the subject, the general issue is the same. Science may be defined as the attempt to discover the courses and conditions of uncontradicted experience, and upon this basis to establish over these regions of life an absolute prevision of the future. Exact science, experimental science, knows what is, and it knows what to expect.

When one reaches the spiritual level this law of existence is not changed. If a man is sure of an uncontradicted experience of the love of God, he is justified in his expectation of its continuance. The twenty-third psalm is an example : —

> " The Lord is my shepherd ; I shall not want.
>   He maketh me to lie down in green pastures :
>   He leadeth me beside the still waters.
>   He restoreth my soul :
>   He guideth me in the paths of righteousness for his name's
>   sake."

Here is the uncontradicted experience, and as the warrantable deduction from it, here is the expectation : —

" Yea though I walk through the valley of the shadow of death,
  I will fear no evil ; for thou art with me :
  Thy rod and thy staff, they comfort me."

In the second half of this psalm the same fundamental soundness of thought is evident : —

" Thou preparest a table before me in the presence of mine
  enemies :
  Thou hast anointed my head with oil; my cup runneth over."

Once more from this uniform experience issues
the just prevision of the future : —

" Surely goodness and mercy shall follow me all the days of
  my life :
  And I will dwell in the house of the Lord forever."

In so far as experience under God, or at the
hands of the universe has amounted to an uncontradicted experience of essential good, expectation of essential good in the future rests upon
a scientific basis.

Social life stands in a great expectation.
"England expects every man to do his duty"
is an expression of the world's expectation. It
is disappointed in a multitude of cases; and yet,
on the whole, it is supported by fact. Upon this
basis of experience business expects faithfulness
in its servants, families believe in the permanence of the love out of which they have risen,
institutions of learning and religion look for the
devotion of their friends, nations rely upon the
loyalty of their citizens, humanity is assured
that it will keep faith with itself. Here the

experience is far from uniform, and therefore
the expectation is far from certain. Yet upon
the whole experience is of faithfulness, and upon
the whole hope is wise.

It appears, then, that prevision is part of
man's life, and that its soundness depends upon
the experience upon which it is based. On
account of the complexity of experience and
the impossibility of comprehending it, there is
inevitable a certain vagueness in forecast even
when it is upon the whole sound. This is the
case with the Hebrew prophets. They knew life
to a great depth and over a wide expanse; and
out of this amazing insight they were able to
forecast the general movement of mankind. In
general they are right: in particulars they are
wrong. Where they are definite they are undone
by history; where they are vague they are supported by the march of civilization. The outline, the trend, the general result, the large and
vague issues, were all that even their insight
could provide. And the spiritual expectation
can never be anything more than this, a faith
born out of experience, in the general shape of
the coming time. The preceding interpretation
of the leading moods of the nineteenth century
tends to raise expectation. And it may not be
wholly vain to indulge a little the spirit of prophecy. It is part of the spirit of man; it is at
work over the entire field of human interest; its

persistence in the universal trust in nature and its intensity in scientific activity are contagious. Since Prometheus is awake in all other souls, he must not be allowed to slumber in the disciple of faith.

It is expected that the sense of humanity will more and more envelop all human interests, and among them the forms of religious belief. Humanity in the sense of a hierarchy of powers in the individual man, holding positions according to ideas of worth, with moral perception and moral feeling as sovereign; and humanity in the sense of an inclusive human brotherhood, where the good of each is seen to involve the good of all, and where the good of all can never be at the permanent sacrifice of any single soul, — this is the consciousness that is more and more to envelop the sum of man's interests. The brutal aspects of industry, social forms, political management, and philosophical thinking are subject to this unsparing judge, and responsive to this unceasing influence. It cannot be that man shall always strive with man in all these fields of endeavor. The method of life in so far as it is brutal is a survival from a past to which it was wholly suited; to-day it meets the protest of the new evolution in man. The protest, while far enough from being sufficiently availing, is nowhere entirely unavailing. Over government during the last hundred years it has wielded

controlling power. The organized industry of
the world is its strongest foe. The food problem
is primarily an animal problem; it is the hardest, or at least one of the hardest, to raise into
a human problem. The family life of man has
been largely left to the guidance of instinct.
Nowhere is it so important that the animal
should be transformed into the man. The per-
petuation of human life is the supreme human
responsibility; and less than any other great
interest it has been subject to moral reason.
Round these interests, however, and those of art
and science and philosophy, stands a militant
humanity. They may indefinitely resist its
influence, but they cannot escape from its presence. And this isolation of human interests
from their league with brute interests must be
followed, after long delay it may be, by surrender. The apostle's cry, " Depart from me;
for I am a sinful man, O Lord," [1] is the cry of
the brute interests in the presence of the human.
The Lord remained, and Peter became a new
man; the sense of humanity is here to stay; the
brutality of the race can never again be left to
itself. It must remain in the tormenting presence of the human ideal. When the human
cannot be driven from the field, sooner or later
the brutal must seek an end of its pain in a great
reconciliation. Man's total nature is not some-

[1] Luke v. 8.

thing fixed; the new creation in the spirit is a truth of history. The new man has been an individual fact for ages; the new social man is slow in coming, yet is he on the way hither. It is upon the arrival of this new humanity, as much superior to the present humanity as that is superior to the tiger, that the new heavens and the new earth shall appear. They will chronicle the fact that the old man with his old order has passed away; they will bear witness to the full advent of the creative power of the new man.

Religious belief is subject to this process of change. What served well a patristic, a mediæval, and a puritan humanity cannot in all respects serve the new humanity. The criticism of life is upon belief, and if it is to last it must be able to approve itself to that criticism. What is unworthy of man cannot continue to seem to be worthy of God. Beliefs are for man and not man for beliefs. They must conform to the laws of his nature; his nature must not be run in their moulds. As the criticism of reason has, during the last hundred years, gone everywhere, so now the criticism of man's humanity is going everywhere. In the critique of reason the mind itself was the first to appear in court; finally the summons went forth to ethics, jurisprudence, history, literature, and theism. The Bible as history and literature was the last to respond to

the warrant. But it had to come. Over all the
critical process has passed, with the general result that every essential interest of man has
acquired a new certificate of worth, and with the
special result that the Bible now makes its appeal no longer in a tongue that no man understands, but in the irresistible idiom of reason.
Man, in like manner, has been taking the measure
of himself, and with the sense of his own stature
and dignity he has made a fresh investigation of
his relations and possessions. Again, over all,
this criticism of humanity is passing. Religious
belief should be the first to welcome this new
mood. But whether it shall meet it in friendship or in hostility it cannot escape its presence
or shun its judgment. Like all the other interests of man, religious belief is born out of life;
and when the old product is confronted by the
new and mightier creative spirit, it must either
grow into the new character and use, or pass
utterly away.

It is expected that the humanity of Jesus
Christ will become more and more controlling in
all thinking about the character of God and the
nature and destiny of man. The great opportunity of Christianity is yet to come. It has so
far been the faith of which the world was not
worthy. The history of human thought about
it is largely a history of distortion. The evident
obsoleteness of patristic, mediæval, and puritan

theology as even a working hypothesis for the modern man, is a strange sight in the presence of the morning freshness and serviceableness of the teaching of Christ, and its transcendent and yet wholly sane idealism. The cable of the centuries by which the gospel has been towed down the stream of time, it is now seen, was attached to much besides the gospel. It was attached to a whole fleet of errors and inadequate notions, and thanks are due to the Providence that takes care of its own, that in such a convoy the hope of man did not sink. That old cable is now broken, and the gospel comes steaming in its own name, and at length, with another convoy, the needy and mighty humanity of the world.

From the action of humanity upon the sum of man's interests much is to be expected; from the action of Christianity upon humanity much more is to be expected. More and more Jesus Christ must become the organ through which God is conceived, and through which man's worth for God is determined. And this is no longer the importation of a foreign standard into thought. Jesus Christ is not an alien in man's world. In him more than in any other that world comes to know itself. He is the highest humanity at work upon the lower and the lowest. The way in which he thought and felt about God and man are supremely normal; the way in which he behaved is ideal behavior

for man. Jesus Christ is man at his best thinking about God's nature and his own, and standing to the task of life. The signs of the times
disclose a growing sense of humanity; the same
signs declare an increasing readiness for a new
appreciation of Christianity. The gospel of the
Incarnation of the Son of God in Jesus Christ
confronts a larger opportunity than it has ever
yet confronted. For the comprehension of its
content and spirit, for wider fields of influence,
and for transmission through a more consistent
humanity, it looks confidently to the future.
For a new construction of its theism and its
anthropology, and for a profounder and happier
consciousness of its world-renewing grace, the
centuries have gathered into a vaster hope.

It is expected that the idea of human life in
this world as an education will more and more
take the place of the idea of probation. As
Thomas Erskine insisted a generation ago, and
like one crying in the wilderness: " No education
can go on without trial; but we are tried that
we may be educated, not educated that we may
be tried." [1] Or as one with equal insight and
felicity, and with wider response to his words,
has written in this generation: " Man is under
probation, not because he is a sinner, but because he is a moral being, undergoing a forma-
tive process. It should, therefore, not be treated

[1] *The Spiritual Order*, p. 59.

in a harsh, doom-like way, but as a gracious
feature of a gracious system." [1] The idea of
probation relates man to God as to a judge. In
the total relation of man to his Maker this idea
has an unquestionable place. Without judgment
the universe could not be moral; without judgment man's life could have no ascertained worth.
The universe as a universe of moral values implies a Supreme moral appraiser; it also implies
that man is subject to this appraisal. God is
doubtless judge of the quick and the dead, but
he is more. He is the Father of men, and, therefore, the judicial relation is instrumental to the
paternal passion expressed in the ancient words:
"Like as a father pitieth his children, so the
Lord pitieth them that fear him." [2] Probation
is a truth overstated, isolated from other truths
that hold the key to its meaning. It is discipline
detached from the benign purpose in which it
lives; it is the rod described as if it were not in
a father's hand. Human life is here on trial,
but this is not the whole story. It is on trial in
order that through the judicial process it may
come into the greater consciousness of itself;
and that it may feel that its evolution into richness and strength is but its response to the inspiration of the Divine education. By itself the
judicial relation to God is hopeless. "Any con-

[1] *The Freedom of Faith*, p. 42.   T. T. Munger.
[2] Psalm ciii. 3.

fidence . . . that I can have in the award of a righteous judge is in fact a confidence in myself — a confidence that I have right on my side, and that it would be unrighteous to condemn me. But in very truth I have no such confidence." [1] And the supplementation of the judicial by the filial relation in Christ shows that in the traditional theology the idea of probation as a finality was really neutralized. Its principal use was in scaring men into the acceptance of Christianity; its subsidiary office was in securing the condemnation of the non-Christian world without compromising the justice of God. It was employed as motive, and it was built into a theodicy; and in neither office was it of much account with reasonable men. In the place of supreme importance the idea of existence as a probation was a calamity; in the place of a servant, and under the authority of the idea of life as a Divine education, it is of permanent utility.

The educational view of life is likely to commend itself more and more, not only on account of its worthiness considered in relation to God, but also on account of its conservative force in relation to human experience. Upon the judicial theory everything is worthless but the perfect product. Nothing that is less than ideal has any business to be. This is the parallel to the literary severities of Meister: "Either a

---

[1] *Spiritual Order*, p. 60.

poem is excellent or it should not be allowed to
exist. Because each man who has no gift for
producing first-rate works should entirely abstain
from the pursuit of art, and seriously guard himself against every deception upon that subject." [1]
In art, perfection or nothing; in life, sainthood
or nothing. Thus the life of the world is wasted;
few are called and fewer still are chosen.

Not thus will sane-minded men look upon life.
The nursery, the school, the college, the early
years in all the trades and professions, have
their chief value as educational forces. The
product is of secondary consideration, the discipline received is the main thing. The awakening of the man is the grand aim of existence,
the worth of his output in work is of subordinate concern. Thus the great moods that seem
to be outside of faith are finally covered by it.
The moods of doubt, denial, and despair; those
of ignorance and perversity and suffering; the
paths of shame and waste, — all lie inside the
circle of the Divine education of man. Thus
the forms of interest that are necessarily temporary have a permanent value. Science and art
are for this world; literature is a monument to
man's life upon the earth, government is the
necessity of the present order; the same is true
of the industrial system. All this ceases for
the individual at death, and unless one dwells

[1] *Wilhelm Meister's Apprenticeship*, vol. i. p. 79.

upon the educational worth of it, it must seem vanity and vexation of spirit. When this whole temporal order in which men live shall dissolve and pass " like the baseless fabric of a vision," its worth shall remain in the souls that have won through it the freedom of the sons of God. Nothing is final but human persons in domestic and social fellowship and God's action upon them ; and yet all circumstances, moods, interests, experiences, and powers that have borne a part in the education of the human spirit become an abiding value. To a redeemed humanity the remembrance of existence here should be like music, — a grand march that meant an immeasurable conquest. Everything that exists may be turned to account in the production of everything that ought to exist. The actual in its natural environment, and under the power of the Holy Spirit, may be converted into a servant of the ideal. The world that humanity in its higher mood expects will come through the prophetic nobility of part of the present world, and through revolt from the part that is base.

It is expected that an ethical view of life of the utmost rigor, combined with an unrestricted hope for man, will more and more dominate the Christian mind. This would seem to be the inevitable consequence of the profounder sense of law and the purpose of law that now obtains. The operation of law is without respect of persons, uniform, irreversible, absolute; it is exaction of the utmost farthing. The purpose of this rigor is love. In the certain revelation of order, in the elimination of confusion, in the exclusion of all unrighteous hope, and the call to trust in the absolutely trustworthy, this purpose of love is manifest. The broad way that leads to death and the narrow path that leads to life remain eternally unconfounded. In the unalterableness and awful plainness of the moral order lies its benignity. The mistake that righteousness leads to woe and that unrighteousness issues in bliss is impossible for a reasonable man. Where it exists, this delusion is the product of passion; against it is the whole witness of life. For the brave and good there is, at least, the foretaste of the peace that passeth understanding; for the wicked there is no such thing as peace. Burke's definition of law covers both the rigor of its operation and the benignity of its purpose: "Law is beneficence working by rule."

In this stern decisiveness is the ground of hope for man. An uncontradicted experience of the folly of unrighteousness cannot but tell upon a reasonable being. An unlimited opportunity for trial would seem to warrant the hope that the sinner will at length be convinced of the error of his ways. Nothing but dust and ashes through endless time would seem to be too much for the stoutest vagrant. Conduct that issues always in Dead Sea fruit would seem finally to discredit itself. Sisyphus is the embodiment of an impossible mood for a reasonable creature. To confront forever a uniform experience of failure and to endeavor forever to make headway against it is the supreme example of idiocy. Law is the silent argumentation of God with men. Where ignorance is polluted with perversity, it is not easy even for God to overwhelm the human debater. Infatuation can fabricate a universe of its own, and install it in the place of the real universe. The resources of an evil will are many, and its courage and pride are great. It is this aspect of the situation that forbids a fixed opinion upon the issue, and that sobers the Christian mind into a high and serious hope. The endless years are the unrighteous man's opportunity for testing his way of life. It would seem that an uncontradicted experience of failure, of eonian length, might convince him that his way is an impossible way. In the grand debate between God and the wicked soul, conducted through the awful rigor and eternal kindness of law, and in the terrible logic of human sensibility and suffering, it would appear that the foolish and perverse soul would at last allow itself to be redeemed.

It is expected that the assumptions with which this book opened will more and more verify themselves in the life of man. It is anticipated that the religious view of the world will commend itself as the truth to an increasing multitude of thinkers, and that the Christian version of this view will vindicate itself as the highest and best. That God will be seen to be in the organism and life of humanity a moral spirit in ceaseless communion with men ; that he will be known as working for ends, and ends that are worthy of himself ; that his advance in human history is not a dream but a reality ; that man's world is an imperishable value for God, and that in an endless process of expansion and transfiguration it will continue an order for itself, and a habitation for God, are profound and confident expectations.

It is expected, finally, that all contradictions of human hope will prove but mightier fulfillments of it. Men are doubtless deceived in many ways, and life is an undeceiving process. Still, hopes may be too meagre and mean, as well as too large and happy. Men are deceived. in the world and they are deceived in God ; but in the first instance the reality is less than expectation, in the second it is infinitely more. Men are deceived in God " as they are in the lights of heaven." The Hebrew Messianic hope, in the letter, met with blank contradiction. No such king came as the prophets foretold. The Hebrew Zion is desolate, Jerusalem is a by-

word, the land is a reproach, and the people are
strangers in all parts of the world. Read according to the letter, nothing is more tragic than this
utter disappointment of Hebrew expectation.
But while that which they expected did not
come, something did come immeasurably better.
Christ and his gospel are the answer to Hebrew
hope ; they are other and more and better infinitely than prophetic genius could divine. In the
New Testament there is an equally impressive
hope, contradicted, in the letter, in an equally
overwhelming way. The expectation of the
Lord's return within the limits of the first century was universal. It was not fulfilled. The
epistle to the Hebrews was written about the
time when despair began to settle in the mind
of the church. It was written to show that the
Lord's promise made to the spirit had been
translated into the letter, to prove that the
need, and not the expectation, had been honored. The contrast between what the early
believers expected that Christ would do, and
what he has done, is an example of the way in
which God keeps his covenant with man. The
contradiction of the early hope was in the interest of a vaster hope and its realization. For
Christ in the flesh we have Christ in the process
of the Eternal spirit. The expectation was common for the first ten centuries of our era that
the world was working toward its end. In the

tenth century the gloom of this forecast was
upon all Europe, and it was like the shadow of
death. The end of that old world did come, and
a new order appeared in its place. The form of
the expectation was all wrong ; the sense that
something great was coming was right, and
when it arrived it proved to be an immeasurable thing. King Alfred was wise and good,
Cromwell was far-seeing and true-hearted, and
their hopes for England were great. Yet they
would not know the land that they loved and
served, and whose future they fondly dreamed
about, not because their hopes were too high for
God's providence, but because they were too low.
Between the United States of Washington, and
even of Lincoln, and the nation of to-day there
is a wide contrast. Another reversal of expectation has occurred in the interest of a vaster
realization.

Thus the world rolls in the grooves of time.
God has set his promise not only in the clouds,
but also in the human heart, and in the depths
of the social process. The greatest of all hopes
is the hope of a new heaven and a new earth
wherein dwelleth righteousness. Delays that
appear to be permanent disappointments are the
long sad record. The expectation that is from
God has often seemed to be the least regarded,
the most completely ignored. God's prophets
have been left to perish, while iniquity has gone

on its triumphant way. In the tumult of the ages every voice has seemed to be audible but God's. In death the hope of the righteous has appeared to meet with its final contradiction. It is manifest that God does not run this world according to our mind, but according to his own. It is clear that his thoughts are not our thoughts, nor his ways our ways. But herein is the promise of a vaster hope than man can now entertain, and a realization worthy of the perfecter of that hope. History makes it clear that the contradiction of human expectation is for the sake of a sublimer realization, and that this contradiction comes because as the heavens are higher than the earth, so are God's thoughts higher than man's thoughts and his ways higher than man's ways.

INDEX

INDEX

Alcott, Bronson, anecdote of, 139.

Allen, A. V. G., quoted, 93, 135 note; 142.

Amiel, chief value of his journal, 251.

Aristotle, his "Posterior Analytics," 3; fundamental defect of his philosophy, 13; his universe derived from his idea of God, 30; indicates will as the centre of moral experience, 40; his optimism, 215; his remark on man, 246; represents the historic mood, 293; growth of his fame, 322.

Arnold, Matthew, 96, 240, 242.

Assimilative capacity, 75; as an evidence of vitality, 78; shown by the idea of humanity, 79.

Atheism, rejected by faith on three explicit grounds, 272; rendered impossible by humor, 323.

Atonement, the, considered, 146; the real truth of, obscured by misunderstandings, 148.

Baptism, its symbolic meaning, 159.

Beecher, Henry Ward, 286.

Berkeley, his philosophic passion supplied by theistic faith, 31; his sacramental view of the world, 161.

Bible, the, its loss and gain under the higher criticism, 171; value of its translation into modern languages, 365.

Brooks, Phillips, 286.

Brotherhood of man, no explicit part of Hebraism, 53; connection with the Jonah story, 54; foreign to Greek civilization, 57; more favored by Rome, 59; its progress in the Reformation, 60; forced on man by his own nature, 306; as an authentic part of the order of things, 309.

Browning, Robert, 96; the century's supreme humanist, 69, 257.

Bruce, Prof. A. B., cited, 129, 141.

Brutality, as an obstacle to man's moral progress, 35.

Burke, Edmund, quoted, 24; his failure in interpreting the French Revolution, 64; his dictum on man, 246; his definition of law, 397.

Burns, Robert, Emerson's statement regarding, 62; his expression of the meaning of the French Revolution, 67; song of his quoted, 68; greater than Scott, 322; his terrible humor, 328; quoted, 383.

Bushnell, Horace, 119, 286, 353.

Butler, Bishop, his "Analogy," 105, 110.

Byron, Lord, 69.

Caird, Principal, on the origin of evil, 51.

Calvinism, its defects, 262; its form of theism rejected by the new faith, 275.

Carlyle, Thomas, 23; his interpretation of the French Revolution, 65; his assimilative capacity, 77; his books first read in America, 95; his reply to Bronson Alcott, 139; his profound belief in the authority of righteousness, 154; on the Church of England, 188; his fondness for the Book of Job, 200; sar-

The Riverside Press

Electrotyped and printed by H. O. Houghton & Co.
Cambridge, Mass, U. S. A.